Intermedial Dialogues

Edinburgh Studies in Film and Intermediality

Series editors: Martine Beugnet and Kriss Ravetto
Founding editor: John Orr

A series of scholarly research intended to challenge and expand on the various approaches to film studies, bringing together film theory and film aesthetics with the emerging intermedial aspects of the field. The volumes combine critical theoretical interventions with a consideration of specific contexts, aesthetic qualities, and a strong sense of the medium's ability to appropriate current technological developments in its practice and form as well as in its distribution.

Advisory board
Duncan Petrie (University of Auckland)
John Caughie (University of Glasgow)
Dina Iordanova (University of St Andrews)
Elizabeth Ezra (University of Stirling)
Gina Marchetti (University of Hong Kong)
Jolyon Mitchell (University of Edinburgh)
Judith Mayne (The Ohio State University)
Dominique Bluher (Harvard University)

Titles in the series include:

Romantics and Modernists in British Cinema
John Orr

Framing Pictures: Film and the Visual Arts
Steven Jacobs

The Sense of Film Narration
Ian Garwood

The Feel-Bad Film
Nikolaj Lübecker

American Independent Cinema: Rites of Passage and the Crisis Image
Anna Backman Rogers

The Incurable-Image: Curating Post-Mexican Film and Media Arts
Tarek Elhaik

Screen Presence: Cinema Culture and the Art of Warhol, Rauschenberg, Hatoum and Gordon
Stephen Monteiro

Indefinite Visions: Cinema and the Attractions of Uncertainty
Martine Beugnet, Allan Cameron and Arild Fetveit (eds)

Screening Statues: Sculpture and Cinema
Steven Jacobs, Susan Felleman, Vito Adriaensens and Lisa Colpaert (eds)

Drawn From Life: Issues and Themes in Animated Documentary Cinema
Jonathan Murray and Nea Ehrlich (eds)

Intermedial Dialogues: The French New Wave and the Other Arts
Marion Schmid

edinburghuniversitypress.com/series/esif

Intermedial Dialogues
The French New Wave and the Other Arts

Marion Schmid

EDINBURGH
University Press

Pour Julien Azérad,
passionné de la Nouvelle Vague

Edinburgh University Press is one of the leading university presses in the UK. We publish academic books and journals in our selected subject areas across the humanities and social sciences, combining cutting-edge scholarship with high editorial and production values to produce academic works of lasting importance. For more information visit our website: edinburghuniversitypress.com

© Marion Schmid, 2019, 2021

First published in hardback by Edinburgh University Press 2019

Edinburgh University Press Ltd
The Tun – Holyrood Road
12 (2f) Jackson's Entry
Edinburgh EH8 8PJ

Typeset in Garamond MT Pro by
Servis Filmsetting Ltd, Stockport, Cheshire

A CIP record for this book is available from the British Library

ISBN 978 1 4744 1063 2 (hardback)
ISBN 978 1 4744 8137 3 (paperback)
ISBN 978 1 4744 1064 9 (webready PDF)
ISBN 978 1 4744 1065 6 (epub)

The right of Marion Schmid to be identified as author of this work has been asserted in accordance with the Copyright, Designs and Patents Act 1988 and the Copyright and Related Rights Regulations 2003 (SI No. 2498).

Contents

List of Figures vi
Acknowledgements viii

Introduction 1
1 Celluloid and Paper: Rivalries, Synergies, Crossovers 12
2 The World as Spectacle: Cinematic Theatricalities 53
3 Painterly Hybridisations 86
4 Architecture of Apocalypse, City of Lights 127
5 Still/Moving: Photography and Cinematic Ontology 163
Conclusion 204

Bibliography 209
Index 220

Figures

1.1	Antoine Doinel's Balzac chapel in *Les Quatre cents coups*	30
1.2	Colin decrypting the literary riddle in *Out 1*	33
1.3	Natacha holding Éluard's *Capitale de la douleur* in *Alphaville*	38
1.4	Book burning in *Fahrenheit 451*	40
1.5	Language as visual sign: *Bande à part*	46
1.6	The authorial signature: *Pierrot le fou*	48
2.1	The play-within-the-film in *L'Année dernière à Marienbad*	58
2.2	Outdoor rehearsal in *Paris nous appartient*	63
2.3	Theatrical experimentation in *Out 1*	71
2.4	Vietnam protest skit in *Pierrot le fou*	77
2.5	Guillaume re-enacting the Chinese student's performance in *La Chinoise*	79
3.1	Arthur, Odile and Franz's run through the Louvre in *Bande à part*	92
3.2	Piero della Francesca, *Portraits of the Duke and Duchess of Urbino*	96
3.3	Agnès Varda, *La Pointe courte*	97
3.4	Pablo Picasso, 'Sculptor at Rest with his Model, Anemones and Small Torso'	103
3.5	Agnès Varda, *Lions Love (. . . and Lies)*	104
3.6	Abstracting the body into pure form in *Une femme mariée*	111
3.7	Wall graffiti in *Au pan coupé*	120
4.1	The paradoxical beauty of industrial landscapes in *Métamorphoses du paysage*	136
4.2	'There is a menace hovering over Paris': modern architecture in *Le Joli Mai*	140
4.3	Architecture of reconstruction: Pierre Vivien's *buildings* in *Muriel*	145
4.4	Juliette and the 'cité des 4000' in *Deux ou trois choses que je sais d'elle*	148
4.5	Play of lights over Paris in *L'Amour à la mer*	157
5.1	The *punctum* of photography: freeze-frame ending in *Les Quatre cents coups*	168

5.2	*Nostalgérie*: colonial-era postcards in *Le Clair de terre*	174
5.3	The photo shoot in *Le Petit Soldat*	179
5.4	Figuring liminality: the Sibyl's cave in *La Jetée*	188
5.5	Benny Moré dancing in *Salut les Cubains*	197

Acknowledgements

The origins of this book go back a long way. Nebulous though initial ideas always are, they can probably be pinned down to a screening of Jean-Luc Godard's *Le Mépris* at the Cambridge Arts Cinema, in the late 1990s, which I remember as a kind of epiphany. Stunned by the film's bold auteurist style, I felt vindicated in my conviction that film is an art no lesser than literature, theatre or painting. But it was also face-to-face with this New Wave classic that I realised that cinema can engage other artforms, not least the modernist architecture of Adalberto Libera's Casa Malaparte, against whose striking Mediterranean setting the film's final dramas unfold.

Bringing me back to an enduring passion – somewhat like Ulysses returning to Ithaca in *Le Mépris*'s final sequence – the journey of this book has been nourished by new discoveries, encounters and exchanges. My first thanks go to my students at the University of Edinburgh, who have accompanied my immersion into the New Wave with cinephile fervour. I am also grateful to the Department of European Languages and Cultures for having granted me a semester's research leave during which I completed the manuscript of this book and for the unwavering support and good humour of my colleagues in the French and Francophone Section. I am indebted to the Arts and Humanities Research Council for their award of a Research Networking Grant, which has funded the international research group 'Film and the Other Arts: Intermediality, Medium Specificity, Creativity'. The members of the network have deeply enriched my understanding of intermediality, helping me develop the transdisciplinary outlook of the book. I would like to thank them all here.

I could not have wished for a more supportive team at EUP. I am grateful to the series editors Martine Beugnet and Kriss Ravetto-Biagioli for their thorough reading of the manuscript and stimulating comments. I also wish to thank Gillian Leslie, the Senior Commissioning Editor for Film and Media Studies, and Richard Strachan, the Assistant Commissioning Editor, who have expertly accompanied the project from its inception. In my research, I have been kindly assisted by the staff of the Bibliothèque du Film, the Bibliothèque du Cinéma François Truffaut and the Forum des images (all in

Paris) – *un grand merci pour leur aide*. I am indebted to the editors of *French Studies* for their permission to use a section from my article 'Between classicism and modernity: Éric Rohmer on urban change', published in volume 69.3 (2015) of the journal, in Chapter 4.

On a more personal note, I would like to extend my warm thanks to several friends who have been particularly involved in the conception of this book: Sylvia Pereira from the Cinémathèque française to whom I owe the discovery of Guy Gilles; Tony McKibbin, who is always willing to share his encyclopaedic knowledge of cinema; and Kim Knowles, who was a brilliant Co-Investigator on the 'Film and the Other Arts' AHRC project and whose own work on intermediality is a constant source of inspiration. I am especially grateful to Marie-Josèphe and Julien Azérad, who have welcomed me to many a writing retreat in their house in the Berry, lending me the *Cahiers du cinéma* from their library and sustaining me physically and intellectually. With their ever-youthful enthusiasm they are the living embodiment of the spirit of the New Wave. My most heartfelt thanks go to my husband Hugo Azérad for sharing this journey, and for his encouragement, warmth and inspiration all along the way. As always, he is my first and best reader. This book owes more to him than can be put in words.

Introduction

> The cinema is not an art which films life: the cinema is something *between* art and life. Unlike painting and literature, the cinema both gives to life and takes from it, and I try to render this concept in my films. Literature and painting both exist as art from the very start; the cinema doesn't.
>
> Jean-Luc Godard[1]

Cannes 1959. In his closing speech at the festival, André Malraux, the French Minister of Cultural Affairs, celebrates cinema as 'the first global art' – an art that unites humanity in a shared dream, transcending differences of language, ideology and culture. Exalting the powers of the moving image, Malraux is less flattering about the contemporary novel and painting, which he describes as being in decline. 'If the novel gets weaker every year and if even figurative painting has abandoned fiction', he speculates, 'this may be because no fiction can vie with that of cinema'.[2] His carefully crafted speech alludes to rivalries and frictions between the more established arts and cinema. It points to hegemonic struggles and shifting spheres of influence, positions held and lost. Refusing to confine cinema to the status of a technological medium particularly apt at imitating reality, Malraux proclaims its place in French culture at a pivotal point in the history of modern film. For Cannes 1959 wasn't just another year of a prestigious festival. With the combined success of François Truffaut's *Les Quatre cents coups* (*The 400 Blows*, Best Director Award) and Alain Resnais's *Hiroshima mon amour* (*Hiroshima, My Love*, International Critics Prize), it is regarded as the birth of the French New Wave, the legendary movement that revolutionised cinema in the course of the 1950s and 1960s, ushering in a profound renewal of cinematic themes and forms.[3]

That a Minister of Cultural Affairs, who was also a distinguished writer, art critic and filmmaker, should have felt compelled to make such an assertion in 1959 may seem surprising. Almost half a century after Ricciotto Canudo's 1911 manifesto 'The Birth of a Six Art', followed by his influential essay 'Reflections on the Seventh Art' (1923), and decades after the 1920s, often regarded as 'the golden age of cinema as art',[4] was it still necessary to insist on the medium's artistic credentials? Had the bold originality of directors such as Abel Gance, Germaine Dulac or Jean Epstein, and – later – Jean Renoir, Robert Bresson and Jean Cocteau, to list only a few prominent names of French film, not proven cinema's unquestionable place as the seventh art? Malraux's speech is evidence that such achievements were not widely recognised in the 1950s, a period in French film that – as Truffaut denounced in 'A Certain Tendency of French Cinema' (1954) – concerned itself less with originality than with technical mastery, with cinema as industry rather than art.[5]

Cinema's struggle for legitimacy was discontinuous, as Philippe Mary points out in his sociological study of the New Wave.[6] The medium underwent an intense first phase of legitimisation in the 1920s under the aegis of the classical avant-garde, which liberated cinema from its origins as a fairground attraction.[7] Where Canudo had defined film as a synthesis of the rhythms of space (the plastic arts) and those of time (music and dance) into a new form of theatre he called 'plastic art in motion', most filmmakers and critics in the 1920s were engaged in a search for cinematic specificity, seeking to define what makes the medium unique compared to the other arts. Though most of them considered film to be representational in nature, the idea of 'pure cinema' – a cinema concerned above all with the medium's expressive potential and with techniques specific to film – began to impose itself in the second half of the decade, in opposition to mainstream narrative cinema.[8] Yet, despite its name, 'pure cinema' did not operate in isolation from the other arts: many avant-garde directors incorporated music, theatre, poetry, opera, dance and painting into their works.[9]

With its new possibilities for characterisation and plot development, the sound revolution relegated the formal experimentation of the historical avant-garde to the background and rang the death knell for pure cinema. As film moved to the so-called 'era of the script' (privileging subject matter over formal experiment), directors once more turned to literature and theatre in search for inspiration. Post-war French film, as diagnosed by Truffaut, was stifled by the so-called 'Tradition of Quality', whose formulaic adaptations of classical texts and insipid productions devoid of personal style put cinema in the shadow of its literary ancestor. Still considered in its infancy by many commentators, film only slowly gained cultural recognition in the course of the 1940s and 1950s with the foundation of ciné-clubs, the introduction of film analysis courses at the Sorbonne and – not least – its tireless promotion by film journals, above all *Cahiers du cinéma*, soon to become the main organ of the New Wave.[10] Bernard Chardère, of the rival journal *Positif*, explains to what extent, even in the 1950s, cinema lacked cultural recognition:

> I wanted to show that, as in past centuries, film had a history and an aesthetic and was able to *bear comparison* [with the other arts]. We were being a bit naive and juvenile, but more than that we were outraged to see cinema not being taken seriously. Important periodicals existed for literature, for music, but not for cinema.[11]

It is with the New Wave's affirmation of the auteur as the creator of a highly personal vision, in opposition to the technically perfect but formulaic productions of the Tradition of Quality, that cinema conquered a field of autonomy already traced by the classical avant-garde, asserting its place among the traditional canon of the arts. In a crucial second phase of the medium's legitimisation as art, the New Wave – as the epitome of the 'new avant-garde' that Alexandre Astruc foresaw in his article 'The Birth of a New Avant-Garde: La Caméra-stylo' (1948) – achieved the widespread cultural recognition sought by the classical avant-garde.

With the *Cahiers* critics Truffaut, Godard, Rohmer, Rivette and Chabrol soon to take to the camera, a new idea of cinema emerged in France in the late 1950s: no longer seen as a carefully crafted collective enterprise led by a director with technical expertise, cinema became the more personal and spontaneous expression of an auteur, who, like the author of a literary text, captures and shapes reality in an original signature style. No longer the product of a highly specialised mass entertainment industry, cinema affirmed itself as an art form able to vie with the more established arts. The New Wave drew a map for cinema as *the* art of the twentieth century, a medium both artistic and popular, accessible to a large public.

Studies of the New Wave traditionally frame the movement in the context of both the dominant cinema it positioned itself against – the so-called 'Tradition of Quality' – and the coming of age of a new generation with changed values and cultural practices, famously called the 'New Wave' by journalist Françoise Giroud, which gave the movement its name.[12] As an 'artistic revolution' echoing a profoundly altered socio-cultural landscape, the New Wave is conceptualised as a generational shift: upending the sclerotic cinema of the Tradition of Quality, a new generation of filmmakers invents a vibrant cinema perfectly in tune with the attitudes, beliefs and desires of young people. This framing is indispensable for understanding the new cinema that emerged in France in the course of the 1950s and 1960s. Yet, to fully grasp the movement's discursive construction and aesthetic practice, I argue, it is necessary to consider a connected factor, which most histories of the New Wave address only tangentially: the movement's relation with the more established arts, which were enlisted as allies in the creation of a new cinematographic art, while also, to a certain extent remaining rivals.[13]

Focusing on a diverse range of directors, both well established and lesser-known, this book examines the role of the other arts in the New Wave's critical discourses and filmic practice. Teasing out the rivalries, border crossings, media dialogues and hybridisations between New Wave cinema and its neighbouring arts – literature, the theatre, painting, architecture and photography – it probes the movement's ambivalent relationship with these arts in the context of the medium's wider struggle for recognition and self-legitimisation. As we shall see, their roles as models to emulate and authorities to challenge gave the more established arts a central position in the critical discourses that legitimised New Wave cinema. They also had a key role in the movement's diverse artistic output. Referenced and incorporated, self-reflexively foregrounded or tacitly alluded to, adapted or reframed, they helped cinema affirm its credentials as art while allowing a new generation of filmmakers to extend the medium's expressive powers, define its properties and set out new aesthetic agendas. The central thesis guiding my investigation is that the New Wave engaged in the 'impure cinema' the theoretician of the movement, André Bazin, advocated in opposition to the 'pure cinema' of the classical avant-garde.[14] Letting itself be 'irrigated' – to use Bazin's botanical metaphor – by the 'formidable resources' of its neighbouring arts, the New Wave forged an intermedial aesthetic, that is, an aesthetic open to dialogue and exchange with other art forms.

The term 'New Wave' is of course quite elastic and has evolved considerably over the years. My selection of films follows the more extended temporal delineations of the movement that have emerged in recent scholarship. While there is a consensus that the first, most significant phase of the New Wave took place between 1959 and 1963, its vanishing point now tends to be situated around May 1968, when the rise of a new political agenda fractured the movement's aesthetic positions and thematic concerns. After 1968, as Ginette Vincendeau explains, some New Wave directors

> became ultrapoliticised and/or experimental – Godard, Marker – or worked collaboratively, in a challenge to individual authorship [. . .]. Others, on the other hand, like Rohmer with *Ma Nuit chez Maud* (1969) or Truffaut with *La Sirène du Mississipi* (also 1969) turned their back on politics.[15]

If current periodisations of the movement go beyond the narrow 1959–63 timeframe, there is also a tendency to extend the label to later works of core New Wave directors or, indeed, to directors hitherto considered peripheral.[16] Noël Simsolo's *Dictionnaire de la Nouvelle Vague* is emblematic of a considerable extension of the term in that he not only includes forerunners such as Roger Vadim and Jean-Pierre Melville, but also what he calls the 'second generation' of the *Nouvelle Vague*: directors such as Philippe Garrel and Jean Eustache, traditionally considered 'post-New Wave'. While stopping short of Simsolo's 'second generation' – a concept that seems unduly broad[17] – my selection of films aims to offer a more diverse, inclusive view of the movement in tune with recent periodisations. Most of the films I investigate belong to the period between 1959 and 1968. But I also include predecessors such as Varda's *La Pointe courte* (1955), a work poised at the crossroads of theatre, painting and photography, and later works such as Rivette's monumental *Out 1* (1971), which can be seen as a culmination of the director's engagement with the stage. My choices challenge rigid distinctions between the 'Young Turks' (the *Cahiers du cinéma* critics-turned-filmmakers Éric Rohmer, Jacques Rivette, François Truffaut, Jean-Luc Godard and Claude Chabrol) and the 'Left Bank' group directors Alain Resnais, Agnès Varda and Chris Marker. One of my aims is to question the assumption, still widely held, that the Left Bank group were more engaged in, and inspired by, other art forms – especially drama, literature and the visual arts – while the Young Turks drew inspiration above all from personal experience and other films.[18] I also mean to give visibility to hitherto neglected 'satellites' of the New Wave, in particular the unjustly forgotten 'secret child of the New Wave', Guy Gilles.[19]

Rather than opting for a case studies format, which would have focused on a small selection of directors and films, I have organised the book as a series of interfaces between cinema and one of its sister arts. This organisation follows the New Wave's own theorising about cinema's relations with the other arts, which privileges artistic interfaces. Thus, Éric Rohmer, in a polemical series of articles published in subsequent issues of *Cahiers du cinéma* (1955), evaluates the other arts – the novel, painting, poetry, music and architecture – from the vantage point of the youngest, cinema. Positing cinema as the superior art of the second half of the twentieth century, Rohmer takes to task the more established arts which, anticipating Malraux's speech at Cannes, he considers to be in inevitable decline. In a less judgemental vein, André Bazin engages in an extensive reflection on cinema's relations to the other arts in a series of articles written in the course of the 1950s, later to be regrouped in the second volume of his four-volume *What is Cinema?* (published posthumously, 1958–62), entitled *Cinema and the Other Arts* (1959). Like Rohmer, Bazin privileges individual art forms, namely literature, theatre and painting, in his discussions, though he is equally attentive to cinema's situation amongst the other arts more broadly.[20]

Each chapter of the book illuminates a particular interface – literature, theatre, painting, architecture and photography – as a site where media rivalries, encounters and hybridisations are being enacted. As useful operational parameters, these interfaces will allow us to consider specific concerns thrown up by cinema's interaction with one particular art, such as the tension between the verbal and the visual, the notion of performance, cinema's reckoning with space, time and motion, or its reflection on its own materiality. It is important to emphasise that the particular interfaces traced in this book are in no way binary or exclusive. The understanding of the New Wave that underpins this study is that of a heterotopic field where different artistic practices intersect and intermingle, an in-between space where manifold connections and pathways between the arts are being orchestrated. The intermedial space of the New Wave analysed in this book is made up of contact zones, frictions, tensions, absorptions and remediations: it is a space of plurality and heterogeneity.

Readers may wonder why I have not included a chapter on dance and music, especially in light of the renewed interest in the work of Jacques Demy. Although they were without doubt a fertile interface for the New Wave, as more popular art forms, dance and music are less relevant to the question of artistic legitimacy that I take as a starting point in this book. Conspicuously, in the fourth of Rohmer's 'Celluloid and Marble' articles, entitled 'Beau comme la musique' ('Beautiful like Music'), dance is brushed away as a form of 'entertainment', while music is relegated to a 'pure' sphere 'that doesn't care about the evocation of the visible world'.[21] This is not to say that dance and music were not important for the New Wave. Beyond Demy, short choreographies are incorporated into, for instance, Varda's *Cléo de 5 à 7* (*Cléo from 5 to 7*, 1962), Godard's *Pierrot le fou* (1965) and Pollet's little known *La Ligne de mire* (*Line of Sight*, 1960). The dance routine in Godard's *Bande à part* (*Band of Outsiders*, 1964) is one of the iconic scenes of New Wave cinema. The role of music, likewise, cannot be underestimated. One only need to think of Louis Malle's famous collaboration with Miles Davis in *Ascenseur pour l'échafaud* (*Elevator to the Gallows*, 1958) and Godard's collaboration with the jazz pianist Martial Solal for *À bout de souffle* (*Breathless*, 1960); or of Georges Delerue and Giovanni Fusco's very contemporary score for Resnais's *Hiroshima mon amour*.[22] While, within the confines of this project, I have not been able to accommodate them as a full artistic interface, dance and music are touched on in the final chapter, in my discussion of Varda's *Salut les Cubains* (1963).

This brings me to the wider question of the approach of this study. As the theoretician of the New Wave and an intermedial thinker *avant la lettre*, Bazin will be central to my enquiry. Bazin's notion of 'impure cinema' laid the foundation for modern theories of cinematic intermediality, which are concerned with the cross-fertilisation and hybridisation between the arts.[23] In my readings, I will draw on Bazin alongside a more contemporary framework of intermedial theory, drawing on theorists such as Marie-Claire Ropars-Wuilleumier, Jacques Aumont, Angela Dalle Vacche, Ágnes Pethő, Brigitte

Peucker, Alain Badiou and Raymond Bellour, who have enriched our understanding of cinema's interactions with the other arts. Pethő sets out what is at stake in intermedial analysis:

> Although the idea that film has indissoluble ties with other media and arts is one of the oldest concerns of theorising about the movies, it is the theory of intermediality that has brought into the spotlight the intricate interactions of different media manifest in the cinema, emphasising the ways in which moving pictures can incorporate forms of all other media, and can initiate fusions and 'dialogues' between the distinct arts.[24]

As the study of the relations between the arts, intermediality will provide the heuristic template for exploring the rich artistic dialogues at work in New Wave cinema. While attentive to historical context – in particular cinema's quest for artistic legitimacy which stretches from the classical avant-garde to the New Wave – my approach is above all anchored in close film analysis. I take Dalle Vacche's project 'to carve out a space of close reading' as an inspiration for my own analyses of intermedial figurations and significations in New Wave cinema.[25] Revisiting the New Wave through the lens of intermediality, my aim is to revitalise a field of study which may have become all too familiar and to offer fresh new readings of New Wave films. I hope that *Intermedial Dialogues: The French New Wave and the Other Arts* will be seen as an invitation for others to explore further, as a theoretical framework that gives new stimulus and direction for thinking about the New Wave.

The book is organised into five chapters, each focusing, as already mentioned, on a specific interface between cinema and one of its sister arts. The arrangement of the chapters to a certain extent reflects the influence the other arts have had on film: the verbal arts, literature and theatre, come first as the most direct models; painting holds centre stage as the art which, as Dalle Vacche puts it, 'for the cinema constitutes a forbidden object of desire'; architecture and photography are placed at the end as, respectively, an art form that, like cinema, is collective, and the medium that constitutes film's direct technological ancestor.

Chapter 1 explores New Wave critics and filmmakers' ambivalent relationship with literature as both the main model to emulate and the major authority to challenge. Literature resurfaces not only in screen adaptation, but, more diffusely, in the myriad citations, inscriptions and allusions punctuating the cinematic text, as well as in the graphological tropes used to legitimise film as an art form ('politics of the authors', 'cinematic writing', 'camera pen'). The chapter assesses novel attitudes of the New Wave directors to adaptation and to questions of cinematic purity, revisits the collaboration between *Nouveau roman* writers and *Nouvelle Vague* directors, and analyses the manifold

– sometimes irreverent, sometimes celebratory – incorporations of literature in a selection of films. Particular attention will be paid to the incorporation of the written word in Godard's New Wave films as a symbol of media tensions in the director's work, and as a crucial example of his interstitial aesthetic, which breaks down traditional media boundaries.

Chapter 2 examines theatre's double role as both rival and tutelary figure for New Wave directors, who conjugate its forms and figures in many guises. From Resnais's theatrical fictions to Godard's Brechtian conception of the cinematic medium, not forgetting Rivette's incorporation of theatre rehearsals and theatrical plots into the filmic fabric, the theatre takes centre stage in the New Wave as cinema's embodied 'other'. The chapter explores the manifold interactions with theatre and theatricality in New Wave film, focusing on intermedial tropes such as mise-en-abyme and metalepsis, but also interrogating the theatre's capacity – as postulated by Rivette – to reveal cinema to itself. We will see that the collective practices of avant-garde theatre of the 1950s and 1960s, absorbed into the cinema, open up the concept of the auteur, creating a new space for improvisation and creative collaboration.

While the avant-garde of the 1920s had fully explored cinema's nature as a plastic (as opposed to a merely narrative) art form, the advent of sound relegated film's painterly qualities to the background. Godard famously reclaims the painterly ascendance of cinema through multiple borrowings, citations and incorporations of a wide range of art works in his films. An 'exercise in browsing through (a mediated) art history', as Steven Jacobs puts it,[26] his New Wave works playfully (and often allegorically) stage word and image relationships as a struggle for media dominance. Chapter 3 revisits Godard's iconoclastic use of painting, comparing and contrasting it with the intermedial practice of two directors who were trained in the visual arts, Agnès Varda and Guy Gilles. The chapter will investigate seminal intermedial figurations such as the *tableau vivant*, as well as chart the three directors' varied engagement with tradition and modernity in the visual arts.

The inception of the New Wave coincided with a profound mutation of the French urban fabric: parts of historic city centres were razed in post-war modernisation schemes, while 'new towns' were planned outside major cities to relieve the pressure of population growth. Chapter 4 analyses New Wave filmmakers' diverse engagement with architecture – old and new – and urban change in both fictional and documentary genres. Taking Rohmer's article 'Architecture of Apocalypse' as its starting point, it explores urban space as a privileged terrain on which New Wave cinema asserted its modernity by grappling with the forms and textures of the material world. Themes for discussion include New Wave directors' ambivalent representation of the new forms of architectural modernity that emerged in France in the 1950s and 1960s; their interrogation of the living conditions on modern housing estates; and their examination of the relationship between the built environment, affect and memory. We will also consider the movement's fascination with the tactile textures and surfaces of the city, which serve as a self-reflexive mirror in which the filmic medium can reveal itself.

As a medium grounded in photographic technology, cinema retains a deep fascination with photographic images. New Wave cinema explores the boundaries between the photographic and the cinematic in manifold guises, from the inclusion of photographs, freeze-frames or 'found' photo albums to the animation of photography in a 'photo-novel' such as Chris Marker's *La Jetée* (1962) or a cinematic photomontage like Varda's *Salut les Cubains*. Playing on the tension between stillness and movement, the use of photographs interrogates the cinematic medium's particularities, yet also serves as a privileged intermedial tool for grappling with questions of modernisation, colonialism and revolution amid major social and political change in France. Focusing on films by Truffaut, Varda, Gilles, Godard and Marker, Chapter 5 explores the intersection between cinema and photography in the context of wider theoretical debates about their relationship with death, the deceptive realism of technological media of reproduction and what Raymond Bellour calls the new type of 'pensive spectator' solicited by the incorporation of immobile images in film.[27] In examining photograms – the building blocks of film – this final chapter brings us right back to the beginning, bringing more sharply into relief the question that underpins the book and which is central to the New Wave's engagement with the other arts: 'What is Cinema?'

Notes

1. Cited in Roud, *Godard*, p. 6 (emphasis in original). All translations are mine, unless otherwise indicated.
2. Malraux, 'Le Premier art mondial . . . (1959)', p. 468.
3. Malraux personally supported the burgeoning New Wave during the selection for the 1959 festival, defending *Les Quatre cents coups* and *Hiroshima mon amour*. For his politics in support of cinema and his relationship to the New Wave see Jeannelle, *Cinémalraux*, ch. 3, and de Baecque, *L'Histoire-Caméra*, pp. 168–72.
4. See Mary, *La Nouvelle Vague*, p. 20.
5. Significantly, it was only in 1959 that cinema came under the control of the Ministry of Cultural Affairs whereas, previously, it fell under the Ministry of Industry and Commerce. For Malraux's reflection on cinema's relationship to the other arts see his *Esquisse d'une psychologie du cinéma*. On the relationship between literature and cinema in Malraux's work see Jeannelle, *Cinémalraux*.

6. Mary, *La Nouvelle Vague*, p. 21.
7. Ibid.
8. For the wide spectrum of 'pure cinema' ranging 'from Survage's "colored rhythm" and Vuillermoz's "musical analogy" to Gromaire and Léger's "plastic compositions" and Faure's "cinéplastics"' see Abel, *French Film Theory and Criticism,* vol. 1, pp. 329–32 (p. 330).
9. See Nagib, 'The politics of impurity', p. 27.
10. See Ostrowska, *Reading the French New Wave*, p. 25. For the emergence of a cinephile culture in France see de Baecque, *La Cinéphilie*.
11. Cited by Frémaux, 'L'aventure cinéphilique de *Positif*', p. 23.
12. For classic studies of the New Wave see, *inter alia*, Marie, *The French New Wave*; Douchet, *Nouvelle Vague*, de Baecque, *La Nouvelle Vague* and Neupert, *A History of the French New Wave Cinema*.
13. Dorota Ostrowska has paved the way for a comprehensive study of the New Wave's relationship to the other arts with her seminal volume on the connections between the cinematic and the literary avant-gardes in the 1950s and 1960s, *Reading the French New Wave*.
14. Bazin, 'In defense of mixed cinema', p. 74 and p. 75. In my discussion, I will use the original title, 'Pour un cinéma impur: défence d'adaptation' ('For an impure cinema: defense of adaptation'). For Bazin as the theoretician of the New Wave see Marie, *The French New Wave*, p. 47.
15. Vincendeau, 'Introduction: fifty years of the French New Wave', pp. 13–14.
16. See for instance Roloff and Winter (eds), *Theater und Kino in der Zeit der Nouvelle Vague* and Winter and Schlünder (eds), *Körper-Ästhetik-Spiel. Zur filmischen écriture der Nouvelle Vague*, which both contain articles that considerably stretch the temporal boundaries of the Nouvelle Vague, including films such as Rivette's *La Belle noiseuse* (1991), Resnais's *On connaît la chanson* (*Same Old Song*, 1997) or Rohmer's *Conte d'automne* (*Autumn Tale*, 1998). Kline includes a chapter on Bresson in *Screening the Text*.
17. As Simsolo states himself, the directors of what he terms the 'second generation' are the inheritors (or '*ciné-fils*') of the New Wave, rather than a part of the 'core' New Wave. See *Dictionnaire de la Nouvelle Vague*, pp. 9 and 12.
18. See for instance Greene, *The French New Wave*, p. 44.
19. The term is Pichard's, in 'L'oubli et la mémoire'.
20. In the original four volume publication of *What is Cinema?*, vol. 2, *Cinema and the Other Arts*, contained the seminal articles 'For an impure cinema: defense of adaptation', 'Theatre and cinema', 'Painting and cinema', next to articles interrogating the practice of literary adaptation, filmed theatre, and the art film through the analysis of specific films.
21. Rohmer, 'Beau comme la musique', in *Le Celluloïd et le marbre*, p. 60 and 64.
22. For music in the New Wave see Douchet, *Nouvelle Vague*, pp. 256–7.
23. For Bazin as a precursor of more recent intermedial studies see Nagib and Jerslev, 'Introduction', pp. xx–xxi. Nagib and Jerslev understand Bazin's 'impure cinema' not as an *object*, but a *method* (p. xxi, emphasis in original).

24. Pethő, *Cinema and Intermediality*, p. 1.
25. Dalle Vacche, *Cinema and Painting*, p. 11.
26. Jacobs, *Framing Pictures*, p. 116.
27. Bellour, 'The pensive spectator'.

CHAPTER ONE

Celluloid and Paper: Rivalries, Synergies, Crossovers

> In making people accept the principle that a film by Hitchcock, for example, is just as important as a book by Aragon, we've won. The auteurs of film, thanks to us, have definitely entered the history of art.
>
> Jean-Luc Godard[1]

As a medium traditionally associated with the art of telling stories, literature has long been both a major source of inspiration and the main authority to challenge for the younger medium of film. While early cinema readily turned to the classics of literature as sources to adapt and narrative models to emulate, filmmakers and critics of the historical avant-garde sought to define and develop the specificity of the filmic medium outside literary frameworks. They considered both the script and the novel as hindrances to cinema's development of its artistic potential. Thus, the painter and filmmaker Fernand Léger postulated in a 1925 essay:

> The error of painting is the subject. The error of cinema is the scenario. Freed of this negative weight, the cinema can become the gigantic microscope of things never before seen or experienced. [...] Subject, literature, and sentimentality are all negative qualities which weigh down the current cinema.[2]

For Léger and Elie Faure the nature of cinema was not dramatic or psychological, but 'cineplastic' – that is, film was above all concerned with the representation of forms.[3] Other avant-garde theorists such as Léopold Survage drew on music to envisage a cinema in which forms, colours and rhythms can generate emotions. 'Under the influence of experimentalists Walter Ruttman, Hans Richter and Viking Eggeling', Lúcia Nagib explains, 'the adepts of "cinéma pur" proposed to draw exclusively on the techniques inherent in the film medium, such as movement, lighting, contrast, rhythm and [...] montage'.[4] Though not necessarily abstract, 'pure' cinema carved out an alternative path for the medium detached from the strictures of narrative organisation and classic storytelling.

Yet with the advent of sound, the avant-garde's non-narrative conceptions of film quickly lost momentum. The 'sound revolution', writes Richard Abel, 'imposed a different kind of transformation on the French film industry, one that altered the material bases of film production and exhibition, and, in turn, threatened to reorder the very terms of discourse on the cinema'.[5] Replacing theories that focused on cinema's uniquely expressive means, the dominant model for film in the era of the scriptwriters became once more literature, as emphasis shifted back to questions of story and character action. Under the Tradition of Quality that dominated post-war cinema in the 1940s and 1950s, the French film industry found itself not only in the grip of a system that had abdicated creative inventiveness, but also of a practice of adaptation which kept cinema tightly tied to mainly classical literary sources.

Both in the foundational discourses and the cinematic practice of the New Wave, literature is ubiquitous as the model which cinema seeks to live up to or even surpass, the predecessor whose cultural prestige it enlists to valorise film's credentials as art, as well as a rich source of inspiration to be cited, adapted or reworked. If it is true, as T. Jefferson Kline argues in his study of intertextuality in New Wave films, that 'film [. . .] would no longer be the handmaiden of literature, but stand as its rival',[6] the movement's relationship to literature can neither be contained in a psychoanalytical model of repression and return – Kline focuses on the 'conscious and often unconscious relationships that French New Wave filmmakers developed to a constituted-and-then-repressed authority'[7] – nor is it confined to intertextual referencing and reworking of literary texts. Central to a number of seminal texts, frequently referred to in the critical writings of the Young Turks, and omnipresent in New Wave directors' practice, literature is manifestly the single most important interface with which the movement grappled, against which it rubbed up, and which irrigated its shores. As we will see in this chapter, the New Wave's ambivalent relationship to its literary ancestor is inseparably bound up with the notion of the film auteur and the movement's novel attitude to adaptation. Informing New Wave directors' diverse appropriations and refashionings of literary texts and models, it also finds expression in the insertion of written text into the filmic image as a link between literature and cinema.

USURPING THE LITERARY: THE INVENTION OF THE AUTEUR

From its inception in the early twentieth century, French film theory and criticism had hotly debated the role of the director within the wider team of film professionals that contribute to the collective enterprise of filmmaking: was she or he considered to be the author of the filmic oeuvre or merely the *metteur en scène* who translates an already existing text into cinematic language? One of the pioneers of cinema, Georges Méliès, had claimed that the filmmaker 'must be author [scriptwriter], director, designer and often an actor if he wants to obtain a unified whole', but, as Abel notes, 'his essentially auteurist position seems to have fallen into disrepute along with his career'.[8] Most writers of the period considered cinema as essentially a 'new form of theatre', thus contending that the real author of the film is the scriptwriter to whom directors must subordinate themselves.[9] The industry-based model of filmmaking underpinning the post-war Tradition of Quality similarly granted little creative freedom to the director. With scriptwriting delegated to professionals, as Truffaut put it, once the script is submitted, 'the film has already been made'.[10] Far from being the creator of a filmic vision, the filmmaker was reduced to giving visual form to a script. Even legally, in France, the so-called *metteur en scène* (literally 'the one who stages') enjoyed an inferior status compared to the scriptwriter until 1957, when a new law designated directors as co-authors of a film, alongside the author of the script, the adaptation, the dialogue and the music.[11]

It was in reaction to a film industry stifled by a strict separation of labour – most importantly the division between professional scriptwriters and filmmakers – and ossified by an outdated ideal of technical perfection that the New Wave imposed the concept of the auteur as the creator of an individual, highly personal film style. Alexandre Astruc famously paved the way with his manifesto 'The Birth of a New Avant-Garde: La Caméra-Stylo' (1948), which, together with Truffaut's 'A Certain Tendency of French Cinema' (1954), constitutes one of the cornerstones of the French New Wave's 'politics of the authors'. Astruc argues that cinema – previously considered a fairground attraction, a simple distraction or a means of conserving images of the past – is about to become a language: that is, a form as apt at expressing any kind of thought and affect as the essay or the novel. Freed from the tyranny of the visual and the confines of narration that hindered its development, it will 'become a means of writing just as flexible and subtle as written language'.[12] The critic-director predicts that the cinema will soon produce its own masterpieces comparable in depth of reflection to the novels of Faulkner and Malraux or the essays of Sartre and Camus. Indeed, he cites an example of such a development: Malraux's *L'Espoir*, a work in which 'perhaps for the first time ever, film language is the exact equivalent of literary language'.[13] Yet, although the term 'new avant-garde' in his title manifestly harks back to the classical avant-garde of the 1920s, he explicitly rejects surrealism (and what he calls 'abstract films'), which he accuses of merely adapting their experiments in painting and poetry into filmic form. In the same breath, he discards the cinematic specificity to which the classical avant-garde aspired, stating that the new avant-garde, on the contrary, seeks to broaden the domain of cinema, making it 'the most extensive and clearest language there is'.[14]

If prestigious contemporary writers and thinkers trace the horizon of expectation for cinema's future, so does literature more generally provide the metaphorical and conceptual framework for promoting the new avant-garde heralded in Astruc's manifesto. With its cognate figures and terms – the author, writing, language, the pen – the literary bestows authority upon the cinematic. Yet by the same token Astruc undermines the older medium's prestige to make way for what he presents as *the art* of the twentieth century: cinema. Just as he declares the historical avant-garde to be 'already old hat',[15] so literature also is presented as a spent force already superseded by the new art of film. Outdoing Maurice Nadeau's statement that '[i]f Descartes lived today, he would write novels' from an article in the newspaper *Combat*, Astruc wittily paints the picture of Descartes as a filmmaker: 'a Descartes of today would already have shut himself up in his bedroom with a 16mm camera and some film, and would be writing his philosophy on film: for his *Discours de la Méthode* (Discourse on Method) would today be of such a kind that only the cinema could express it satisfactorily'.[16]

Astruc's attitude to both literature and the historical avant-garde is exemplary of a wider double-bind with regard to tradition that characterises New Wave theorising and creative practice. The movement 'combines a simultaneous double move, of claiming traditions while at the same time renouncing those same traditions, a double move directed simultaneously towards literature and the history of cinema', Jean Cléder explains.[17] As prestigious ancestors, literature and the historical avant-garde are enlisted in cinema's struggle for cultural legitimacy, but, by the same token, brushed away to make place for what Astruc terms a 'different and individual kind of filmmaking'.[18] For Astruc, as for Truffaut, who cemented the concept of authorship in his incendiary 'A Certain Tendency of French Cinema' some six years later, the realisation of a new, more personal type of cinema is predicated upon one condition: that directors write their own scripts, that '[d]irection is no longer a means of illustrating or presenting a scene, but a true act of writing'. Extending the literary analogy further, Astruc coins the famous notion of the 'author' creatively engaged in writing: 'The film-maker/author writes with his camera as a writer writes with his pen'.[19]

'Authorship' understood as the signature style of directors who propose a highly personal vision and who shape the filmic process all the way from its inception to post-production, was to become the one defining discourse – not to say the foundational myth – of New Wave filmmaking. Both the ultimate criterion by which to measure a director and a powerful tool in New Wave directors' self-definition, auteurism played a crucial role in cinema's struggle for recognition in a still largely literary culture, while also providing ammunition for the rebellion against the 'scriptwriters' films' of directors like Claude Autant-Lara, Jean Delannoy and Yves Allégret that Truffaut lambasts in his 1954 manifesto. Detracting from the collective, professional nature of cinematic production upheld by the Tradition of Quality, auteurism promoted the author as a singular, indeed, a solitary figure: 'Cinema isn't a trade. It's an art. It's not a team. You're always alone; on-set as before the blank page', proclaimed Godard in a Romantic exultation of the creative act that elevates the director to the status of artist.[20] To compare the act of filmmaking to that of literary writing became a way of asserting the director's artistic independence within a tightly controlled industry with its hierarchies, demand for professional accreditation and aesthetic credos (notably narrative coherence, psychological realism and verisimilitude).

Thus, when Agnès Varda coined the term *cinécriture* (ciné-writing) to describe her work, or when another pioneer of the New Wave, Jean-Daniel Pollet, declared in an interview that he wanted to make *La Ligne de mire* (1960) 'with the same liberty as a writer writing a novel',[21] the literary trope they evoke is a way of signalling their creative investment as directors who not only write their own scripts, but develop a personal style. Varda writes,

> [t]he cutting, the movement, the points-of-view, the rhythm of filming and editing have been felt and considered in the way a writer chooses the depth of meaning of sentences, the type of words, number of adverbs, paragraphs, asides, chapters which advance the story or break its flow, etc. In writing it's called style. In the cinema, style is cinécriture.[22]

Philippe Mary points out that Chabrol, Truffaut and Godard deliberately downplayed the technical aspect of filmmaking to foreground instead the originality, resourcefulness and signature style of the auteur. Pitting the technical mastery of the Tradition of Quality against the freshness of the young cinema, they substituted inspiration for *savoir faire*, creativity for professionalism.[23] Transferring the symbolic capital of literature to the cinema, the 'politics of the authors' not only cemented the concept of the auteur, it served to establish a canon of directors who, like the consecrated literary greats, shape the filmic medium with their personal vision and style. Coined by Truffaut in his polemical article 'Ali Baba and the "politics of auteurs"', which asserted that even the failed work of a great director is still to be defended on grounds of the auteur's genius, the term implies relations of power as well as the capacity to exercise influence.[24] The frequent comparisons between directors and writers in the articles of the Young Turks – Godard, for instance, asserts '[Robert Bresson] is French cinema, the way Dostoevsky is the Russian novel', or 'I am not afraid to grant him [Joseph Mankiewicz] a status just as important as that held by Alberto Moravia in European literature'[25] – were instrumental in this canon formation. Mediated by literature, the promotion of the film auteur, as Godard could declare triumphantly in a 1959 article in *Arts* that I have quoted in the epigraph, secured a place for cinema in the history of art.

Godard's first feature, *À bout de souffle*, as Cléder demonstrates, translates the concept of the auteur into cinematic practice through its extensive use of improvisation that short-circuits the shooting script and, by extension, the literary-based practice that underpins traditional filmmaking.[26] *À bout de souffle*'s title credits do not cite specialist film professionals but Truffaut and Chabrol, that is, two film auteurs, as, respectively, the film's scriptwriter and technical advisor. Yet, as is well known, neither of the two had any extensive involvement in the film (apart from Truffaut signing over his initial idea for the film to Godard). This hoax, then, playfully enthrones Godard as the 'complete author',[27] who, in one person, unites the various functions hitherto assigned to specialised film professionals. The authority of literature as the narrative model for cinema is not only undermined; it is symbolically transferred to film in the scene in which a writer of fiction named Jean Parvulesco is interviewed by a group of journalists, including the female lead Patricia (Jean Seberg). Ironically, the literary author Parvulesco is played by a prominent film auteur, Jean-Pierre Melville, one of the predecessors of the New Wave, who, intriguingly, had adopted his artistic pseudonym in homage to the American novelist Herman Melville. Although Parvulesco responds to the onslaught of questions with remarkable poise and cool, the rapid editing of the scene and Godard's attention to the off-frame space, in the words of Cléder, 'gives him a position that is certainly central in terms of the dialogue, but utterly superfluous and parodistic in terms of the mise-en-scène'.[28] In a parodic enactment of the rivalries between the two media, cinema eclipses the verbal art of literature.

Indeed, for Godard, as he notes in an interview upon being awarded the Prix Jean Vigo in 1960, *À bout de souffle* was proof of the vitality of cinema at a time when its artistic siblings had already become a spent force. When asked by a journalist whether prizes for cinema are important, the director – ever the provocateur – declared: 'Yes because they attract attention to cinema at the expense of other art forms that today I consider less significant, art forms that have breathed their last [*qui sont à bout de souffle*] while cinema hasn't'.[29]

AT THE CROSSROADS OF FILM AND LITERATURE: ADAPTATION NEW WAVE-STYLE

If literature provided the conceptual model and symbolic capital for inventing the film auteur, New Wave theory and practice also had to position itself towards its narrative ancestor with regard to adaptation, a practice that was both the favoured genre of the Tradition of Quality and the privileged territory of the scriptwriter. It is in confrontation with this practice poised between literature and film that the movement developed some of its key aesthetic principles, crystallised in two seminal texts, Bazin's 'For An Impure Cinema: Defense of Adaptation' (1951) and Truffaut's aforementioned 'A Certain Tendency of French Cinema'. Ushering out the classical aesthetics of the Tradition of Quality, these articles – highly divergent though they are in tone and scope – point to a new relationship with literature that no longer confines cinema to its shadow. More broadly, Bazin's article, with its advocacy of an 'impure cinema', can be seen as the manifesto of the New Wave's intermedial aesthetic.

Reflecting on early film criticism's fight for the autonomy of the Seventh Art, Bazin asks himself whether the medium is not now 'in process of becoming an art derived from and dependent on one of the traditional arts'. Can contemporary cinema survive 'without the twin crutches of literature and theatre'?[30] In an intricate meditation on the evolution of the arts inspired by Malraux's *Le Musée imaginaire* (1947), Bazin argues that, as the youngest art, cinema cannot escape the influence of literature, theatre, music and painting.[31] Far from being a sign of its decline, cinema's conquest of the theatrical repertoire and numerous adaptations are, on the contrary, a sign of its maturity: henceforth in full possession of its means of expression, film can do justice to the works it transposes thanks to an intimate knowledge of its own aesthetic structures. If commercial adaptations have a tendency to flatten and vulgarise literature, directors of genius like Jean Renoir remain by contrast true to the spirit of a source text while also remaining completely independent of the original. In opposition to the advocates of a 'pure cinema' who guarded against artistic border crossings, Bazin therefore promotes an 'impure cinema' that enriches itself in contact with the other arts, even though his ultimate goal remains the medium's autonomy:

> While we wait until color or stereoscopy provisionally return its primacy to form and create a new cycle of aesthetic erosion, on the surface cinema has no longer anything to conquer. There remains for it only to irrigate its banks, to insinuate itself between the arts among which it has so swiftly carved out its valleys, subtly to invest them, to infiltrate the subsoil, in order to excavate invisible galleries. [. . .] As it awaits the dialectic of the history of art which will restore it this desirable and hypothetical autonomy, the cinema draws into itself the formidable resources of elaborated subjects amassed around it by neighbouring arts during the course of the centuries. It will make them its own because it has need of them and we experience the desire to rediscover them by way of the cinema . . .[32]

Dealing with more than just the question of adaptation, this complex, meandering article makes an eloquent case for cross-fertilisation between the arts within the broader framework of cinema's struggle for legitimisation and, ultimately, emancipation. Bazin's geological metaphor offers an apposite trope for cinema's conquest of and commerce with the other arts, which it appropriates and makes its own. Yet, cinema, he insists, also offers us the opportunity to rediscover the other arts in filmic form. Hence, intermedial dialogue for him is reciprocal, benefiting all the arts. Bazin further interrogates the dialectic between literature and the cinema at work in adaptation in another fundamental piece, '*Le Journal d'un curé de campagne* and the stylistics of Robert Bresson'. Stressing the creative aspects of adaptation, he argues that it can neither be understood as translation, nor as 'free inspiration with the intention of making a duplicate'. 'In no sense is the film "comparable" to the novel or "worthy" of it. It is a new aesthetic creation, the novel so to speak multiplied by the cinema'.[33]

Centred more narrowly on the adaptive practices of the Tradition of Quality, Truffaut aggressively takes to task its scriptwriters – in particular the influential Jean Aurenche and Pierre Bost – whom he holds responsible for the alleged mediocrity of the majority of 1950s cinematic production. His attack revolves in essence around three points: first, the scriptwriters' profound contempt for cinema, reflected in their search for 'equivalences' between literary and cinematic procedures, a practice which presupposes that cinema is less protean in its means of expression than its literary ancestor; second, Aurenche and Bost's ideological recuperation of their literary sources, notably through additions that convey their own anti-clerical, left-leaning world view; and, third, the scriptwriters' uninspired and formulaic adaptive practice, which turns great literary works into insipid, second-rate films. Opposing directors and scriptwriters, men of the cinema and men of letters (the word 'littérateurs' in the original is a derogatory term, which, unlike 'écrivain', implies writing as a profession), looking to Astruc and the cinematic lineage of Renoir, Bresson, Cocteau, Jacques Becker, Abel Gance, Max Ophuls, Jacques Tati and Roger Leenhardt, Truffaut promotes the film auteur as no longer a mere executor of a filmic script, but the creator of a personal film style. It is noteworthy that at no point in this polemical essay does Truffaut condemn the practice of adaptation as such. Rather, he reclaims the territory of adaptation from its colonisation by professional screenwriters; for him, a good adaptation can only be written by a 'man of the cinema'. Seeking to rescue both cinema and literature from the clutches of professional screenwriters, his vociferous attack on the Tradition of Quality belies a deep love, as well as an impressive knowledge of literature: not only does Truffaut evoke a diverse range of texts from Flaubert to Bernanos via

Gide and Colette, his assessment of Aurenche and Bost's adaptive practice relies on a profound familiarity with literature in addition to a vast knowledge of contemporary cinema.

The New Wave did not turn its back on adaptation as is sometimes hastily assumed;[34] nor did New Wave directors systematically write their own scripts as Astruc and Truffaut advocated, though they remained more involved in the script-writing process and often collaborated closely with their script-writers.[35] And yet, just as it marked a rupture with the script-based, heavily literary-inflected Tradition of Quality, so too did the *Nouvelle Vague* herald a new practice of adaptation that fully exploited the expressive powers (mise-en-scène, editing, lighting, framing, music) of the cinematic medium. Where directors such as Claude Autant-Lara or Jean Delannoy relied on the prestige of literary classics to valorise their films, New Wave filmmakers largely shied away from the French literary canon in their adaptations. It is hardly a coincidence that, when approached by Nicole Stéphane about adapting *In Search of Lost Time*, Truffaut – despite a lifelong love of Proust's novel – first hesitated, but eventually declined. Instead of adapting major works that threatened to eclipse film with their heavy cultural baggage and to stifle directors' creativity, New Wave directors either resorted to original (many of them autobiographically inflected) stories or turned to lesser known, often contemporary writers.

Truffaut's first short, *Les Mistons* (*The Mischief Makers*, 1957), is based on a collection of stories by Maurice Pons, *Virginales*; the film noir pastiche *Tirez sur le pianiste* (*Shoot the Piano Player*, 1960) is adapted from the American David Goodis; *Jules et Jim* (*Jules and Jim*, 1962) reworks Henri-Pierre Roché's little-known eponymous novel, while *Fahrenheit 451* (1966) is transposed from Ray Bradbury's dystopian science fiction and *La Mariée était en noir* (*The Bride Wore Black*, 1968) filmically recasts a crime novel by William Irish. In both *Les Mistons* and *Jules et Jim*, Truffaut uses a voice-over narration that injects the literary voice into the filmic text, thus offering a homage to the adapted authors.[36] Godard, letting himself be inspired more loosely by literary works, draws on Dolores Hitchens's *Fools' Gold* in *Bande à part*; on Beniamino Joppolo's eponymous play in *Les Carabiniers* (*The Carabineers*, 1963); on Lionel White's *Obsession* for *Pierrot le fou* (1965); on the Maupassant novellas *La Femme de Paul* and *Le Signe* for *Masculin féminin* (1966) and *Deux ou trois choses que je sais d'elle* (*Two or Three Things I know about Her*, 1967); and on Julio Cortázar's *The Southern Highway* for *Weekend* (1967). Only *Le Mépris* (*Contempt*, 1963) qualifies as an adaptation in the sense of a clearly identifiable proximity between the source – Alberto Moravia's eponymous novel – and its filmic rewriting; though, as we will see shortly, Godard's interrogation of adaptation in *Le Mépris* is used to affirm the originality of film.

More classical in his literary tastes, Rohmer adapted two early films, *Les Petites filles modèles* (1952, unfinished) and *Bérénice* (1954) from nineteenth-century sources: the children's writer Comtesse de Ségur and Edgar Allan Poe. His six *Contes moraux* are auto-adapted from a series of novellas in the style of Henry James and Stevenson which he wrote after the Liberation.[37] In his preface to the printed version of the texts, Rohmer insists on the marked literariness of his films (enhanced by the use of a narrator), but also on cinema's unique capacity of bringing the written words to life fully: 'They've had a steadfastly literary appearance from the first throw. They and the things they convey – characters, situations, words – needed to affirm their anteriority to mise-en-scène, even though it alone possessed the virtue of making those things come fully into being'.[38]

Where Rohmer deliberately foregrounds the filmic works' literary antecedents, Rivette, by contrast, in his adaptation of the only genuinely canonical work adapted by a New Wave director, Diderot's *La Religieuse*, is eager to efface the origin of both source text and film, giving primacy to the filmic medium as an auto-generating entity: 'the idea [in *La Religieuse*] was not to make an adaptation, rather [the main idea] was that there was no author at all [and] film was something that has already existed [prior to shooting]'.[39]

If the New Wave refuses to be confined to the shadows of literature, for the most *auteurist* of the Young Turks, Godard, the contested terrain of adaptation becomes a battleground of media tensions, played out in *Le Mépris*, his first big-budget film with an international star.[40] Inverting traditional hierarchies between literature and the cinema, the director asserts provocatively that his film constitutes an aesthetic improvement of its literary source, which he contemptuously qualifies as a 'vulgar and pretty airport novel'.[41] Reminiscent of Truffaut's 'A Certain Tendency', *Le Mépris* is an overt attack against the screenwriter embodied by the opportunistic protagonist Paul (Michel Piccoli), who sacrifices his aesthetic ideals – and ultimately his wife – to the Hollywood dream machine, embodied by the brutish producer Prokosch (Jack Palance). In contrast, the figure of the auteur is elevated through the presence of the legendary Fritz Lang, playing himself as a director adapting the *Odyssey*. As the assistant to Lang, Godard, in a cameo role, places himself – and, by extension, the New Wave – in the noble lineage of cinema's greats whilst at the same time usurping the older director's place as it is he who is responsible for the filmic extracts ascribed to Lang, which exhibit a distinctly Godardian aesthetic. The film-within-a-film structure, as in Fellini's *8 1/2* two years earlier, self-reflexively celebrates the cinematic medium through emphasis on filmmaking as a process rather than a product.

As Marie-Claire Ropars-Wuilleumier shows in a brilliant article, *Le Mépris*'s dynamic is based on the principle of rewriting: if Godard cinematically recreates the Moravia text, in the filmic mise-en-abyme Lang rewrites the *Odyssey*, yet his film, shortly before completion, is also rewritten by Paul to satisfy the commercial imperatives of the American producer.[42] If artistic creation is thus presented as a quasi-infinite play of exchanges and transformative re-enactments, the very notion of originality is called into question. The impossibility of distinguishing between copy and original is hinted at through Lang's status as actor who *plays* a director, as well as through the multi-lingual exchanges at Cinecittà where words uttered in one language are instantly substituted for another. No longer an attempt at faithfully reproducing a source, translation becomes itself original in the numerous instances where the producer's assistant Francesca (Giorgia Moll) mistranslates, censors or adapts, whilst Lang's citations of Dante in German, or Paul's of Brecht in French further destabilise the concept of original source. The simulacrum, Ropars-Wuilleumier explains, becomes the very motor of the film: 'Itself conceived as a simulation, adaptation will serve as a boomerang to establish the film by establishing the simulacrum as the generating principle of the filmic work'.[43] Displacing the origin of art into an incessant channel of recycling – five years before Roland Barthes's 'The Death of the Author' – Godard does away with any literary authority that might debase cinema to the status of a derivative waste product. Taken as an opportunity for affirming the filmic medium and asserting its expressive powers, adaptation – no longer an imitative practice in the service of canonical literature – becomes proof of cinema's creativity and modernity.

Cross-fertilisations at the Vanguard: New Novel/New Cinema

If the Young Turks heralded a new practice of adaptation, it fell to a director of the Left Bank group, Alain Resnais, to align filmic with literary modernity through collaboration with some of the most innovative writers of his time. Having previously worked with Paul Éluard on the short *Guernica* (1950), with Jean Cayrol on his acclaimed Holocaust documentary *Nuit et brouillard* (*Night and Fog*, 1955) and with Raymond Queneau on the commercial short *Le Chant du styrène* (1958) (for all three films, the writers wrote the voice-over commentaries), Resnais opened a new chapter in the relations between literature and film with *Hiroshima mon amour*, based on a screenplay by Marguerite Duras, a writer who had established herself as one of the most original, highly personal voices of contemporary literature. Premiered at Cannes the same year as Truffaut's *Les Quatre cents coups* and Marcel Camus's *Orfeu Negro*, *Hiroshima* became one of the figureheads of the New Cinema of the late 1950s as well as a trailblazer for a modernist film language defiant of the classical dogma of narrative coherence and character psychology. While it would be beyond the scope of this book to discuss the relationship between the *Nouveau roman* (New Novel) and the *Nouvelle Vague* in any detail (it has already been examined extensively by critics such as Ostrowska, Murcia and Stam),[44] it is worth revisiting Resnais's collaboration with Duras, and, two years later, with Alain Robbe-Grillet, as crucial examples of a 'literary cinema' in which literature and film are treated as equals. The underlying principles that have shaped the two films will then be contrasted with the *Cahiers* critics' reception of *Hiroshima*, which once more throws up the discursive tensions between literature and film that interest us here.

Pierre Kast comments in a 1959 *Cahiers du cinéma* round-table discussion of *Hiroshima mon amour* that Resnais's and Duras's collaboration was grounded in a mutual esteem for each other's art: 'Resnais didn't ask Marguerite Duras for a piece of second-rate literary work meant to be 'turned into a film', and conversely she didn't suppose for a second that what she had to say, to write, might be beyond the scope of the cinema'.[45] Both here and in the later *L'Année dernière à Marienbad* (*Last Year at Marienbad*, 1961) – made in collaboration with Alain Robbe-Grillet, the leader and theorist of the *Nouveau roman* movement – the director and his collaborating authors worked unburdened by any implied hierarchies or hegemonic tensions between the respective media. Stam lucidly sums up what was at stake in *L'Année dernière à Marienbad* (and the same could be said about the partnership between director and writer in *Hiroshima mon amour*). The film, he asserts, constitutes a 'collaborative effort by two artists trying to instantiate their vision of a radically modernist art, while still respecting the specific traits and potentialities of their respective media'.[46]

Duras's and Robbe-Grillet's dismantling of the linear plots of traditional novels, together with their questioning of stable characterisation and psychological coherence, not forgetting their emphasis on the fluid, subjective time of memory and fantasy, allowed Resnais to import into cinema the modernist features of some of the most avant-garde writing of the period. It is important to note here that the *Nouveau roman* movement spearheaded by Robbe-Grillet did itself hark back to the modernist experiments of authors such as Proust, Faulkner, Dos Passos, Joyce and Kafka who, some thirty years earlier, had abandoned realist narrative models in favour of a new type of writing acutely attentive to mental phenomena of consciousness. Similarly, the New Cinema of the late 1950s, propelled forward by Resnais, gave a new lease of life to the historical avant-garde's quest for new filmic forms outside the constraints of traditional realist narrative. Tellingly, when Rohmer, in the *Cahiers du cinéma* round-table discussion, asks whether Resnais will be remembered as 'the first modern filmmaker of the sound film', he is quick to qualify this epithet, reminding his colleagues of the great modern directors of the silent period (he mentions Eisenstein, the Expressionists and Dreyer), and insisting on the altogether more classical, conservative nature of sound as opposed to silent film.

Both *Hiroshima mon amour* and *L'Année dernière à Marienbad* can be qualified as 'literary' films, not only because their screenplays were written by renowned authors of fiction, but because of the uninhibitedly literary inflections of the dialogues and voice-over and of their narrative complexity. 'Literary film', a quintessentially French genre, Francis Vanoye explains, is characterised by:

> the presence of a very written text, given to read or to be understood according to a mode of reading deliberately sophisticated, not to say ostentatious, as well as complex narrative forms. [. . .] But cinematic writing concedes nothing to the literary, in these works, and it is this which ensures this textual doubling that to us seems to typify the genre[47]

In the wake of Robert Bresson, a filmmaker who exercised a great influence on the New Wave, Resnais opts for a Brechtian, non-naturalistic approach to speech. The theatrical style of delivery in *Hiroshima* or, in contrast, the flattened-out, monotonous dialogues in *Marienbad* preclude any passive absorption in the filmic illusion, encouraging viewers to engage with the filmic world on screen at a deeper, more reflective, level. Resnais's extensive use of voice-over – a technique habitually considered as un-cinematic – emphatically ties the filmic works to their origins as literary texts, while the often disjunctive relation of sound and image reminds us of the coexistence between two different media (one verbal, the other audio-visual). The fact that the screenplays for the films were published by their authors (Robbe-Grillet published his script as a *ciné-roman* simultaneously with the release of the film; Duras published her screenplay in 1960) draws attention to their autonomy as literary objects, yet also signals the hybrid nature of both the films and their underlying texts. The original edition of *L'Année dernière à Marienbad* was illustrated by forty-eight still photographs from the film, signalling the interconnectedness between the two works.

How then was *Hiroshima*, this landmark of the New Wave, received by the *Cahiers* critics; or rather, how did they deal with its hybrid status as 'literary cinema'? It is interesting to note that in a previous *Cahiers du cinéma* roundtable discussion on the state of contemporary cinema, in 1957, Rivette had categorically warned against cinema following the path of literature:

> The only possibility that the cinema has of doing something important [. . .] is in *not* following literature, whether it's the literature of fifty or fifteen years ago. [. . .] But it's not a question of following the literature of a few years ago. It's perhaps not even a question of trying to keep up with new literature: the real function of the cinema should be to go further than literature.[48]

Two years later, in the aforementioned follow-up roundtable focused on *Hiroshima*, Godard declares provocatively that *Hiroshima* is literature; but he is instantly reminded of the compromised relations between literature and cinema by Pierre Kast: 'literary people have a kind of confused contempt for the cinema, and film people suffer from a confused feeling of inferiority'.[49] In the course of the discussion, *Hiroshima* is singled out as an exception, since neither Resnais nor Duras distinguished between literary expression and cinematic creation. In other words, this hybrid film at the crossroads of literature and cinema is considered a work that transcends traditional notions of medium specificity. But very quickly medium specificity and media tensions come back into the debate. After asserting that Resnais has achieved something which, hitherto, was considered to be the strict domain of literature, Godard challenges contemporary literary production by declaring that the director has written the novel 'that the young French novelists are all trying to write, people like Butor, Robbe-Grillet, Bastide and of course Marguerite Duras'.[50] Not only is authority shifted once more from the literary author to the film auteur (significantly, in the process, the film is labelled as 'novel'); in a discursive tour de force, *Hiroshima* is heralded as the cinematic avant-garde work that paved the way for avant-garde writing. Rohmer, who had forcefully argued cinema's superiority over the other arts in the second half of the twentieth century in his series of articles 'Le Celluloïd et le marbre', brings the point home:

> To sum up, it is no longer a reproach to say that this film is literary, since it happens that *Hiroshima* moves not in the wake of literature but well in advance of it. There are certainly specific influences: Proust, Joyce, the Americans, but they are assimilated as they would be by a young novelist writing his first novel, a first novel that would be an event, a date to be accorded significance, because it would mark a step forward.[51]

As Rivette had demanded in the first roundtable, cinema gets ahead of literature; though, ironically, in the exercise of inverting traditional hierarchies, the film's literary origin – that is, Duras's screenplay – is swept under the carpet . . .

To what extent Resnais's cinematic experiments did indeed prove influential for the literature to come must remain open to debate. What is undeniable, however, is that, just as the classical avant-garde had attracted writers such as Benjamin Fondane, Blaise Cendrars and Philippe Soupault, who crossed over into filmmaking, so too in the course of the 1960s and 1970s did some of France's most original writers – Duras, Robbe-Grillet, Georges Perec – take to the camera after writing filmscripts. While the New Wave fractured and fizzled out post-1968, these amphibian writer-directors carved out a niche in the margins of mainstream cinema with their small-budget, formally innovative films. As for *L'Année dernière à Marienbad*, it was recycled as a cinephile reference in Truffaut's *Domicile conjugal* (*Bed and Board*, 1970) where a strange neighbour, nicknamed 'the Strangler', troubles the lives of Antoine (Jean-Pierre Léaud) and his wife Christine (Claude Jade), until, one evening, they see him performing a comic spoof of *Marienbad* on television. As is implied in this mise-en-abyme pitting the big screen against the small screen, cinema – once the belittled newcomer among the arts – henceforth faced another rival: television as the new popular medium of mass culture.

RHIZOMATIC INTERTEXTUALITIES: BALZAC *AVANT TOUTE CHOSE*

Famous for its cinephile references to other films, New Wave cinema equally abounds in literary citations – some fully acknowledged, others more tacit and subterranean – which form a vast network of allusions, quotes, borrowings and rewritings that attest to New Wave directors' grounding in and passion for the literary medium. Indeed – perhaps paradoxically, as Serge Daney points out – as film emancipates itself from its ancestor literature, the written not only resurfaces in the film text, but becomes one of the movement's defining characteristics: 'At a time when the young filmmakers seem proud to no longer confuse cinema and literature, image and writing, film and book, the importance of the written word among all the people of the "new wave" appears, with hindsight, as their strength and uniqueness.'[52] It is of course Godard who is best known for his extensive use of literary citations in his films, from the ludic Aragon and Apollinaire montage in *À bout de souffle*, to the sustained Malrauxian intertext that nourishes the political intrigue in *Le Petit Soldat* (*The Little Soldier*, 1963); the cinematic homage to Rimbaud in *Bande à part* and *Pierrot le fou*; Fritz Lang's recital of a Hölderlin poem in *Le Mépris*; not to mention the literary subtexts in *Une femme est une femme* (*A Woman is a Woman*, 1961) and *Alphaville* (1965) plus a raft of other allusions, (mis)quotations, unacknowledged citations and rewritings that make his films a repository of literary culture.[53] Susan Sontag observes:

> from the numerous references to books, mentions of writers' names, and quotations and longer excerpts from literary texts scattered throughout his films, Godard gives the impression of being engaged in an unending agon with the very fact of literature – which he attempts to settle partially by incorporating literature and literary identities into his films.[54]

If the director never published a novel with Gallimard, as was his early ambition,[55] he invented a new type of cinema in the lineage of Proust, Joyce and Faulkner, suffused with and in constant dialogue with literature. Broken down into fragments, the materials of literature are assimilated into the intermedial fabric of Godard's films. Georges Didi-Huberman, in a wider study of Godard's citational practice as a summoning and taking to trial of the past, argues that citations are 're-authorised' only to be 're-authorised' by the filmmaker-auteur, who asserts his position of authority by putting them into relation with a much broader body of knowledge that circulates freely in his films.[56] Citation in Godard's films is an act of admiration, but it also involves a degree of rivalry; indeed, it is driven by a desire to surpass the literary medium it invokes. The scene in *Pierrot le fou* in which Ferdinand (Jean-Paul Belmondo) dreams of a new form of writing – one that inserts itself into the tradition of the modernist novel but goes even further in its capturing of 'life itself' – is emblematic of a wider vying for the preeminence of cinematic expression. Godard, Sontag asserts, is speaking 'for himself as a filmmaker, and he appears confident that film can accomplish what literature cannot'[57] through his male protagonist's monologue: 'I've found an idea for a novel. I won't describe people's lives, but life itself, just life. Everything that takes place between people: space, sounds and colours. It should be possible. Joyce tried to do it, but I should be able to improve on him.'

Rohmer, compared to Godard, was less given to citation and more conservative in his artistic tastes (in the series of articles 'Le Celluloïd et le marbre', he strikes a deliberately anti-modernist pose, mischievously accentuated in a follow-up interview with Noël Herpe and Philippe Fauvel in 2009). Yet he too engaged in a sustained dialogue with literature in his filmic oeuvre. Together with Chris Marker, who similarly wrote a novel before becoming a filmmaker, Rohmer holds a particular position in that he crossed over into cinema after making his artistic debut with a novel in the tradition of Gide and American behaviourism, *Elisabeth* (1946). Trained in the classical literary tradition, but with an interest in the modernist works of Proust, Faulkner and Céline and not insensitive to the experiments of the *Nouveau roman*, Rohmer's literary tastes vacillated between classicism and modernity.[58] Heavily inflected by the literary – most evident in *Ma nuit chez Maud* with its Pascalian intertext, but also, in his later career, in his adaptations of Chrétien de Troyes, Kleist, Grace Elliott and Honoré d'Urfé – Rohmer's characters famously 'speak like books', the intricacy and intellectual depth of their conversations aligning his dialogues with written rather than oral forms of expression. The director himself, drawing attention to his characters' propensity for auto-analysis, places his films, in particular the six *Contes moraux*, in the tradition of seventeenth-century French 'moraliste writing':

> From a literary perspective, the moralist is he who formerly studied morals and characters. Seen from this angle, my films treat certain states of the soul.

> My *Contes moraux* are the story of characters who like to analyse their thoughts and state of mind.[59]

Coupling cinephilia with an avid passion for books, Truffaut in essence considered writing and filmmaking to be interchangeable activities. While the story of his life remained unwritten, he imagined himself as a writer of autofiction through his filmic alter egos Antoine Doisnel (Jean-Pierre Léaud) and Bertrand Morane (Charles Denner): in *L'Amour en fuite* (*Love on the Run*, 1979), the former has a certain success with an autobiographical novel, *Les Salades de l'amour*, and prepares another book based on his relationship with Sabine (Dorothée); in *L'Homme qui aimait les femmes* (*The Man Who Loved Women*, 1977), the latter is shown penning the story of his love life which forms the basis of the film – a mirroring device also employed in *L'Histoire d'Adèle H.* (*The Story of Adele H.*, 1975). Other characters like Dr Itard (played by Truffaut), who keeps a scientific logbook based on his educational experiment with the 'wild child' in *L'Enfant Sauvage* (*The Wild Child*, 1970), or Claude (Jean-Pierre Léaud), who appropriates Muriel's intimate diary in *Les Deux Anglaises et le continent* (*Two English Girls*, 1971), are filmed in the process of writing.[60] More generally, in Truffaut's films – as indeed in those of Rohmer, Godard, Rivette and Chabrol – characters can often be seen buying books, reading, writing or discussing literature: their bookishness summons the literary medium from within the filmic text.

If a shared passion for literature links the Young Turks, one author in particular reappears in their theoretical writings and filmic works: Balzac, the very author against whom *Nouveau roman* writers positioned themselves and who, in critical discourses of the 1950s and 1960s, was considered the epitome of an outmoded narrative tradition. In his article 'De la métaphore' from the 'Le Celluloïd et le marbre' series, Rohmer pits the ingenious storyteller of the nineteenth century against contemporary authors whose predilection for technical language and abstraction he denounces as a cul-de-sac for modern literature.[61] As Rohmer's declared writer of choice,[62] Balzac inspired the overall organisation of the director's work into cycles (the *Contes moraux*, *Comédies et proverbes* and *Contes des quatre saisons*) that were modelled after the *Comédie humaine*.[63] More explicit intertextual references to Balzac punctuate films by Chabrol, Godard, Truffaut and Rivette; though, as we will see, each filmmaker engages with the author in a highly personal way that is to a certain extent emblematic of their positioning towards tradition and modernity.

Chabrol's second film, *Les Cousins* (1959), inserts itself in the narrative tradition of the nineteenth-century *Bildungsroman* à la Balzac, with its trajectory of a naive young man from the provinces freshly arrived in Paris to study law, but whose hopes and ideals will soon be crushed. As Godard remarked wittily in a preview, the film extends the writer's multi-volume opus, 'adding an unpublished chapter to the *Comédie humaine*. Indeed, we can see Rubempré living with Rastignac.'[64] Balzac as the literary model underpinning the narrative is referenced in the scene in which the librarian (Guy Decomble) offers the sensitive law student Charles (Gérard Blain) – a twentieth-century filmic alter ego of Balzac's Lucien de Rubempré – a copy of *Les Illusions perdues* as if to warn him of his impending destiny.[65] Largely classical in terms of his narrative construction and film language, excelling above all in the dissection of bourgeois mores that would become his trademark, Chabrol thus explicitly positions himself as a heir to the nineteenth-century novelist to whom he owes the nickname the 'Balzac of the cinema'.[66]

Frequently referenced in Godard's critical writings during the *Cahiers* years alongside Dostoevsky, Racine, Aragon and other authors, Balzac also makes an appearance in *Pierrot le fou* – a film that is the stylistic opposite of *Les Cousins* – among a wealth of other literary, pictorial and philosophical citations. In light of the film's radical deconstruction of narrative models borrowed from the realist novel – manifest in its subversion of linear plot, notably in its playful use of chapters arranged in non-chronological order – any reference to the author of the *Comédie humaine* may seem of necessity ironic. Yet rather than assigning him the role of an anti-model, Godard – not devoid of a certain nostalgia – showcases Balzac's hidden riches with a narrative aside. Irritated that a friend uses the number '225' instead of 'Balzac' to make a phone call, Ferdinand (Jean-Paul Belmondo) bursts out: 'Haven't you read Balzac? How about César Birotteau and the 5th Symphony resounding in his head?' On a superficial level, the allusion to this little-known novel sets the imaginative, artistically minded Ferdinand apart from his materialistic wife and her social set, while announcing his tragic end (aurally reinforced through the premonitory musical motif that follows the literary reference). On a deeper artistic level, the incorporation of a literary intertext that itself ekphrastically summons another art – in *César Birotteau*, Balzac at length describes the eponymous character's emotions at hearing Beethoven's Fifth Symphony – draws attention to the intermediality at play in this polyphonic film, where cinema incessantly remediates other art forms. Balzac is summoned a second time shortly before Ferdinand's suicide when the protagonist scorns the switchboard operator: 'You've forgotten who Balzac is too?' Threatened by oblivion in the rational world of modern communications – one of Godard's major thematic concerns that will be explored in *Alphaville* – it falls to cinema to keep literature alive through quotation and incorporation.

More intimately personal is the homage to Balzac that Truffaut makes in his autobiographically inspired *Les Quatre cents coups*, in which we see the rebellious Antoine (Jean-Pierre Léaud) relishing his reading of *La Recherche de l'absolu*, a novel about the conflict between personal passion and responsibility. A shot of the cigarette-smoking adolescent engrossed in the book, accompanied by the novel's ending spoken in voice-over by Truffaut, evokes the director's own impassioned discovery of Balzac as a child. The camera lingers on the last page of the book before cutting to a close-up of the boy's enchanted face. Reading here not only has the power to entrance; it becomes a vital means of subtracting the child from a family environment that offers little love or affection. The world of books serves as a sanctuary and quite literally becomes a chapel where the boy can worship the powers of the imagination, even if the candle he lights for Balzac only further ignites existing family feuds. Philippe Mary reads Antoine's rewriting of Balzac in a class exam and subsequent accusation of plagiarism by his teacher as an expression of Truffaut's cultural complex towards a dominant culture that he conquered as an autodidact.[67] But, beyond the conflict with regard to what Mary calls 'legitimate culture', the plagiarism scene, I would argue, also asks wider questions about influence and originality.

Antoine has not strictly speaking plagiarised Balzac: he unconsciously reworks the novel he has read the night before. But is this inadvertent rewriting not also a form of inauthenticity? The process of borrowing and appropriation that is at stake here throws into relief the issue of originality that was central to an auteur like Truffaut: how do artists find their own language among the numerous art works that have nourished their imagination? Does the process of artistic emancipation necessarily imply burning one's former heroes, in just the way that Antoine – albeit unwittingly – sets ablaze his Balzac altar? Revealingly, the fire metaphor resurfaces in the allusion to Rivette's *Paris nous appartient* (*Paris Belongs to Us*, 1961) (in reality only released two years later), which the family, in one of their happier moments, go to see:

Figure 1.1 Antoine Doinel's (Jean-Pierre Léaud) Balzac chapel in *Les Quatre cents coups* (François Truffaut, 1959).

'but the Gaumont Theatre doesn't like arsonists', comments the stepfather in a cinephilic pun that links Antoine's burning of the Balzac chapel to the subversive posture of New Wave filmmaking. The Balzacian intertext suggests that evolution in the arts – predicated upon the assimilation and reworking of earlier works – also necessitates symbolic acts of rupture to make way for the new, setting ablaze cinematic tradition as well as burning down literary models.

Balzac also informs the themes of Truffaut's third film, *La Peau douce* (*The Soft Skin*, 1963), a melodramatic story of adultery revolving around the critic and publisher Pierre Lachenay (Jean Dessailly), a renowned authority on the novelist. The topic of one of Lachenay's papers, 'Balzac and money' – though indeed a central theme in the *Comédie humaine* – speaks volumes about the different sensibility of the artistically minded but emotionally deprived adolescent drawn to 'the quest of the absolute' in *Les Quatre cents coups* and the well-heeled man who has made a profession of criticism and publishing without, however, accessing the status of a genuine author.

Widely referenced in the films of the Young Turks, Balzac plays a particularly prominent and sustained role in the filmic work of the most enigmatic of the group, Rivette.[68] According to his own testimony, the director was spurred to read Balzac by Rohmer, but was at first put off by the author's famously detailed descriptions.[69] He eventually adapted two Balzac novellas, *Le Chef-d'œuvre inconnu* (freely transposed to *La Belle noiseuse*, 1991) and *La Duchesse de Langeais* (in *Ne touchez pas à la hache*, 2007). Some twenty years before these explicit reworkings, Rivette embarked on a more loose intertextual play with Balzac in his prodigious film experiment *Out 1*. It is worth dwelling a little on this project, which, in the words of Rohmer, constitutes 'a monument in the history of modern cinema and an important milestone for cinematography'.[70] The film was shot during six weeks in the spring of 1970, relying largely on improvisation. In the absence of any preliminary script or dialogues, actors were invited to invent and shape their characters in a collective creative act. Although *Out 1* was part of a longer tradition of improvised filmmaking, Rohmer explains that it was the only film where the technique has been used so systematically, without any safety net. Rivette himself acknowledges his debt to Rouch's *Petit à petit*, a film similarly based on improvisation, which he saw in an eleven-hour rough cut in July 1969. The director and his actors developed the parts in casual conversations over several weeks. Shortly before the start of production, Rivette and the screenwriter Suzanne Schiffman devised a diagram setting out the meetings between characters in the course of the film. Their encounters, they decided, were going to be linked by the parallel stories of two young people, Colin (Jean-Pierre Léaud) and Frédérique (Juliet Berto) who, without knowing one another, get embroiled in the workings of a mysterious group inspired by Balzac's *Histoire des Treize*.

One of the legendary 'films maudits' of the twentieth century, the film exists in two versions: a thirteen-hour rough cut (broken down into eight episodes) called *Out 1: Noli me tangere*, destined for television; and a four-and-a-half-hour edited 'short' version for the cinema, *Out 1: Spectre*. Shown once in Le Havre in 1971, the long version was out of circulation for some twenty years until German television allowed Rivette to restore and complete the film in 1990. While the long version is divided into episodes, the shorter one is intended as a 'cinema block' to be seen in one sitting. It essentially preserves the same plot in more condensed form, though several events have been changed and the order of scenes is not always the same. My reading is based on *Out 1: Noli me tangere*.

The film's fictional plot takes off when Colin receives three cryptic messages, including a text that he will decode as an allusion to Lewis Carroll's *The Hunting of the Snark* and Balzac's *Histoire des Treize*. In the meantime, we hear about a mysterious group, one of whose members, Igor, has disappeared, leaving, in the words of one of the characters, 'the remaining twelve'. Convinced that Paris is in the grip of a secret society modelled after Balzac's *treize*, Colin consults a Balzac specialist, played by none other than Rohmer in the cameo role of an erudite, albeit somewhat pedantic, professor. Amusing as it is in its ironic self-representation of the man of letters (Rohmer started out as a secondary school teacher and later lectured at the Sorbonne), the scene with the literary scholar also highlights the film's underlying mise-en-abyme. Asked about the role of the *treize* for Balzac's *Comédie humaine*, the professor explains that they have a crucial narrative function in nourishing the intrigue and propelling it towards its conclusion. As will become evident in the course of the film, this is precisely the role the *Histoire des Treize* (of which Rivette, according to his own account, only knew the preface)[71] plays in *Out 1*, where it motivates the comings and goings of the characters, providing a loose narrative thread for the actors' improvisations. As the subterranean link in an otherwise fragmented and organically evolving film, the Balzac intertext sets the characters in motion, keeping the labyrinthine narrative afloat.

When questioned about Balzac's indebtedness to real-life events and about the possible existence of a secret organisation modelled after the *treize* in modern-day Paris, the professor exercises caution, urging Colin to re-read Balzac. As in *Les Quatre cents coups*, the question of influence is thus once again raised, but deferred in a boomerang-style argument that returns to its source: the text. A different interpretative grid is opened up when the professor cites a passage from Balzac's *L'Envers de l'histoire contemporaine* evoking a group that is organised like *les treize*, but committed to a good cause. Could

Figure 1.2 Colin (Jean-Pierre Léaud) decrypting the literary riddle in *Out 1* (Jacques Rivette, 1971).

the modern-day *treize* in the filmic fiction, who count several artists among their members, be just such a 'conspiracy for good'? Such a reverse reading in tune with the title of the new Balzac source (*The Reverse of Contemporary History*) proves all the more productive if we consider that the *Cahiers* critics compared themselves to a secret society.[72] Are the *treize* in *Out 1* an allegory for the Young Turks and their colleagues at *Cahiers du cinéma*? Rivette himself points in this direction in an interview with German television, explaining that the film engages with the aftermath of May 1968 and, in particular, with the fracturing of the *Cahiers* group.[73]

The message Colin receives takes the form of a literary riddle: it is composed of ten verses, alternating heptasyllabic and octosyllabic lines. By decomposing and recomposing the text, and through analysis of its poetic form, the young man realises that the first words of the uneven lines form an address, 2 Place Sainte Opportune, where he finds a shop tellingly named 'L'Angle du hasard'. With its Surrealist overtones, 'Chance corner' is emblematic of the crisscrossing narratives, chance encounters and unexpected twists in *Out 1* that testify to the director's absurdist vision of a universe devoid of reason or order. It is here that Colin meets Pauline/Émilie (Bulle Ogier), whose double name inspired by the characters from Corneille's *Polyeucte* and *Cinna* intertextually associate her with unrequited love and political complots. But unlike a Cornelian drama or a Balzacian novel, the filmic plot simply fizzles out without any attempt at a narrative resolution. The love-struck Colin eventually abandons his quest, considering that the *treize* were a mere adolescent fantasy; the less fortunate Frédérique is killed while attempting to save one of the members of the group.

But who, then, are the *treize* and what was their goal? As in the earlier *Paris nous appartient*, another complot story revolving around a theatre rehearsal, the film refuses any answers to the questions it raises. In sharp contrast to the nineteenth-century realist novel with its causality-driven plots and – to use a term from Barthes – its 'prattle of meaning', Rivette's film remains steeped in mystery as reality dissolves into a paranoid vision. Ironically, Balzac, the epitome of what Barthes, in his own assessment of literary tradition and modernity, *S/Z*, terms the 'readerly' text – that is, the sort of works in which 'everything holds together [. . .] with a kind of logical "paste"'[74] – serves as the catalyst of a film that eschews causality and closure. Revisited and cinematically rewritten by Rivette, the largely classical assembly of texts regrouped in *Histoire des Treize* provides the loose narrative thread that makes the bold experiment of total filmic improvisation possible.

LITERATURE AS SALVATION: *ALPHAVILLE* AND *FAHRENHEIT 451*

If literature is omnipresent in New Wave cinema as a source, reference, narrative catalyst or tacit subtext, the movement also produced two of the most impassioned homages to the literary medium in cinematic form: Godard's *Alphaville* and Truffaut's *Fahrenheit 451*, released within a year of each other. In the footsteps of Marker, who had given a highly artistic twist on science fiction films with his medium-defying 'photo-novel' *La Jetée* (1962) – of which more in Chapter 5 – the two directors recast the futurism of science fiction in a contemporary setting. Situated in an undefined future in which artistic expression has been banned and emotional experience and the ability to think critically have been all but effaced, *Alphaville* and *Fahrenheit 451* are dystopias in the tradition of Huxley, Orwell and Zamyatin. *Fahrenheit 451*, Truffaut's only English-language film, was adapted from Ray Bradbury's eponymous dystopian novel written during the McCarthy era, while *Alphaville* was written by Godard himself, inspired by Cocteau's *Orphée* (1950). Beyond their grounding in a specific genre and artistic heritage revitalised through the personal vision of the film auteur, what links these stylistically divergent films on a thematic level is their fervent advocacy of literature as a tool of resistance against totalitarianism. As we will see, each director will define his own way of incorporating and reworking, dismantling and reassembling the literary text in filmic terms.

In the stylish *Alphaville*, Godard transports Eddie Constantine, popular star of the Lemmy Caution French detective series, to an outer-space galaxy masterminded by a computer, Alpha 60. Rather than drawing on the futuristic props and sets habitually used in science fiction filmmaking, in true New Wave fashion, Godard constructs the galaxy's capital out of the urban landscape of contemporary Paris and its rapidly developing suburbs. The glass-fronted high rises with their vast, minimally furnished vestibules, lengthily scrutinised by the camera, in conjunction with the strict geometrical pattern of Haussmannian boulevards, provide a fitting setting for a city of the future in the grip of a regime committed to the principles of logic and efficiency. Thanks to fast film stock, cinematographer Raoul Coutard was able to shoot at night without any special lighting devices, creating a melancholy cityscape where the liquid, hazy exteriors are made to contrast with the brightly lit interiors of modernist buildings in a wider confrontation between light and darkness that informs the film's central theme of thought control and surveillance. In Alphaville, human emotions, as well as the language to express them, have been banned, together with artistic creativity and independent thinking. Strongly reminiscent of Nazi terror and Stalinist repression – evoked through a wealth of references ranging from the sign 'SS' on the elevator buttons to the regime's five-year plans – dissenters are eliminated in show-style public executions, electrocuted in specially equipped movie theatres, or, at best, re-educated in ironically named HLMs (glossed as 'Hôpitaux de la longue maladie' instead of 'Habitation à loyer modéré', that is, France's rent-controlled housing schemes). The few remaining artists live in insalubrious ghettos, in permanent fear for their lives. Language is reduced to pure functionality, the regime's 'Bible' – in fact a dictionary of permitted terms – being regularly updated to replace words that convey feeling or thought with technical terminology.

Alphaville catalyses Godard's anxieties about the technocratic turn of Western societies while playing out his broader concerns with language and communication as well as his interest in semiotics, explored further in *Deux ou trois choses que je sais d'elle*. Intriguingly, he had offered Roland Barthes the part of Professor von Braun – the scientist who keeps control over the dehumanised city – but the semiotician declined, because (according to the director) 'he was afraid of being made to appear ridiculous'.[75] For Godard, the antidote against the sterile functionalism of a technological society lies in the medium that creatively shapes and reinvents language: literature. As a visitor from the 'outer countries' (i.e. earth), Lemmy Caution is from the outset associated with a cultural heritage that the forces of darkness led by von Braun (aka Leonard Nosferatu) are seeking to eradicate. As Allen Thiher puts it, Lemmy is 'another of Godard's characters who carry a heavy valise full of the debris of past culture and who never hesitate to pull out the famous quote when necessary'.[76] Citing Pascal, Nietzsche and Bergson and referencing Borges and

Céline, he is aligned with a prestigious tradition of writers who shaped modern consciousness, or, in the case of the latter, who revolutionised literary writing with his use of slang, ellipsis and parataxis. In a typically Godardian mix of high and low culture, the straight-talking, fast-shooting detective doubles as a figure of cultural memory whose capacity to connect to the ideas and writings of the past contrasts sharply with the amnesia that threatens Alphaville. For, as is widespread practice in totalitarian regimes, the powers that control the city seek to erase all traces of former civilisations: 'Before us, there was nothing here. No one', Alpha 60 proclaims in a lecture in the Institute for General Semantics. 'The meaning of words and of expressions is no longer understood.' Deleted from dictionaries and sanctioned by punishment, affective words such as 'tenderness' or 'crying', by dint of no longer being spoken, lose their meaning. With their disappearance, the emotions they used to describe are gradually eroded: deprived of the language to express feelings, the citizens of Alphaville are conditioned into thoughtless functionality.

How to save this robotic humanity alienated from itself, if not through language? On his death bed, fellow agent Henri Dickson (Akim Tamiroff) bequeaths Lemmy a copy of Paul Éluard's 1926 collection of poems *Capitale de la douleur* together with a cryptic message on how to destroy Alpha 60. Poetry – as the genre associated with a particularly expressive, often metaphorical use of language; and Surrealist poetry in particular with its refusal of logic, its incongruous combinations of words and images and its celebration of dreams and the unconscious – is enlisted as the key weapon against a system that cannot tolerate irrationality. It is easy to see why Godard should have chosen this particular work as the iconic text of salvation in his futuristic fable: with its evocative title, *Capitale de la douleur* instantly resonates with the theme of a city in the grip of state terror, while also articulating a more intimate, personal drama that was alluded to in the collection's original title, *L'Art d'être malheureux* (*The Art of Being Unhappy*). Éluard's anguished poems, inspired by his passion for his wife Gala whom he was afraid of losing (she eventually left him to live with Salvador Dalí whom she married in 1934), resonated with Godard's feelings for Anna Karina, whom he divorced in 1965, but whose love he hoped to rekindle during the making of the film. But, just as importantly, Éluard as a famous Resistance poet – thousands of copies of his poem 'Liberté' were parachuted by Royal Air Force planes over French soil in 1942, making it one of the best remembered symbols of French opposition against the German occupation – comes to embody the struggle against an oppressive regime with overtly fascist overtones. Godard himself recalled the effect that discovering Éluard's 'Liberté' and poems from Aragon's *Crève-coeur* at school had on him: 'these resistance fighters resisting with language were an enormous discovery for me'.[77]

In the film's central sequence, Lemmy has Natacha read extracts from *Capitale de la douleur* in an attempt to make her recover her memory and reconnect with her feelings through poetry. Karina's marked accent in French, combined with her slow delivery and skipping between poems, further accentuate the inherent strangeness of Éluard's work. In a close-up on a page from the book, the camera hesitantly tracks from left to right, back to the left in a shaky move down to the next line, and slowly to the right again before panning back to the title. The gliding movement imitates that of the eyes on the page, in a simulation of the slow deciphering of a reader who has difficulty in understanding the words of the poem and penetrating its meaning. With its ambiguous, highly imaginative use of language Surrealist poetry restores Natacha's capacity to question, feel and, eventually, remember. If the young woman was previously confined to mere reciting (be it the hollow phrases she has been conditioned to reiterate or the verses she reads from *Capitale de la douleur*), she now accesses the poetic and affective dimensions of language in one of the most beautiful – and supremely discreet – scenes of lovemaking of Godard's oeuvre. In a 'magical fold'[78] in the narrative – reminiscent of Éluard's pure present – time breaks free from its hinges as the two lovers dance around one another in an oneiric ballet of tenderly caressing hands and gazes. If language, sound and the image are often disjointed in Godard, signalling the near-impossibility of any kind of transparent communication, here we witness a rare moment of grace, in which words, images and music are in perfect unison. What was fragmented becomes unified in the enchanted night of love while a man and a woman find a common language that overcomes difference through touch, looking and speech. With its emphasis on sensual experience, the scene is strongly embodied; and yet the diaphanous flashes of the transfigured lovers, rhythmically punctuated by a black screen – a device evoking photography – also imbue it with an ethereal, spiritual quality. Drawing on the topos of romantic fusion epitomised in the love duet from Wagner's *Tristan and Isolde*, with its incantation of the *Nacht der Liebe*, Godard reinvents Éluard's poetic chant in filmic form. As Thiher points out, the 'montage creates an image poem in which Godard, echoing surrealist myth, shows the couple to be the locus of salvation'.[79] The dissolving images of the lovers dancing around each other are sutured by the voice-over of Natacha (the filmic version of an interior monologue) which poetically speaks the unison of two separate beings through love. A coda shot of her looking out on the city with *Capitale de la douleur* pressed against the window seems to attribute the love poem spoken by Natacha to the collection. Yet, as several commentators have signalled, her recital is in fact composed of a collage of verses assembled from a wide range of Éluard's poems from different volumes and periods, including one of his last works, *Le Phénix* (1950).[80]

Figure 1.3 Natacha (Anna Karina) holding Éluard's *Capitale de la douleur* in *Alphaville* (Jean-Luc Godard, 1965).

Godard, then, does not merely pay homage to literature in a passive, reverential kind of way in *Alphaville*. Rather, as in the earlier *À bout de souffle*, which intertwines poems by Aragon and Apollinaire, prefacing them with an apocryphal line and putting them in the mouths of the characters in the movie,[81] *Alphaville* recomposes Éluard's work through devices that are eminently cinematic: découpage and montage. Godard's assembly of poetic fragments into a new creation asserts the creativity of the film auteur over the authority of the literary writer. The process of recreation is double here in that Godard not only rewrites Éluard's poems, but also refashions his work into a multi-sensory audiovisual poem: the two artforms of literature and film fuse into a new, original creation that palimpsestically recalls its origins. It is worth pointing out that Éluard lends himself perfectly to such intermedial intervention, as the poet himself frequently incorporated and refashioned other art forms in his work. *Capitale de la douleur*, for instance, contains several poems on painters – amongst others De Chirico, Picasso, Paul Klee and Miro – reworking their motifs. Like other members of the Surrealist movement, who often worked in more than one medium or crisscrossed between media, Éluard was eager to establish pathways between the arts, or, as he would have put it, 'establish relations'. In the wake of a movement that favoured artistic encounters, Godard's image poem – more than merely an affirmation of the filmmaker's creative powers – celebrates mobility between artistic forms and their capacity, just like the lovers in the poem, to enter into dialogue;

indeed, metaphorically speaking, to make love with one another. Across media boundaries, the film auteur exalts the powers of poetry to resuscitate that which makes us most deeply human, in defiance of the anaesthetised existence to which a technological society without culture would condemn us. Uniting film and cinema in one long embrace, it elevates art, and poetry in particular, to a sacred space.

Stylistically different (and variably successful in aesthetic terms) though they are, there are striking parallels between Godard's dystopic fable and Truffaut's *Fahrenheit 451*. The latter also features an oppressive political regime that numbs its citizens into a conformist existence by means of brainwashing, tranquillisers and indoctrination through technology. Where, in *Alphaville*, computers exercise thought control, in Bradbury's unspecified city of the future it is interactive television games that keep spectators in the grip of an elective 'family', which supplants more meaningful relations of kinship or friendship. The raft of antennas the camera zooms in on one by one in the title credits becomes the visual signifier of an omnipresent system of surveillance. Here the declared enemies of the state are books, banned (under the pretext that they make people antisocial) and destroyed in public book burnings by pyromaniac firemen. Like Godard, Truffaut chose a contemporary setting – the film was partly shot in studio conditions, but also features two English housing estates as well as the French monorail test track in Châteauneuf-sur-Loire – for his visionary fable. And, as in *Alphaville*, the totalitarian regime has strongly fascist overtones, first and foremost through the echoes to Nazi book burnings, but also in more subtle allusions to the censorship, terror and denunciations during the French Occupation (chapter titles such as 'Un pays occupé', 'Résistance' and 'Délation', used for the DVD, make the analogy more explicit).[82]

Diana Holmes and Robert Ingram point out that in *Fahrenheit 451* 'both narrative and visual image focus obsessively on books'; 'they come to represent in themselves all the human values which the film defends'.[83] Just as Natacha regains her humanity through Surrealist poetry, so the fireman Montag (Oskar Werner) is metaphorically reborn by reading *David Copperfield*: in a close-up recalling the one in *Alphaville* in which Natacha reads *Capitale de la douleur*, we see him deciphering the novel, the camera tracking his finger as it slides along the lines, while he hesitantly pronounces the words in voice-over. Just as she is able to reconnect with her memory thanks to Éluard, so too for Montag do books allow him – in an allusion to Proust – to 'catch up with the remembrance of the past'.

Both in the dialogues and the mise-en-scène of *Fahrenheit 451*, books are anthropomorphised: 'books are my family', Montag affirms defiantly to his brainwashed, apathetic wife (Julie Christie); 'these books were alive, they spoke to me', protests the dissenting lady as the firemen are about to destroy her library. Several entirely wordless scenes record the firemen's search for, brutal handling and destruction of secret libraries, the camera lingering in close-up on the books as they are consumed by fire. Crumpling under the flames, the parchment-like pages disturbingly resemble human skin, their personification through voice and image conferring an even more sinister meaning to the fire brigade's motto, 'We burn them to ashes and then we burn the ashes'. Truffaut seems to suggest that the Nazi book burnings – already referenced in the film-within-a-film sequence in *Jules et Jim* where the protagonists watch a newsreel documentary about the 1933 book burnings in Germany – were a first step in the wider process of dehumanisation that led to the crematoria of Auschwitz. We are reminded of Heinrich Heine's prophetic remark from his play *Almansor* (1821): 'Where they burn books, they end up burning people too.' A regime that attacks culture and independent thinking does not value human life either, as becomes painfully clear from the sacrifice of the lady who chooses to immolate herself with her books rather than renounce reading: a female figure of resistance, she is associated with Joan of Arc through images evoking Dreyer's *The Passion of Joan of Arc* (1928), as well as through the presence of a book on the mythical heroine among the titles to be burnt.

The wide range of books visible in the film, encompassing fiction, philosophy, (auto)biography, art books, history and even an issue of *Cahiers du cinema* (as well as, more cynically, a copy of Hitler's *Mein Kampf* that the fire captain, with a gesture of regret, condemns to the flames), is testimony to Truffaut's own vast and eclectic reading tastes. The covers of Melville, Twain, Kafka,

Figure 1.4 Book burning in *Fahrenheit 451* (François Truffaut, 1966).

Cocteau, Balzac, Turgenev, Genet – to name only a few authors – are lovingly filmed in close-up: together they form a global, multi-lingual repository of memory and experience about to be destroyed. Intriguingly, as in *Alphaville*, Surrealism holds pride of place in Truffaut's celebration of human creativity. Among the many works of the lady's library stacked up for burning, the camera rests on an illustrated art book entitled *The World of Salvador Dalí*, its pages, as if turned by an invisible hand, revealing image after image of iconic paintings. As in Godard's film, Surrealism's dismantling of reason and logic opposes resistance to a dehumanising system. And here also, a humanity alienated from itself can be rescued through the emotions literature can revive. Doris's tears as she listens to Montag reading *David Copperfield* and her comment that she had forgotten all those feelings are strangely reminiscent of Lemmy's mission to 'save those who weep' (first jotted down as the feminine singular 'celle' on his notebook, but then crossed out). Did Godard, knowing that his friend Truffaut was about to adapt *Fahrenheit 451*, make a deliberate nod to Bradbury's book; or is this just another thematic convergence between two films with strongly related concerns? Curiously, in the French context, Bradbury's book people (that is, the dissidents who become figures of a collective cultural memory by memorising and embodying books) resonate with the poetry subtext that underpins *Alphaville*: during the Occupation, people all over France learnt the poems published in underground journals by Aragon, Éluard and many other resistance poets by heart.[84]

In both films, literature preserves human memory, but it is ultimately through film that literature can be remembered and kept alive. Lemmy's and Natacha's recitation (or, rather, creative reworking) of Éluard, and Truffaut's wordless shots of piled-up books (later followed by the redemptive images of the book people reciting their texts) quite literally bring the literary works of the past to life. Film, like literature, thus ensures a cultural transmission, extending the mission of literature in a different medium. At a time when screen media was already more popular than literature, prompting widespread concern about mass media reducing interest in reading, Godard and Truffaut suggested that film would not be a substitute for books. Rather, cinema makes literature accessible to a broader audience, alerting spectators to the vital function of reading as the very means to preserve our humanity. To quote Bazin's article 'For an Impure Cinema': 'Who will complain of that'?[85]

THE AESTHETICS OF THE IN-BETWEEN: JEAN-LUC GODARD'S 'CINEMATO*GRAPHIES* OF WRITING'[86]

Although Godard's work in particular is nourished by the voices of literature which he cites, disassembles, rewrites, evokes or (mis)appropriates in a truly polyphonic intermedial practice, the director, perhaps paradoxically, has a highly ambiguous attitude towards the written word. Philippe Dubois signals that Godard 'continuously insisted that writing is his "supreme enemy", that "writing embodies the Law" and thus "death" (as opposed to the image, which embodies "desire" and "life")'.[87] Indeed, in a 1980 interview, the director states: 'For me, images are life and text is death. You need both: I'm not against death. But I'm not that much for the death of life, especially during the time it must be lived.'[88] Not only does Godard repeatedly associate the image with life, he also accords primacy to seeing over writing, as is evidenced in his video poem *Scénario du film Passion* (1982) in which he asks: 'Are we able to see the Law, was the Law written first of all or was it first of all seen and then Moses wrote it on the tablet? I think we first see the world and write it thereafter.' Inverting the biblical 'In the beginning was the word', Godard postulates the anteriority of the visual over the verbal. Yet despite his oft-expressed distrust of writing, language and even literature, his films not only abound with literary and other quotations, but frequently incorporate written text into the filmic image. Dubois provides a long list of the recurring figures through which the filmmaker represents written text in and through images: representations of the acts of reading and writing, epistolary videos and film-letters, postcards, book covers, newsletters, posters, fliers, neon signs, graffiti, credit titles, intertitles, inserts and subtitles, verbal collages, electronic graphics, direct inscriptions on the screen, puns and even the image screen as visual-writing. His brief article on Godard's 'written screen' is supplemented by a 'scripto-visual essay', based on a composition of frame enlargements, which visually traces the written in a number of emblematic films.

This final section on the relations between literature and film in the New Wave will seek to shed light on Godard's insertion of text into the filmic image from an intermedial point of view. As a trace of that which precedes film – that is, literature and the script – writing is a priori associated with the medium of literature, and, thus, with the textual regime of reading. Yet in its evocation of the visual gesture of film, the gesture of writing also becomes a figuration of the motion picture, as the film and media scholar Joachim Paech explains. At the interface of literature and film, writing serves as a link: Paech calls it a 'trace of transitions and of the establishing of relations between different media, forms, figures and fragments of meaning'.[89] Writing, then, in its double incarnation as both a discursive and a figurative space, is a privileged means of playing out differences between the verbal and the visual, but also of crossing the boundaries that separate text-based from image-based media.[90] To what extent are the figurations of the written in Godard's films of the New Wave period emblematic of the rivalries, encounters and exchanges between literature and film which have interested us in this chapter? How does the written as a mediator between the verbal and the visual transcend media difference? What new kind of cinematic writing emerges in the interstices between textuality and visuality explored by the director?

In a famous deconstructivist reading, Ropars-Wuilleumier has highlighted the profound ambiguity that characterises representations of the written in Godard's first feature *À bout de souffle*, a film that persistently mobilises both the graphic and semantic aspects of writing.[91] Gliding between image and sign, the written penetrates the film text in numerous figurations, from the cinema posters that self-reflexively reinscribe the filmic medium, to the newspapers, neon signs and book covers that multiply signs of the protagonist Michel's (Jean-Paul Belmondo) impending death, not forgetting Patricia's (Jean Seberg) implication in the deadly circuit of the written in her status as an aspiring journalist and writer. Even inside the darkroom of the cinema, the written haunts the filmic – albeit as an aural trace – in the montage of the Aragon and Apollinaire poems that substitute for the filmic dialogue. The activity of writing, Ropars-Wuilleumier concludes, 'is from Godard's first feature film profoundly linked to cinema's auto-representation'. And later: 'the development of a cinécriture, at least with Godard, assumes a direct consideration of the written form'.[92]

The interpenetration between the filmic and the written in *À bout de souffle* provides the matrix that informs all of the director's later work, culminating in *Histoire(s) du cinéma*, Godard's history of the twentieth century through the history of cinema. In this project, which exists in two media (print and film), the written is not only frequently superimposed on the filmic image, but writing and the filmic image are indelibly intertwined in a sustained dialogue. Published in Gallimard's prestigious 'Collection blanche' series, the print version consecrates Godard as an *écrivain-cinéaste* in the tradition of Malraux, an intellectual figure to whom, as George Didi-Huberman has shown, he is deeply indebted.[93] In Godard's first period, the cross-overs between the written and the filmic analysed by Ropars-Wuilleumier in *À bout de souffle* are played out in multiple figurations, becoming more accentuated as the director formulates his cinematic critique of the lures of advertisement and consumer culture. Given the omnipresence of writing and signs in this large corpus of works, it would be impossible to offer any exhaustive analysis here. What follows is intended to identify emblematic migrations between the written and the filmic with a view to highlighting the wider liminal aesthetics at play in Godard's work.

In *Vivre sa vie* (*My Life to Live*, 1962) and *Une femme mariée* (*A Married Woman*, 1964) – two films drawing on literary intertexts without ever naming them explicitly (respectively, Zola's *Nana* and Flaubert's *Madame Bovary*) – Godard inserts himself in a literary tradition through the use of chapter headings presented in the form of intertitles. The recourse to a literary device 'textualises' the filmic narrative, yet, at the same time, the written text of the intertitles is visualised as it becomes a *picture* of writing inserted amongst other images.[94] Reminiscent of the medium of literature, the use of intertitles also recalls the devices of silent cinema, often considered a 'purer' form of the medium – Godard himself states in dialogue with Youssef Ishaghpour that sound cinema is 'like a child who has been perverted'.[95] Silent cinema's mobilisation of the written to convey dialogue or thought is playfully appropriated in a scene in *Une femme mariée* in which Charlotte (Macha Méril) eavesdrops on two girls discussing their first sexual experience. Charlotte's thoughts, functioning as some kind of echo chamber for the girls' conversation, are printed on the screen image, inserted between the three women. As we move from the printed words of a magazine Charlotte is leafing through, to the dialogue between the girls and, enmeshed within it, Charlotte's thoughts transcribed into words grafted on the filmic image, a wider transmigration between written, oral and visual forms of representation is enacted. Not only does thought become visible in writing, but the written is assimilated into the filmic image, where it occupies the central position of the screen as a sign amongst other visual signifiers.

The duality of written language as both visual sign and semantic signifier, which is at the heart of Godard's cinemato*graphies*, is explored to comic effect in the slapstick performance – once again reminiscent of silent film – in *Une femme est une femme* where Angela (Anna Karina) and Émile (Jean-Claude Brialy) have a fight through the medium of literature. In disagreement about Angela's wish to have a child, the two lovers have become entrenched in stubborn muteness until they enlist books from their library in a silent, burlesque war of words. Partly masked with their hands or extended with added-on text, the lovers let the titles of the books *speak* for them, but, for the communication to be successfully conveyed in a film, the covers must also be *shown*: captured in close-up, they alternate in the shot/countershot procedure habitually used for dialogue. Whilst most of the couple's jibes take the form of one-letter words ('Monstre', 'Sardine', 'Bourreau' . . .), Émile's more elaborate repartee, composed of the title 'Eva', completed in handwriting with 'te faire foutre', requires a phonetic reading, 'Et va te faire foutre', to signify. (In English the recomposed message translates as 'Bugger off').

The phonetic as the third component of language alongside its graphic and semantic aspects – and one that underpins many a Godardian pun – is also creatively explored in *Bande à part*, another work suffused with literary references, starting with the three protagonists' names, which all allude to literary figures: Franz (Sami Frey) evoking Kafka; Arthur (Claude Brasseur) citing 'Rimbaud' as his surname; Odile (Anna Karina) taking her name from the eponymous Raymond Queneau novel referenced in the film. In one of the film's first scenes, revolving around literature and translation, Arthur slips a seduction note to the ingénue Odile while their English teacher dictates a passage from Shakespeare. Phonetically transliterating and creatively extending the famous *Hamlet* dictum, his note, filmed in close-up, reads: 'Tou bi or not tou bi contre votre poitrine, it iz ze question.' The written, the oral and the visual cohabitate in this irreverent rewriting of one of literature's most memorable quotations, calling into question any monolithic perceptions of the written as an unalterable form frozen in a stable orthography, but also of literature as a revered form of 'high' art not to be tampered with.

Oscillating between graphic sign and semantic signifier as well as between its printed form and phonetic actualisation, the written in Godard is subject to manifold interventions, deconstructions and transfers, notably in the filmmaker's signature-style filmic decompositions and re-compositions of written language. Under the seemingly smooth surface of words, other meanings are teased out as Godard deconstructs the word as a stable semantic entity. Thus, for instance, among the many signs that 'speak' to Charlotte as she makes her way to Orly airport to secretly meet her lover, the road sign DANGER, zoomed-in by the camera, contracts to ANGE (ANGEL) whilst the word PASSAGE, filmed in a slow tracking movement with a marked pause between the syllables decomposes into PAS SAGE (NAUGHTY). In *Pierrot le fou*, behind the cheerful 'OASIS' written on the walls of Marianne's (Anna Karina) flat, set off in red, lurks the acronym 'OAS' (for 'Organisation armée secrète'), and with it, the spectre of the Algerian war that cast its shadow on French cinema well beyond Algerian independence. In a similar vein, but here making an ironic statement on gender relations, in the trailer for *Masculin Féminin* the word 'MAS CUL IN', broken down into its syllables, provocatively posits sex as quite literally the centre of masculine preoccupations (one of the informal meanings of 'cul' in French being 'sex').

Like the (post)structuralist thinkers who came to prominence in the 1960s – notably Lacan, Derrida and Barthes – Godard destabilises fixed meanings, relishing instead language's hidden and double significations, in the semantic glidings and shifts that can be excavated within words, not least his prodigious surname, broken down into GOD ARD on posters and in trailers. The omnipresence of letters, words and other symbols incorporated into the filmic image, Godard's verbal and visual puns, use of intertitles and heterogeneous montage aesthetics equally recall the subversive practices of the Lettrist avant-garde of the 1950s, to which he had some exposure. In her book on Lettrist film, Kaira M. Cabañas suggests that New Wave directors, at least in part, owe some of their techniques – disjunction between sound and image tracks, chronological dislocations, hybridity of the filmic image incorporating text, use of imageless sequences with voice-over – to the experiments of directors such as Isidore Isou and Maurice Lemaître. It is worth noting that Lemaître in particular repeatedly accused Godard of plagiarising his films.[96]

The playful deconstruction of language at work in Godard's films does not stop at the level of the word as the smallest component in a syntactic unit. The title credits for *Bande à part* and *Pierrot le fou* are emblematic of a further stripping down of words into their constituent letters that radicalises the procedure we have already observed: in the former (black and white) film, the title appears letter by letter, starting from the 'À' in the centre, while alternating shots of the three protagonists flicker on the screen; in the latter, the credits gradually unfold as groups of letters appear in alphabetic order. No sooner assembled, the title decomposes, applying the same principle in reverse order. The assignment of a specific colour to different letters of the alphabet evokes Rimbaud's synaesthetic poem 'Voyelles', thus announcing the Rimbaldian intertext that underpins the film's aesthetic of cinema as poetry, but also pointing to the work's conception as impure cinema, where different art forms, each invoking a particular sense, will be put in relation. The French bleu-blanc-rouge colour coding – a recurrent feature of Godard's films –, combined with the dismantling of words into letters once more draws attention to written language's double status as a figurative sign that falls under the regime of showing as well as a semantic signifier inviting a process of reading. Transcending any clear-cut dichotomy between word and image,

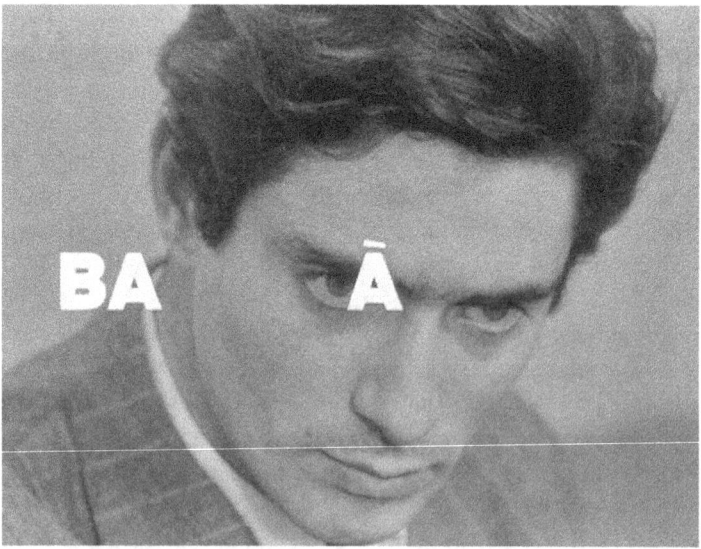

Figure 1.5 Language as visual sign: Jean-Luc Godard, *Bande à part* (1964).

the written partakes in a double system of signification where boundaries between the readable and the visible are broken down.

Raymond Bellour, in an article on the relations between text, spoken language and the image in Godard's films, thus describes the porosity between the verbal and visual: 'The screen is treated like a page of writing, and the word like material that develops between meaning and non-meaning, according to a multiplicity of meanings.'[97] The filmmaker, he elaborates, withdraws its readability from writing 'to make it the object of a visible-legible, guaranteed by its plasticity *in vivo* at the time of inscription and of unfolding'.[98] To conclude this reflection on Godard's exploration of the interface between the visible and the readable, it is useful to examine in detail one particularly prominent instance of such a plasticity *in vivo*: the gesture of writing as a figure of intermediality. Numerous are the instances in Godard's films where characters are engaged in the act of writing: consider for instance Bruno's and Arthur's love declarations penned on a piece of paper in *Le Petit Soldat* and *Bande à part*; Nana's careful composition of a letter to solicit work in a brothel in *Vivre sa vie*; Ulysse and Michelangelo's postcards to their wives in *Les Carabiniers*; Camille's farewell letter to her husband in *Le Mépris*; Ferdinand's diary in *Pierrot le fou*; Bernard doodling in *Deux ou trois choses que je sais d'elle*; the revolutionary students penning ideas on the walls of a bourgeois flat in *La Chinoise*. What is it about the act of writing that so fascinates Godard? Before examining a particularly sustained instance of writing in action – Ferdinand's diary – let us recall Paech's observation that the gesture of writing can serve as an intermedial figuration of the motion picture.[99] Traditionally associated with the medium of literature, writing in motion also evokes the medium of film, making it a privileged liminal space between the two.

Among Godard's *Nouvelle Vague* films, *Pierrot le fou* is undoubtedly the work which most extensively plays out tensions between word and image, in what Angela Dalle Vacche has identified as a technique of cinematic collage.[100] A battleground and a meeting place between the verbal and the visual, the film persistently puts literature and film in relation, not least in the diary the aspiring writer Ferdinand keeps of his turbulent love relationship with Marianne. In a series of insert shots filmed in close-up, a hand – Godard's own – pens words on the page, occasionally deleting text or pausing hesitantly. Emphasis is on the physical act – the corporeal gesture – of handwriting, rather than on the meaning of the text that unfolds before our eyes. The tight framing, which only makes fragments of the diary visible and randomly cuts words, combined with the quick montage, at best allows spectators to grasp a few words or part of a sentence. As in the title credits, the graphic aspect of language is highlighted through colour, here via the use of coloured pens and, later, a coloured background: writing is *visualised* as the text is assimilated into the cinematic image. In one of the insert shots, letters are anagrammatically realigned as Ferdinand decomposes his lover's name into an associative chain of words spaced out like a poem: 'Marianne/ Ariane/ mer/ âme/ amer/ arme'.[101] Just as the words on the page are in constant flux, so significations dissolve and reassemble in a mobile, poetic conception of language as a space of creative association. In the last shot of the diary, just before Ferdinand commits suicide, the letters 'la rt', written in black pen on blue surface (mirroring the blue with which Ferdinand paints his face which, in turn, mirrors a Picasso painting and the portrait of Rimbaud shown earlier),[102] are supplemented with the letters 'mo' added to the second group of lettering: the broken-up 'l'art' (art) morphs into 'la mort' (death) amidst a wider migration between cinema, the visual arts and poetry.

As can be gathered from these transfigurations of the written in Godard's films, the 'life/death' dichotomy that informs his thinking about the visual and the textual by no means enshrines an essentialist view of media difference. On the contrary, in tune with his commitment to montage as a means of putting heterogeneous entities into relation with a view to creating new significations, the written and the visual in Godard's films constantly rub against each other, showing off their differences, but also revealing commonalities and even exchanging their properties. Attentive to language's dual status as both graphic sign and semantic signifier, Godard ceaselessly explores the interstices and possible migrations between text and image, and through them, between the literary and the filmic medium. In a typically intermedial procedure – one we also find in the work of directors such as Peter Greenaway, and which Ágnes Pethő calls 'the double mirror'[103] – writing becomes an image while, at the same time, the screen becomes a site of writing. The gesture of writing recalls the motion picture just as, inversely, the cinematic image takes on the traits of a book. Godard's own handwriting

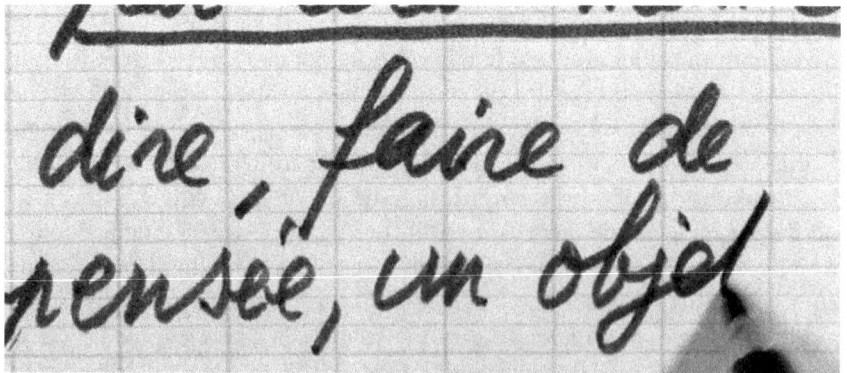

Figure 1.6 The authorial signature: Jean-Luc Godard, *Pierrot le fou* (1965).

in *Pierrot* – also discernible in the trailers for *Made in U.S.A.* (1966) and *Deux ou trois choses que je sais d'elle* – serves as an authorial signature for a new form of *cinécriture* breaking down traditional boundaries between the visual and the verbal, literature and film.

In conversation with Youssef Ishaghpour, the director describes the heuristic moment when the relation between image and text transcends mere illustration:

> the image that you bring enters into the text and [. . .] finally the text, at a given moment, will come out of the images again, [. . .] there's no longer a simple relationship of illustration, [. . .] this allows you to exercise your capacity to think and to reflect and to imagine, to create.[104]

In Godard's intermedial cinema, it is in the exchange between text and image – in their cross-fertilisation and transmigration – that thinking, but also creation more widely, can take place. Transcending traditional hierarchies between literature and film and using tensions between media to creative ends, he inaugurates a truly 'impure' cinema where dialogue with the other arts enables film to achieve its vocation as 'a form that thinks'.[105]

Notes

1. Godard, 'Truffaut représentera la France', p. 194.
2. Léger, 'Painting and cinema', p. 373.
3. See Abel, *French Film Theory and Criticism*, vol. 1, p. 204.
4. Nagib, 'The politics of impurity', p. 23.
5. Abel, *French Film Theory and Criticism*, vol. 1, p. xv.
6. Kline, *Screening the Text*, p. 2.
7. Ibid. p. 4.
8. Abel, *French Film Theory and Criticism*, vol. 1, p. 19.
9. Ibid. p. 19.
10. Truffaut, 'A certain tendency of French cinema', p. 54.
11. See Cléder, *Entre littérature et cinéma*, p. 59.
12. Astruc, 'The birth of a new avant-garde', p. 32.
13. Ibid. p. 34.
14. Ibid. p. 36.
15. Ibid. p. 36
16. Ibid. p. 33.
17. Cléder, *Entre littérature et cinéma*, p. 60.
18. Astruc, 'The birth of a new avant-garde', p. 35.
19. Ibid. p. 35.
20. Godard, 'Bergmanorama', p. 2.
21. Gauteur, 'Un nouvel espoir du cinéma français'.

22. Varda, *Varda par Agnès*, p. 14. I am using Alison Smith's translation from her book *Agnès Varda*, p. 14.
23. Mary, *La Nouvelle Vague*, pp. 113–15.
24. Truffaut, 'Ali Baba et la "Politique des auteurs"'.
25. Godard, 'Dictionnaire des cinéastes français', p. 89 and idem., 'Joseph Mankiewicz', p. 43.
26. Cléder, *Entre littérature et cinéma*, pp. 66–71.
27. Ibid. p. 67.
28. Ibid. p. 71.
29. Antoine de Baecque, Emmanuel Laurent, DVD, *Deux de la vague*, Les Films du Paradoxe, 2011.
30. Bazin, 'In defense of mixed cinema', p. 55.
31. For Malraux's influence on Bazin see Andrew, *André Bazin*, pp. 59–60, 64–5 and passim.
32. Bazin, 'In defense of mixed cinema', pp. 74–5.
33. Bazin, '*Le Journal d'un curé de campagne*', p. 142. See also Bazin's 'Adaptation, or the cinema as digest'.
34. See for instance Kline's statement that 'literature qua adaptation was repressed' in the work of New Wave directors (*Screening the Text*, p. 3).
35. See Marie, *The French New Wave*, pp. 72–7.
36. See ibid. p. 80.
37. See Rohmer, *Le Celluloïd et le marbre*, p. 84.
38. Rohmer, 'Avant-propos', in *Six contes moraux*, p. 7.
39. Aumont, Comolli, Narboni and Pierre, 'Le Temps déborde', p. 19.
40. On Godard's attitude to adaptation in general and in *Le Mépris* in particular see Stam's excellent reading in *Literature Through Film*, pp. 279–99.
41. Godard, 'Le Mépris', p. 31.
42. Ropars-Wuilleumier, 'Totalité et fragmentaire: la réécriture selon Godard'.
43. Ibid. p. 157.
44. See Murcia, *Nouveau roman – Nouveau cinéma*; Ostrowska, *Reading the French New Wave*; Stam, *Literature Through Film*, ch. 6, 'Modernism, adaptation and the French New Wave'.
45. Domarchi et al., 'Hiroshima, notre amour', p. 61.
46. Stam, *Literature Through Film*, p. 262.
47. Vanoye, *L'Adaptation littéraire au cinéma*, p. 126.
48. Bazin et al., 'Six characters in search of *auteurs*', p. 41.
49. Domarchi et al., 'Hiroshima, notre amour', p. 59.
50. Ibid. p. 64.
51. Ibid. p. 65.
52. Daney, 'Truffaut, objectif plume', p. 236.
53. For studies of Godard's use of literary citation see D'Abrigeon, *Jean-Luc Godard, cinéaste écrivain*; Marie-Claire Ropars-Wuilleumier's classic articles 'L'instance graphique dans l'écriture du film. *À bout de souffle*, ou l'alphabet erratique' and

'Totalité et fragmentaire: la réécriture selon Godard'; and Kline, *Screening the Text*, ch. 7.
54. Sontag, 'Godard', p. 419.
55. See Godard, 'L'Art à partir de la vie', p. 9.
56. Didi-Huberman, *Passés cités par JLG*, p. 30.
57. Sontag, 'Godard', p. 421.
58. See his first and third interviews with Herpe and Fauvel in *Le Celluloïd et le marbre*.
59. Elbhar, 'Éric Rohmer parle de ses *Contes moraux*', p. 13.
60. On the ambiguous status of writing and authorship in Truffaut, see also Holmes and Ingram, *François Truffaut*, ch. 6.
61. Rohmer, *Le Celluloïd et le marbre*, pp. 49–52.
62. Ibid. p. 106.
63. Balzac also nourished the plots of several of Rohmer's post-New Wave films: *Le Beau Mariage* (*A Good Marriage*, 1982) is loosely based on the novella 'Le Bal de Sceaux'; *Conte d'automne* (*Autumn Tale*, 1998) was inspired by the novel *Modeste Mignon* (though Rohmer made sure to efface any references to the source in the script); the spying drama *Triple Agent* (2004) draws on *Une ténébreuse affaire*. See De Baecque and Herpe, *Eric Rohmer. Biographie*, pp. 302, 393 and 449.
64. Godard, 'Tournage', pp. 167–8.
65. See also Kline's psychoanalytical reading of the Balzac intertext as a screen memory (*Screening the Text*, ch. 4, 'In the labyrinth of illusions: Chabrol's mirrored films') and, on Balzac's influence on the Chabrolean aesthetic Dousteyssier-Khoze, *Claude Chabrol's Aesthetics of Opacity*, pp. 29–37.
66. Balzac is also briefly evoked in Chabrol's *Les Bonnes femmes* (1960) when the greeting 'honoré' is playfully extended by 'de Balzac' by one of the characters.
67. Mary, *La Nouvelle Vague*, pp. 206–9.
68. On Rivette's reworkings of Balzac see Francesca Dosi's article 'Balzac et Rivette: l'énigme d'une rencontre'.
69. See Lalanne and Morain, 'Entretien avec Jacques Rivette'.
70. Letter to Stéphane Tchalgadjieff, in booklet accompanying 5 DVD Box set *Out 1* (*Noli me tangere*, *Spectre*), Arte Edition, 2013, p. 36.
71. *Out 1*, DVD 2, Bonus, Interview 3: Die Geschichte der Dreizehn/ Éric Rohmer/ Balzac.
72. On this comparison see Lalanne and Morain, 'Entretien avec Jacques Rivette'.
73. *Out 1*, DVD 3, Bonus, Interview 6: Die Gruppe der Dreizehn/ Cahiers du cinéma / Die Zeit nach 1968 / Eine Komödie.
74. Barthes, *S/Z*, p. 156.
75. See Darke, *Alphaville*, p. 72.
76. Thiher, 'Postmodern dilemmas', p. 954.
77. Albéra, 'Cultivons notre jardin. Entretien avec Jean-Luc Godard', p. 87.
78. The term is borrowed from Martin, 'Recital: three lyrical interludes in Godard', p. 263.
79. Thiher, 'Postmodern dilemmas', pp. 955–6.

80. See D'Abrigeon, *Jean-Luc Godard, cinéaste écrivain*, and Martin, 'Recital'.
81. On the reworking of the poems see Ropars-Wuilleumier, 'L'instance graphique dans l'écriture du film'.
82. For a reading of resistance and censorship in the film see Harrison, 'Readers as resistants'.
83. Holmes and Ingram, *François Truffaut*, p. 168.
84. On resistance poetry during the German occupation see Smock, 'The honor of poets', p. 950.
85. Bazin, 'In defense of mixed cinema', p. 75.
86. The term is borrowed from Cléder, *Entre littérature et cinéma*, p. 179.
87. Dubois, 'The written screen'.
88. Godard, 'Alfred Hitchcock est mort', p. 416.
89. Paech, 'Die Spur der Schrift', pp. 45–6.
90. For the written in cinema see also Chion, *L'écrit au cinéma*.
91. Ropars-Wuilleumier, 'L'instance graphique dans l'écriture du film'.
92. Ibid. p. 120.
93. See Didi-Huberman, *Passés cités*, pp. 136–53. What interests Godard in Malraux – and this was particularly important at the time of the New Wave – in Didi-Huberman's words, is the possibility 'of creating a visual form that puts into relation cinema and the novel' (p. 147).
94. For processes of textualisation of the image and visualisation of writing in Godard see also Cléder, *Entre littérature et cinéma*, pp. 27–31.
95. Godard and Ishaghpour, *Archéologie du cinéma*, pp. 81–2.
96. Cabañas, *Off-Screen Cinema*.
97. Bellour, 'L'Autre cinéaste: Godard écrivain', p. 121.
98. Ibid. p. 126.
99. Paech, 'Die Spur der Schrift', p. 46.
100. Dalle Vacche, 'Jean-Luc Godard's *Pierrot le Fou*: Cinema as Collage against Painting'.
101. For a reading of these permutations see Dalle Vacche, 'Jean-Luc Godard's *Pierrot le Fou*', p. 118.
102. See Pethő, *Cinema and Intermediality*, p. 302.
103. Ibid. p. 84.
104. Godard and Ishaghpour, *Archéologie du cinéma*, p. 13.
105. In Godard's *Histoire(s) du cinéma*, in two subsequent images, the words 'une forme qui pense' are printed over the face of one of the figures in Piero della Francesca's *Exaltation of the Cross*, the last episode of his fresco cycle *The Legend of the True Cross* (1452–66) in the Basilica of St Francis, Arezzo. See *Histoire(s) du cinéma*, vol. 3, *La Monnaie de l'absolu. Une Vague Nouvelle*, p. 99 and p. 101.

CHAPTER TWO

The World as Spectacle: Cinematic Theatricalities

> It's the paradox of cinema, which is an art without being an art, a spectacle without being a spectacle, a theatre without being a theatre, which refuses theatre and which makes it.
>
> Éric Rohmer[1]
>
> I prefer to say spectacle, otherwise you're imagining that there is theatre on one side and cinema on the other.
>
> Alain Resnais[2]
>
> You've got to make theatre from cinema, mix things up.
>
> Jean-Luc Godard[3]

Both a source of inspiration and a medium from which cinema sought gradually to emancipate itself, theatre has shaped and enriched filmic expression ever since the younger medium's inception. Film developed in intimate dialogue with its ancestor, drawing on and reworking stories destined for the stage, and taking inspiration in the codes and practices of theatrical representation. As an embodied art form concerned with staging moving bodies in space, the theatre became a natural reference point for set design, composition, lighting and the direction of actors; indeed the very concept of filmic mise-en-scène (literally 'staging') was coined in analogy to theatrical practice. Early cinema found a rich source of inspiration above all in popular theatrical genres such as comedy and melodrama which helped its ascension as a popular mass entertainment. At the same time, certain theatrical genres that had fallen out of fashion – such as farce and the *commedia dell'arte* – were resuscitated in slapstick cinema.[4] With the majority of French and American comedians during cinema's early days coming from music hall or boulevard theatre, typically theatrical conventions such as the direct address to the audience, or the aside, were imported into film.[5]

The foundation in 1908 of the production company 'Le Film d'art', while helping to establish cinema as an art form, also put a stranglehold on its creative development. Chaperoned by the *Comédie française*, and wooing more refined theatre and opera audiences, *film d'art* largely drew on stage actors and directors for its productions. Little concerned with the specific properties of film, directors such as André Calmettes and Charles Le Bargy filmed as if they were photographing a play, their actors remaining characteristically poised and the use of fixed camera in their 'cinematographic plays' mimicking the eye of the theatre spectator. It is against this over-reliance on theatrical models – as well as literary ones, as we have seen in the previous chapter – that early film theorists cautioned in their advocacy of a cinema that develops its own expressive possibilities. Ricciotto Canudo's critique of a cinema industry that simply 'plucks' film actors from the theatre and derives its staging from theatrical practices in 'Reflections on the Seventh Art' (1923) is exemplary of a wider cautioning against the pressure of theatrical conventions among film critics and avant-garde filmmakers of the 1920s.[6]

With the development of a more mobile camera and the possibilities of montage, cinema began to emancipate itself from theatrical models. The evolution of a specifically cinematic language and codes of perception (mobile camera, montage, different types of shots and camera angles, pan, fade, dissolve, soft focus, superimposition or distortion of the image) allowed the medium to absorb and transform theatrical models into its own syntax.[7] Yet, with the sound revolution and the ensuing return to narrative models, film's traditional reliance on theatrical models was once more reinforced. In France, under the dual aegis of Sacha Guitry and Marcel Pagnol – two artists who crossed back and forth between the stage and film – filmed theatre returned in the guise of the so-called 'theatre-film', a hybrid genre that, in essence, recycled theatrical productions in cinematic form. As Richard Abel points out, for Pagnol and Guitry film was

> a 'minor art' of recording and communicating or disseminating a work of art already conceived beforehand, primarily for the stage. [...] The director, cameraman, and others were merely technicians in the service of the playwright and his text and the spectacle of the stage actor.[8]

At a time when cinema was still widely perceived as a handmaiden of theatre, Bazin, in a crucial two-part article, 'Theater and Cinema' (1951), rehabilitated the younger medium with regard to its older ancestor, pointing out fruitful connections between the two beyond what he calls the 'canned theatre' of *film d'art* and Pagnol's theatre-films. Reminding readers of the intertwined history of the two arts, the critic posits that there are no unbridgeable ontological differences between them. Not even the notion of presence, usually seen as the essence of theatre – by virtue of the physical presence of the actors on the stage – is unique to the stage arts, as cinema can also put us 'in the presence' of an actor. Rather what is at stake are 'two psychological modalities of a performance':[9] in the theatre, actors and spectators are mutually aware of their presence; film, by contrast, is the solitary contemplation of a spectacle that ignores us. For Bazin, filmed theatre can in no way be a substitute for a stage performance. Rather we should think in terms of 'a complex mechanical aesthetic' by which the original theatrical effectiveness 'is preserved, reconstituted, and transmitted thanks to a system of circuits [. . .], of amplifications [. . .], of induction or interference'.[10] Far from corrupting film, as advocates of a pure cinema would have it, Bazin argues that filmed theatre enriches and elevates the medium, in that it prompts directors to harness a specifically cinematic language: 'The more the cinema intends to be faithful to the text and to its theatrical requirements, the more of necessity must it delve deeper into its own language.'[11] No longer the humble servant of theatre, he concludes provocatively, cinema can breathe new life into theatre; in fact, 'it may [. . .] be that the only possible modern theatrical productions of certain classics would be on the screen'.[12] Although Bazin's main focus in 'Theater and Cinema' was filmed theatre and adaptation, his advocacy of an impure cinema and his confident postulation of cinema as the saviour of theatre made the article fertile ground for the burgeoning New Wave.

The New Wave opened a new chapter in the relations between the two arts at a time when French theatre, just like film, was undergoing a major phase of transformation. In the 1950s and 1960s more traditional forms of theatrical representation coexisted with, and were gradually replaced by, a 'new' or 'avant-garde' theatre.[13] While major figures such as Sartre, Camus and Anouilh, all of whom were associated with a largely traditional dramaturgy, continued to exert a certain influence, theatrical conventions were revolutionised by the Theatre of the Absurd of Beckett, Ionesco and Adamov, with its non-rationalist worldview, demolition of language and interrogation of human thought and communication. Jean Vilar's *Théâtre national populaire* (TNP), founded to make a demanding repertoire accessible to a mass audience, yielded to a more political theatre, especially under the influence of Brecht, whose epic theatre revolutionised French theatrical practice in the late 1950s and 1960s. In 1961, the first production of the Living Theatre at the Théâtre du Vieux-Colombier, Paris, ushered in a new concept of theatre in which the process of putting together a performance becomes more important than the underlying text or its staging. The theatrical experiments of Jerzy Grotowski, which encouraged actors to give themselves to the public without any form of defence in seemingly trance-like or frenetic states, and, in his wake, the improvisational practices spearheaded by Peter Brook, Marc'O and Ariane Mnouchkine shifted emphasis from the finished product to the process of creation. Especially post 1968, the notion of collective creation gained a special resonance as the traditional figure of the stage director was effaced in favour of collaboration and as the public was invited to take part in the theatrical event.

With the New Wave, Volker Roloff suggests, the exchanges between theatre and film became particularly distinct and visible as directors discovered new hybridisations and exchanges.[14]

> Many films of the New Wave show the differences, tensions, and ruptures between the two media, as well as the combinations, pathways and interstices; they refer to the whole of what Paech calls an 'area of tension of synaesthetic experience', which brings theatre and cinema together and which we can describe as an intermedial interplay between different senses, arts and media.[15]

What is more, crossing over into theatre allowed the New Wave to reflect and comment on practices of social interaction:

> What is at stake, and therein lies the critical impulse of the New Wave, is always the theatricality of society, theatricality as a social and anthropological category, as a mode of perception and as daily role play, and thus what Debord calls the 'société du spectacle', the *theatrum mundi* of our time which, paradoxically, finds a stronger expression in film than in conventional forms of theatre [. . .] for film not only shows theatricality, but, at the same time, deconstructs it via a change of medium.[16]

On a formal level, too, theatrical conventions such as the aside or the falling of the curtain were playfully referenced and reworked. The similarities and differences between the two media as regards their negotiation of space, the direction of actors, use of dialogue and voice, construction of looking and seeing, as well as the spectator experience they afford were sounded out with a view to apprehending the limits, but also the expressive possibilities of each medium.

While theatrical inflections can be traced in many New Wave films[17] this chapter will focus on three particularly prominent figures – Resnais, Rivette and Godard – whose incorporation and refashioning of theatrical forms throws into relief the movement's intense engagement with a medium that was itself renewing its language in the mid-1950s and 1960s, as it moved from more classical forms of dramaturgy to a radical form of modernity. As we will see, these three directors absorbed theatrical forms or conventions in manifold guises and with diverse functions, in a manner that was to a certain extent emblematic of the New Wave more widely. Theatre appears in their work as the filmic mise-en-scène of rehearsals and stage productions; as cinema's mirror image or blind spot; as satirical political comedy, Brechtian anti-illusionist spectacle, happening, performance or 'live theatre'; or, in a more allegorical vein, as *theatrum mundi* unveiling the artifice of societal role playing. The recourse to theatrical models not only enabled the three directors to better understand the aesthetic possibilities of film, but to creatively work through tensions inherent in both media: realism versus artifice, classicism versus modernity, the direction of actors versus improvisation, illusion versus truth. Finely attuned to the experiments that revolutionised French theatre, their engagement with the theatre led them to reconsider some of cinema's central questions, not least the figure of the auteur.

ALL THE WORLD'S A STAGE (IN FILM): ALAIN RESNAIS'S *CINEMATRICALITIES*[18]

Like his Left Bank colleagues and friends Agnès Varda and Chris Marker, who will make an entrance in subsequent chapters, Alain Resnais was an outspokenly intermedial director. Echoing the Wagnerian idea of the *Gesamtkunstwerk*, as well as Canudo's famous concept of film as the 'synthesis of all the arts', Resnais's filmic work, according to his own account, aspires to a 'synthesis of all artistic forms of expression'.[19] As Scarlett Winter points out, Resnais – in close collaboration with painters, architects, composers, writers and authors of graphic novels – dissects artistic processes, shaping and adapting techniques borrowed from the other arts into new constellations of image, word and sound.[20] The theatre plays a particularly prominent role in the director's intermedial aesthetic – unsurprisingly, perhaps, given that he began his career as an assistant to Georges Pitoëff, a stage director known for his popularisation of playwrights such as Pirandello, Ibsen, and Shaw.[21]

From the 1980s onwards, Resnais increasingly drew on theatrical plays, notably in the retro-style *Mélo* (1986), based on a play by Henri Bernstein; then in *Smoking/No Smoking* (1993), *Coeurs* (*Private Fears in Public Places*, 2006) and *Aimer, boire et chanter* (*Life of Riley*, 2014), all adapted from plays by Alan Ayckbourn; and culminating in *Vous n'avez encore rien vu* (*You Ain't Seen Nothin' Yet*, 2012) with its double transposition of Jean Anouilh's *Eurydice* and *Cher Antoine ou L'Amour raté*. In their use of theatrical codes to construct cinematic time and space, as well as in the direction of the actors, these works proudly exhibit their theatrical origins in a hybrid aesthetics of the in-between. Yet Resnais's crossings-over into the domain of theatre were by no means limited to adaptation, however creative such an approach may be, nor were they unique to the later stages of his career. Ever since his first feature films under the influence of the New Wave, theatre – as the medium of artifice – was a rich source of inspiration for this director, who was distrustful of any reductively realist conceptions of cinema and who explored theatrical conventions for his 'theatre of the unconscious'.[22] Let us, therefore, quite literally begin with beginnings: the enigmatic play-within-the-film of *L'Année dernière à Marienbad* that sets the scene for many a New Wave theatricality.

The film's overture, with its famous tracking shots along the corridors of a palace and its monotonous voice-over describing the baroque setting, leads us into the space of a theatre. Visually mimicking the trajectory of a spectator on their way to a performance, the camera approaches a door, furtively bringing into view a poster announcing the programme, before entering a salon in which a performance is approaching its end. We can at first neither see nor hear the actors, as the camera hovers along the ceiling and meanders around the auditorium, bringing into sight, one after another, the eerily immobile faces of spectators, while the voice-over continues its monologue. When the stage finally comes into view in a counter-shot, its set reveals itself to be a mirror image of an engraving of the palace we glimpsed earlier in one of the corridors. In the repetition of features which we have already perceived in a different art form, the scene – as Jean-Louis Leutrat points out – 'obliges us to shift from one type of representation to another'.[23] Put differently, it introduces a process of remediation that becomes a structural principle for the whole film.

An actress dressed in nineteenth-century costume stands as rigidly motionless as the audience, frozen in a theatrical pose. The camera cuts back to the auditorium, tracking along rows of spectators, before returning to the stage where a male actor slowly comes into view in a vertical tracking shot. Almost imperceptibly, as the image track cuts forwards and backwards between the auditorium and the stage, a double shift occurs on the level of the soundtrack: the disembodied voice (soon to be associated with the film's male protagonist), hitherto engaged in a monologue, now addresses itself to an unnamed woman. In what Robbe-Grillet, in his screenplay for the film, calls a more 'played' tone,[24] the voice amorously speaks of his waiting for the beloved woman, of another man to whom she is linked by a strong bond. For a brief moment, a dialogue between the voice-over and a female voice, later assigned

Figure 2.1 The play-within-the-film in *L'Année dernière à Marienbad* (Alain Resnais, 1961).

to the stage actress, can be heard before another male voice, assigned to the male stage actor in one of the following shots, continues the exchange. Not only, then, are the sound and image tracks largely desynchronised (although they intermittently come into sync when we hear dialogue from the play), the hitherto disembodied voice changes focaliser, as if it had finally found host in a different body. At the chiming of a clock, with a theatrical gesture of the hand, the actress declaims: 'There. And now I'm yours.' The curtain falls.

As a mise-en-abyme of the filmic action, the play-within-the-film announces the triangular relations between characters that remain unnamed in the film but whom Robbe-Grillet's screenplay designates as X (played by Giorgio Albertazzi), A (Delphine Seyrig) and her companion, possibly husband, M (Sacha Pitoëff). Dialogue and situations from the play reappear in the 'real' world of the film, where they are mirrored, varied and estranged. In a framing device, the theatrical action resumes at the end of the film when the camera penetrates once more into the space of the theatre, where we briefly glimpse an earlier part of the play. The voice-over, by now firmly assigned to X, evokes M's presence in the theatre, his last chance to hold A back if he were to leave before the end of the play. 'In one sense', Anthony Paraskeva remarks, 'the entire film takes place between the two stagings of the play, or possibly during just one.'[25] But just as the performance that frames the filmic action seems to be caught up in a loop where any linear notions of time have been forfeited, so the filmic action remains suspended without any resolution. In many ways, what lies between the two performances is an incessant repetition of the same: a man entreats a woman – whom he pretends to have met last year, but who has no recollection (or denies) that they have been romantically involved – to leave her companion and go with him.

An integral part of the film's dreamlike web of echoes, doublings and mirrorings (visually signalled by the mirrors of the setting through which we perceive some of the action) – indeed the first, most sustained, instance of a game of reflection and refraction that will be perpetuated in manifold guises – the play-within-the-film is instrumental in the weaving of a textual fabric that incessantly turns back on itself in a process of embedding and reduplication. But more than just a mirroring device which invites us to make connections between the diegetic worlds of the play and film, in the film's interpolation of the theatre the two worlds – as signalled by the merging of the disembodied voice-over with the theatrical dialogue – have become intermingled. The boundaries between stage and reality, between theatrical play and the play of love, between interiority and exteriority, appearance and reality, as Winter explains, are dissolved into a world of deceptive appearances: 'the world in Marienbad is a false world of simulacra and puzzle pictures, of deceptions and visions, of shadows and spectres'.[26]

In its transition from the theatre stage to the social stage, from theatrical to social performance, the film creates an interstitial space where the performative nature of social role-play can be examined. Enhanced by the *huis clos* character of the setting, the deliberately stilted performance and non-naturalist diction of the actors visually and aurally construct the filmic world as a *theatrum mundi* where empty rituals are being re-enacted. As the locus of verbal and gestural performances, theatre offers a particularly fruitful interface for dissecting the rites of an upper-class society, which – if not already dead, as suggested in the reference to 'nameless phantoms' served by 'immobile, silent servants, who had doubtless died a long time ago' – has ossified into a ghostly form of non-living. Rigidified in meaningless social routines and out of touch with the world around them, the social actors resemble the statues of the lifeless decor they inhabit. These are no longer the transparent, natural bodies of a Rousseau who had hoped for a world in which the dichotomy between being and appearance will collapse, but, rather, an extreme figuration of the mechanical, socially conditioned body which has become opaque and unreadable, disjointed even from its words which, at times, no longer seem to inhabit the subject who pronounces them.

If theatre becomes the prism through which Resnais denounces an obsolete class alienated from itself and from society at large, theatrical performance in *Marienbad* also – and just as importantly – offers, on a formal level, both a model and a foil for cinematic style. Pitting the real presence of the live performance, where performer and spectator are mutually aware of their presence, against the illusory presence of cinema, where actors are indifferent to the audience, the play-within-the-film interrogates what Bazin calls the 'two psychological modalities of a performance', setting in motion a curious intermingling between the two. Paraskeva writes:

> The lover behaves like a theatrical spectator, while the actress [. . .] performs a filmic spectacle, lit like a Golden Age Hollywood icon in the grand manner of Garbo. The actress on stage playing Ibsen performs for an audience; Seyrig, who mirrors her character, performs for the camera. These shifts between the here-and-now of live performance and the ghostly there-and-then of filmed performance are partly achieved by doubling the camera's point of view, alternately, between the man's and the husband's, and that of an unnameable third person.[27]

In sharp contrast to the staging of the filmed play which is singularly static – were it not for the historical costume and set, it could be mistaken for a contemporary production of Beckett rather than the Ibsen play alluded to in the title[28] – a nimbly mobile camera brings the spectacle to life in a virtuoso exercise of cinema's expressive syntax: vertical and horizontal tracking shots, tilts, close-ups, zooms and the meandering movements we mentioned earlier endow the camera with a physical presence of its own, making it seem more alive than the actors frozen in sculptural poses. It is the virtuosity of a cinema fully aware of its possibilities that animates the theatrical world, giving a new meaning to Bazin's speculation that, henceforth, 'the only possible modern theatrical productions of certain classics would be on the screen'. In the final instance, then, the theatre in its manifold functions – mise-en-abyme and metalepsis, *theatrum mundi*, intertext and source of theatricality – above all allows the filmmaker to forge a film language that, in the best sense of auteurism, is most personally his own. Resnais does not seek to hide the mediations used by cinema for the sake of any kind of transparency; on the contrary, he affirms what Vincent Amiel calls 'the "mediological" characteristics of cinema'.[29] Fusing theatre and film into a hybrid space without frontiers, *L'Année dernière à Marienbad* announces the *cinematricalities* that were to become the director's signature style.

FROM PIRANDELLO TO PERFORMANCE: JACQUES RIVETTE'S INTERROGATION OF THE AUTEUR

If Resnais and Godard, who frame this chapter, extensively engage with theatrical models and forms in their films, centre stage must be given to Rivette as the New Wave director who has arguably gone furthest in his exploration of the interface between the two media. In articles on Mizoguchi and Bergman, or in direct conversation with Otto Preminger and Jean Renoir – artists who draw extensively on theatrical models – the critic Rivette interrogates the specificity of theatre and film in their portrayal of human intimacy, but also shows a particular interest in cinema's incorporation of theatrical forms.[30] In his filmic work from the late 1950s to the early 1970s, theatre becomes a major source of influence, as evidenced in the theatrical mise-en-abyme of his first feature *Paris nous appartient* that is extended into a more complex mirroring structure in the experimental *L'Amour fou* (1967); in the intersection between theatrical and painterly references in *La Religieuse*; or, more radically, in the real-time incorporations of avant-garde theatrical performance in *Out 1*. Later post-New Wave works such as *L'Amour par terre* (*Love on the Ground*, 1984), *La Bande des quatre* (*The Gang of Four*, 1989) and *Va Savoir* (2001) similarly gravitate around and creatively draw on the stage. The phantom of the theatre, in more or less explicit form, haunts all of Rivette's films.[31]

In an interview with *Cahiers du cinema* coinciding with the release of *L'Amour fou*, the director offers a crucial insight into the function of theatre for his cinematic art. As a medium concerned with the truth, yet reliant upon means that are of necessity untruthful (i.e. illusory), he explains, film is akin to the theatre, an art concerned above all with truth and lying. Unlike earlier filmmakers who have used a film-within-a-film structure to self-reflexively look at cinema, he prefers to examine the medium through its older sibling, theatre:

> all films are about theatre: there's no other subject. [. . .] If you take a subject dealing in any way with theatre, you're in the truth of cinema, you're transported [. . .]. Because it's the subject of truth and lies, and in cinema there isn't any other subject: it's necessarily an interrogation of the truth, by means that are necessarily based on lies. [. . .] Cinema has many attempts at films about cinema, and it doesn't work as well, it's more laboured, it feels coquettish. It's weaker, maybe because it only has one level; it's the cinema looking at itself, rather than, if it looks at the theatre, it's already looking at something else: not itself but its older brother. Of course, that is also a way to look at itself in a mirror, but the theatre is the 'civilian' version of cinema, it's the face it shows to the public.[32]

In its use of a theatrical mise-en-abyme, the enigmatic *Paris nous appartient* offers a matrix for the persistent interrogation of the cinematic medium by way of the theatre in Rivette's oeuvre. As in the later works, the director privileges creative process over finished product, giving access to what is normally withheld from audiences: the 'behind the scenes' of planning and rehearsing a play, in this case the preparations for a production of Shakespeare's *Pericles*, directed by the enthusiastic but penniless Gérard Lenz (Giani Esposito). In the film's paranoid plot, the doomed production becomes entangled in a mysterious Cold War conspiracy with distinct echoes of Fascism, the Spanish Civil War and the McCarthy era. As the complot closes in on Gérard and his troupe, the dramatic world of the play spills out into the 'real' world of the film. In the words of Jonathan Romney, 'life itself becomes a sprawling drama without clearly identifiable beginning or end. [. . .] Paris becomes a vast stage in which multiple mystery dramas are forever played out'.[33]

On a narrative level, the unwieldy plot of *Pericles*, a play decried as undramatic and disjointed, difficult to stage and even incomprehensible in parts, becomes a model for the new cinema Rivette is ushering in with *Paris nous appartient*: the play's manifold locations and lack of dramatic unity find an echo in the spatial fragmentation and meandering, often unresolved narrative threads of a film that has foregone any traditional notions of plot or continuity. Narrative incoherence as a means towards a different type of spectator engagement is celebrated in a discussion between Gérard and the literature student Anne (Betty Schneider), in which the stage director explains that it is precisely the play's disjointedness that he finds compelling as it helps project audiences onto another, non-literary, plane. *Pericles*, he asserts, is 'the

Figure 2.2 Outdoor rehearsal in *Paris nous appartient* (Jacques Rivette, 1961).

mise-en-scène of a chaotic, but not absurd world, like the one in which we live'. On the level of artistic creation, the play's status as a probably collaborative text co-written by Shakespeare and at least one other author raises questions about authorship, a notion that was central to New Wave filmmaking, but from which Rivette gradually distanced himself. Unlike Godard, for instance, who likes the 'look' of improvised cinema,[34] but as the embodiment of the auteur who keeps control over all aspects of the creative process, Rivette was increasingly committed to filmmaking as a collaborative act shared by actors and the director, culminating in *Out 1*, which relies largely on improvisation. Although in *Paris nous appartient* we are still some way from the idea of collective creation developed by stage directors such as Ariane Mnouchkine and Peter Brook in the course of the 1960s and 1970s, the filmed rehearsal scenes insist on the team effort of putting on a play, even if the stage director takes responsibility for the overall vision.

With its unknown actors (including the non-professional Anne), recourse to makeshift rehearsal spaces – some of them in outdoor locations – and precarious financial conditions, the theatre troupe is strongly evocative of New Wave filmmaking, giving this first film of the movement (it was begun in 1957, but only completed three years later) a manifesto-like character. Shot by a twenty-nine-year-old director on a shoestring budget, *Paris nous appartient* gives voice to Rivette's own anxieties and tribulations through the double of the stage director engulfed by a raft of financial and logistical problems, yet brimming with artistic passion and ideas. Gérard's loss of actors departing to work for television or radio, that is, media that benefit from more generous funding models, points to the fierce competition between older and newer media in the late 1950s that affected independent theatre just as it did art cinema.

Contrary to the technique of 'method acting' that revolutionised American theatre in the second half of the twentieth century, Gérard subscribes to an anti-illusionist concept of performance rooted in European dramatic and filmic traditions spearheaded by, amongst others, Brecht and Robert Bresson. 'But theatre is not illusion, it's a reality. You're not Gower, you're an actor, don't imagine things, use the stage. You are addressing the audience directly, I want it to be visible', he instructs one of his actors, discouraging any character identification. As a filmmaker committed to a modernist aesthetic – referenced pictorially in the art brut-style drawings that plaster the walls of Philip Kaufman's (Daniel Crohem) room and the Modigliani postcards that adorn Anne's garret – Rivette uses the stage director as a mouthpiece to caution against any naively mimetic attitude to representation. Revealingly, the production's demise comes about when Gérard is hired by an established theatre, which imposes well-known actors and forces him to adopt an illustrative, 'transparent' aesthetic. Within the film world, the provocative demands of actors, lighting and set designers (including the suggested construction of a pirates' galley manned with dwarfs), who seek to take artistic control over the production are part of a wider complot destined to drive the stage director to suicide. Yet, in the wider allegory that links the theatre to New Wave film-making, Gérard's struggle against the world of commercial theatre points to the threat of big production systems – the maligned Tradition of Quality, but also the American studio model – which not only leave little creative autonomy to the director, but whose adherence to a conformist, realist aesthetic straitjackets cinema's creative powers. Compromised in his integrity, Gérard quits, asserting his artistic freedom over the lures of popular recognition and financial gain: 'When you start making concessions, you can't stop', he explains to the similarly uncompromising Anne.

Through its theatrical mise-en-abyme, then, beyond comparing the personal and political machinations of antiquity with those of the contemporary world, *Paris nous appartient* evokes the battle between the small-budget, deliberately amateurish aesthetic of the New Wave and the commercially driven, technique-focused model of big production systems. A romantic ode to creative genius, the film resonates with the agonies and doubts of the independent director working outside traditional funding models, who strikes a singularly lonely figure here, even among a group of melancholy exiles. If the film's title sounds like the triumphant battle cry of a new generation of filmmakers who quite literally take to the streets of Paris, it is almost instantly undercut in the credit titles by a quote from the conservative Catholic author

Charles Péguy, 'Paris belongs to no one'. Ever shifting, cultural, artistic and political territories become the site of contestation and conflict as the film works through tensions between tradition and modernity, conservatism and rebellion, commerce and art. But among all the bleakness of the film's ending with its distinctly Mallarméan overtones – the languid images of swans flying over a wintry lake evoke the sonnet 'Le Vierge, le vivace et le bel aujourd'hui', itself an emblem of obscurity and disjointedness – there is a glimmer of hope and defiance as the destitute members of the troupe gather outside Paris to complete the *Pericles* project: Paris belongs to no one, but art is for the happy few who persist.

Of an altogether different nature is the intersection with theatrical models in *La Religieuse*, Rivette's screen adaptation of Diderot's controversial Enlightenment novel. To circumvent censorship, the project first came to life as a theatrical production at the *Studio des Champs Elysées* in 1963 produced by Godard, staged by Rivette, and with Anna Karina in the role of the eponymous nun. The film version retains echoes of the stage play while also emphasising the inherently theatrical quality of Diderot's novel, produced by an author who moved seamlessly between novelistic and dramatic genres and who is credited with having invented the concept of the 'fourth wall'. From the opening scene with its spatial set-up reminiscent of the proscenium stage and its three knocks announcing the rise of the curtain, as Mary Wiles demonstrates, 'the codes of the theater – architectural, cultural, gestural – are encrypted within the film text'.[35] Settings such as the chapel at Longchamp Convent or Suzanne's apartment evoke the theatre stage and the dressing room where actors get ready for, or unwind from, performances. Suzanne herself likens her singing during Holy Week to the performance of an 'actress in a theatre'.[36] Finding inspiration in Diderot's conception of theatrical staging as a series of tableaux, Rivette intermingles theatrical and painterly references, notably to the Rococo painter Fragonard. In a bold mixing of the arts, the director 'mov[es] from novel, to the theatrical scene, to the pictorial tableau – in full circle to redefine the theatricality of Diderot's novel in his film'.[37]

The intermedial exchanges at work in *La Religieuse* place Rivette in the tradition of Bazin's impure cinema, a concept he evokes in a 1991 press conference:

> It [cinema] is an impure art, complex, between the novel, the theater, painting, music, dance, etc., and it is understandable that in this indeterminate place from within the middle of the traditional arts, we would want to look sometimes in this direction, or in that direction . . .[38]

Rivette's experience of staging *La Religieuse* retrospectively made him reflect on his representation of the theatre in *Paris nous appartient* which, with hindsight, he deemed to be too picturesque, exterior and even clichéd.[39] Working with a group of actors made him realise that 'the work of the theatre was something else, more concealed, more mysterious, with a deeper relationship between the people who are engaged in it, a sense of complicity'.[40] His next two projects, *L'Amour fou* and *Out 1*, open new avenues for the relationship between cinema and theatre in their interlacing of experimental film and theatrical avant-garde practice. If, as Wiles argues, *Paris nous appartient* reflects the spirit of Jean Vilar's *Théâtre national populaire* and draws on the strategies of Situationist theatre developed by Charles Dullin's theatre school *L'Atelier*, *L'Amour fou*, by contrast, is inspired by the ideas and theatrical practice of one of the avant-garde figures of French theatre in the 1960s, the experimental stage director and theoretician Marc'O.[41] A former producer and filmmaker in the orbit of the Lettrist movement, Marc'O was one of the first stage directors to shift emphasis from the literary text – of which, traditionally, the actor was considered to be a mere executioner – to the comedian as creator. Attentive to the internal dynamics within a theatre troupe, he devised a set of improvisational techniques to allow actors to become fully involved in what he considered a collective creative process. Both Bulle Ogier and Jean-Pierre Kalfon worked with the director at the American Center, one of the major Paris hubs for theatrical experimentation and a breeding ground for a new generation of actors, when Rivette discovered them in *Les Bargasses*, a play about sex workers in a bordello putting on an Aeschylus play to pass time while their clients are at war. So impressed was he by the play and the young actors that he gave them the lead roles in *L'Amour fou*, an experimental work that intertwines the relationship of a couple in crisis with the staging of a play. Though rarely screened, the more than four-hour-long *L'Amour fou* counts among the masterpieces of Rivette's filmic work.

At the centre of the film, as in *Paris nous appartient*, is a theatre troupe rehearsing. Stage director Sébastien Gracq (Jean-Pierre Kalfon) recasts Racine's classical piece *Andromaque* in an avant-garde stage language, elaborated in collaboration with his multicultural troupe of actors. What we see on screen constitutes a genuine theatrical experiment, insofar as Rivette gave Kalfon – who was a stage director-cum-actor in real life – carte blanche to choose his actors and to stage the play according to his own artistic vision. The play-within-the-film is itself the subject of a film-within-the-film as, in the filmic plot, the staging of the play is the focus of a television documentary in the making. The 'live' character of the play coming into being is relayed by the use of two cameras: on the one hand, Rivette and his team film the rehearsals with a 35mm Mitchell camera; on the other, a television crew led by André S. Labarthe – a critic for *Cahiers du cinéma* and, since 1964, director (together with Janine Bazin) of the documentary film series *Cinéastes de notre temps* – document the work of the director and his troupe with a hand-held 16mm Coutant.[42] Beyond merely capturing the rehearsals, the television crew seek to penetrate the mystery of theatrical creation by questioning the director and his actors on stage as well as in a series of backstage interviews. Whereas the editing of *L'Amour fou* often simply alternates takes of the two teams, we also see the television team at work filmed by Rivette's crew: in a doubly self-reflexive process, an invisible camera captures the filmic apparatus – clapper, camera and sound recording devices – in the process of documenting a play in progress.

Rivette's team maintains the same distance to the stage as would a spectator seated in the audience; Labarthe's crew, by contrast, gets much closer to the stage, periodically zooming in on the actors to capture their facial expressions and gestures in close-up.[43] The 16mm camera absorbs the theatrical performance by way of the specific syntax film developed in opposition to the stage arts: shot/counter-shot, shifting camera angles, varying shot formats. In their differing point of views and positioning, the two cameras contrast the conditions of spectatorship afforded by the theatre (one stable, unalterable point of view) with those of the cinema (variable camera angles and distance to the stage, mobility of the camera that can penetrate even backstage). In essence, they embody two opposing regimes of vision: the static gaze of the theatre audience versus the mobile gaze of a cinema that has emancipated itself from its ancestor. As a critic from *Cahiers du cinéma* remarks in the aforementioned interview with Rivette, while the takes of the shaky, grainy 16mm constantly remind us that we are watching a film, the 35mm's simulation of the unmediated presence that is characteristic of theatrical performance creates an effect of transparent immediacy:

> This gives the curious impression that it is the 16mm camera in charge of everything to do with the film, and that the 35mm camera doesn't exist, that it is only a transparent filter [. . .]. In the scenes in which the 16mm and 35mm cameras are mixed, it is the 16mm camera which passes for being cinema, with a precise sound, and when it is the 35mm camera, one has the impression of being a spectator of a performance, in the auditorium. In the apartment, one no longer has the impression, on account of the presence of the sole 35mm camera, that one is watching a film.[44]

Revealingly, in the dialogue *L'Amour fou* establishes between three media which each to a certain extent derive from one another – theatre, film and television – the latter (that is, cinema's main rival in the 1960s in the competition for most popular mass medium) appears as a hindrance to theatrical creation. Irritated by the intrusive presence of the TV crew, Sébastien's wife Claire (Bulle Ogier), who was to play the role of Hermione, walks out on the production where she will be replaced by Sébastien's former partner Marta (Josée Destoop). Henceforth, the filmic action moves back and forth between the rehearsals and the couple's home in a mirroring between the space of the theatre and the domestic space as sites where dramas of jealousy and betrayal are being acted out. The theatrical mise-en-abyme generates a complex set of echoes and reflections, notably in the doubling between Marta, who rehearses Hermione on stage, and Claire, who continues her rehearsals at home, but also between the fictional character embodied by Marta and Claire's predicament as Sébastien becomes attracted to Marta again. Not forgetting the stage director Sébastien, who at times resembles Labarthe, at others Rivette. Marta's revelation that her artist's name pays tribute to the actress Marta Abba, that is, the mistress and muse of Sicilian playwright Pirandello, introduces a further mirroring between the love triangle formed by Sébastien, Claire and Marta and that of Pirandello, his wife Antonietta and Marta Abba, culminating in the disturbing scene where Claire attacks Sébastien with a hairpin inspired by Antonietta's affliction with a mental illness that made her physically violent.[45] '[Th]e metaphor of the mirror', Wiles writes, 'determines the relation of repetition and difference that exists between film formats (16mm and 35mm), spaces (inside and outside the theatre), characters (scripted and unscripted), directors (TV and theatre/theatre and film/film and TV) and stories (*Andromaque* and *L'Amour fou*).'[46]

The allusion to Pirandello in this filmic hall of mirrors is far from coincidental. As a dramatist who revolutionised traditional theatre practices with his invention of 'theatre-in-the-theatre' and a playwright famous for his complex metaleptic narratives where different diegetic planes get entangled – notably in his celebrated theatre trilogy *Six Characters in Search of an Author*, *Each in His Own Way* and *Tonight We Improvise* – Pirandello offers both a model and an interpretative framework for a film where characters, actors and 'real' people have become enmeshed. Pirandello's work created a sensation in Paris thanks to Pitoëff's ingenious staging of *Six Characters* at the Théâtre des Champs-Élysées in 1923, introducing a new vein of theatre that, as J. L. Styan explains, would nowadays be called 'metatheater': 'theater which makes its audience conscious of the theater's own elements in order to work'.[47] Anna Paolucci provides a useful analysis of Pirandello's metatheatrical practice:

> He used telescopic techniques to destroy the passive notion of static 'illusion' on stage, superimposing action, moving actors in and out of their 'formal' roles, juxtaposing 'real' events with stage plot, creating a dialectic spiralling of roles within roles, settings within settings, realities within realities. In the fragmentation that resulted, a new force was unleashed that was to revitalise both drama and fiction in the years that followed.[48]

Pirandello's concept of theatre-in-the-theatre would of course have been of great interest to Rivette, who similarly draws on mise-en-abyme to create filmic spaces that allow him to reflect on cinema as a medium. But so would have been the playwright's concept of drama as a 'constant *becoming*',[49] his sustained questioning of the control exercised by the director (especially in *Tonight We Improvise* where the actors rebel against the stage director), and emphasis on creation as a form of collaboration which strongly resonate with Rivette's own concerns regarding the status of the cinema auteur. An implicit double of both Pirandello and the filmmaker, Sébastien's doubts about the production he directs (especially after seeing rushes of the rehearsals), his desire for a less controlling role and wish for greater involvement of the actors in the creative process obliquely give voice to Rivette's interrogation of auteurism and embrace of the new collective practices of the theatrical avant-garde of the 1950s and 1960s which were themselves strongly influenced by Pirandello.[50] Add to that the fact that Pirandello wrote one of the first novels about the cinema, *Shoot* (1915), centring on the work of a cameraman, and we begin to grasp the multiple pathways between theatre and cinema that nourish both the playwright's and Rivette's work.

In *L'Amour fou*, as we have seen, the theatrical and the domestic sphere become permeable through a web of echoes and mirrorings as dramatic plots and filmic 'reality' intersect. Yet, more broadly, theatrical performance can no longer be contained within the four walls of the theatre, as is most evident in a micro-performance enacted by Claire and Sébastien within the space of their home – a scene that was entirely improvised by the two actors. On the verge of breaking up, the couple are taking a 'time-out', which brings a sudden release of libidinal energy at a point where the narrative has become englued in a morbid stasis. Dressed up and masqueraded as if to mark the theatrical nature of the action to come, the two lovers smear their bedroom and each other in paint, rip off the wall covering, and smash the partition door to pieces with an axe. Next comes the television set, which implodes under the impact of the axe in a symbolic destruction of the medium that is at the origin of the crisis that has engulfed *L'Amour fou*.[51] The convulsive orgy of destruction does not cease until the whole living space has been trashed. The performance-style character of the sequence with its emphasis on ritual, wasteful expenditure and sexual release – the aggression against the object world is punctuated by love making – align the time-out with the experimental practices of the 'happening', spearheaded in 1960s New York by Allan Kaprow, Jim Dine and Claes Oldenburg and developed in Europe by groups such as Fluxus and Viennese Actionism.[52] The lovers' tearing and cutting of tactile surfaces and smashing of their domestic interior recall the destructivist *Materialaktionen* (material actions) of one of the Vienna Actionists, Otto

Mühl, who broke up, slashed, hacked and blew up the objects of consumer culture in his theatrical performances. Sébastien's cutting up of his clothes in an earlier scene is reminiscent of Yoko Ono's performance *Cut Piece* (1964) in which members of the audience were invited to cut off the artist's clothes, while the lovers' seclusion from the public space announces John Lennon's and Ono's 'bed-ins' in protest against the Vietnam War which, intriguingly, were filmed and later turned into a documentary movie. It is worth noting that Viennese Actionism did itself tap into some of the sources that inspired Rivette, notably Surrealism and Artaud's Theatre of Cruelty, which informed the notion of acting as a trance-like state and the emphasis on excess in the new theatrical practices of the 1960s. *L'Amour fou* signals its affinity with Surrealism through its title borrowed from André Breton's phantasmagoric, multimedia narrative as well as through the presence of Breton's *Nadja* – a novel revolving around the narrator's love for a mentally disturbed young woman – on the mantelpiece in the couple's bedroom. In *Paris nous appartient*, Rivette had given visual expression to his admiration for Artaud through a photo of the dramatist, actor and theatre director on Philip Kaufman's walls, even if at this point, as Cyril Béghin remarks, Artaud's theories did not yet have any direct resonance in the filmic fiction and the play of the actors.[53] Among this cross-fertilising circulation of tropes and ideas that extend from the classical avant-garde into the new vanguard of the 1960s and 1970s, let us also note that one of the heirs of the New Wave, Chantal Akerman – who like Rivette was intimately attuned to the experimentations of contemporary theatre – pastiches the scene of the lovers smashing the partition door in her feminist fable *Nuit et jour* (*Night and Day*, 1991), where it likewise constitutes the couple's desperate final attempt to make space for a relationship that escapes them before the woman walks out on her companion.

Though questioning the director's exclusive control over the artistic creation and delegating parts of the film to two other directors – the mise-en-scène of the play-within-the-film to Kalfon, the realisation of the film-within-the-film to Labarthe – *L'Amour fou* is still a film that relies to a certain extent on a screenplay (scripted by Rivette and Marilù Parolini). Indeed, in many ways, via the theatrical mise-en-abyme, the film is concerned with how a written text can be transformed into a performance, even if the coming into being of this performance, just like the film itself, is based on collective work with as little intervention of the director as possible.[54] It was with the almost thirteen-hour-long *Out 1*, Rivette's most daring and monumental work and one of the boldest experiments in the history of modern cinema, that the director made the leap to total improvisation, loosely held together by the Balzac intertext we discussed in the previous chapter. Eager to develop his work on filmic duration and to assimilate the new theatrical paradigm of collective creation into his practice, Rivette gave his actors carte blanche to invent and shape their characters according to their own vision. Everything we see and hear on screen was improvised on the spot without any pre-existing script or dialogues. The palpable difficulties of actors less comfortable with the improvisational technique, notably Bernadette Lafont and Françoise Fabian, endow the film with an immediacy and sense of risk traditionally associated with the experience of a live performance.[55] If theatrical creation is once more at the centre of Rivette's preoccupation, here, in a new variation on the double, we witness the work of two theatre groups engaged in staging Aeschylus: Lili's (Michèle Moretti, another actress who had formally worked with Marc'O) troupe of non-professional enthusiasts rehearse 'Seven against Thebes' whereas her former partner Thomas (Michael Lonsdale) directs a professional group engaged in research on 'Prometheus Bound'. The first two episodes of the film, often in real time, document the groups' collective creative practice. Diverse though their approaches may be, both troupes share a belief in the actor as artistic creator that is emblematic of the shift from the staging of a text to the idea of collective creation post 1968.[56]

Merging a Greek chorus with African drum rhythms and a modern flute improvisation, Lili's group recalls the diverse cultural inspiration of theatre collectives such as Ariane Mnouchkine's *Théâtre du soleil* or Peter Brook's *Centre International de Recherches Théâtrales* who fused Western with non-Western sources. Starting from the dramatic text, the group devises physical and vocal exercises in view of creating a spectacle that reconnects contemporary audiences with Ancient Greece. The troupe led by Thomas,

Figure 2.3 Theatrical experimentation in *Out 1* (Jacques Rivette, 1971).

by contrast, subscribes to a rawer form of improvisation destined to overcome the automatisms of everyday life and to release repressed instincts via protracted corporeal exercises. Convulsively rolling on the floor, biting and touching one another while emitting humming and whining sounds in an increasingly animalistic crescendo, the actors seek to access a primordial, presocialised state of being. The twitches and contortions of their trance-like, piled-up bodies are captured by a nimbly mobile, hand-held camera.

In an interview for *Cahiers du cinéma*, Michael Lonsdale recalls that, in *Out 1*, his fictional troupe was engaged in genuine theatrical research rather than just a filmic experiment.[57] Lonsdale's own exposure to the methods of the theatrical avant-garde – he had briefly worked with Peter Brook, using exercises developed by Jerzy Grotowski's Theatre Laboratory and Judith Malina and Julian Beck's Living Theatre – is noticeable in these rehearsal scenes which provide a fascinating insight into contemporary theatrical practices.[58] Bernard Dort's description of the practices of the Living Theatre illuminates the theatrical experiments on which Rivette draws in *Out 1*:

> what is at the centre is no longer the text, nor even the performance as the dramatic actualisation of a text, it's the process of elaborating the performance, it's the actor engaged in an endeavour of personal liberation, it's the group that will become an instrument of this liberation.[59]

In a perceptive article on performance in *Out 1*, Cyril Béghin points out that, while none of the two groups follow any particular practice in an orthodox way, Rivette makes a clear distinction between actors like Lonsdale, Moretti, Ogier and Fabian, who moved forwards and backwards between theatre and film, and the 'pure children of the cinema' Jean-Pierre Léaud and Juliet Berto. This opposition, he argues, 'activates a sort of metaphor of origins': on the one hand, Léaud and Berto, in their respective roles as a (false) deaf-mute relying on gestural language and a reembodiment of a character from a Feuillade serial, pantomime early cinema; on the other, the two theatre groups point to the contemporary avant-garde, which was heavily influenced by Artaud's call for a new theatrical language of ritual, magic and gesture in *Le Théâtre et son double* (1938).[60] With *Out 1*, then, Rivette seeks to reconnect with the richness of gestural expression of silent cinema, while also letting himself be inspired by the experiments of physical expression conducted by the theatrical avant-garde. In its attentiveness to the language of the body, which is in no way presented as subordinate to verbal language, *Out 1* offers a fascinating repository of 1970s gestures and practices of the everyday, from Colin's (Léaud) playing the harmonica in Parisian cafés to the penniless Fréderique's (Berto) passing time in her garret. In its embracing of non-verbal expressivity, the film aligns itself with what Giorgio Agamben has identified as one of the inherent projects of early cinema: a desperate artistic effort 'to evoke what was slipping through its [humanity's] fingers for ever' at a time when rapid technological change and modernisation were threatening to efface gestural richness.[61]

If the world of the theatre and the 'real' world once more become permeable in *Out 1*, here, in a variation on the earlier films we discussed, filmed theatre becomes gradually absorbed by literary narrative. As the fictional plot thickens, the documentary-style rehearsal scenes give way to a more narrative-driven feature propelled forward by the Balzac intertext. The primordial energy of theatrical experiment evaporates, both groups are shown to be in crisis, with their directors contemplating abandoning the productions. Yet the practice of theatrical improvisation showcased in the first two episodes has merely migrated from the theatre stage to the filmic practice. As becomes palpable in Bulle Ogier's visible surprise and pain as Bernardette Lafont slaps her in the face or in the latter's manifest discomfort as she remains silent among her happily improvising fellow actors, we are in the domain of the live event with all its risk and unpredictability. Nowhere more so than in the protracted final scene – metonymically entitled 'Noli me tangere' like the whole film – in which a destitute Thomas, after a wild run along a winterly beach, collapses in the sand, shaken by what at first seems to be tears, but which gradually morphs into a convulsive laughter. The gesturing, trance-like body becomes a landscape to be deciphered, as enigmatic as the unresolved mystery of the 'Treize'. The actor, having given up all defences, becomes a saintly, Christ-like figure – a trope that reappears in the vocabulary of Grotowski and Peter Brook.[62] Theatrical and cinematic improvisation, being 'in' (the world of theatre) or 'out' (the world of film), reveal themselves as the two facets of the same quest for a more truthful expression of what it means to be human.

BRECHT AND BEYOND: JLG'S THEATRICAL POLITICS

Divergent though they are in style and vision, there is much that links Godard and Rivette in the early 1960s: not least, as we have seen, Godard's production of Rivette's stage version of *La Religieuse*, but also, more generally, a sustained passion for theatre as a medium through which cinema can enrich its language and reflect on itself. Having played a small part alongside Karina in Antoine Bourseiller's production of Giraudoux's *Pour Lucrèce* at the 1962 Guingamp theatre festival, Godard became interested in filming a production of the play that he would stage himself. Intended as a 'praise of the theatre through cinema', the project came to an abrupt halt on the first day of production when Godard stepped out on the set to join Karina at a shooting in

Spain.⁶³ Closer still to Rivette, indeed anticipating *L'Amour fou*, is an equally unfinished project for a film based on the staging of Pirandello's *Six Characters in Search of an Author*, which was to enmesh the production's reception by the audience and critics with the process of its coming into being, while also developing a mise-en-abyme between the play and the 'real' lives of the theatre company.⁶⁴ In an interview for *Cahiers du cinéma* of 1967, Godard reiterates his longstanding passion for making a film 'intended to teach the audience what theatre is', in which the filmed process of theatrical creation would be intercut with scenes of the stage director and actors reviewing major dramatic theories from Aristotle to Brecht and Stanislavski.⁶⁵ For Godard, then, if theatre is above all a creative practice, it also needs to be understood as an artistic form whose theories and conventions have evolved and sometimes radically changed over the centuries. It must be grasped as the expression of a personal vision, but also as a collective process shared by a theatre group.

Where Rivette garnered inspiration in Pirandello and the theatrical avant-garde of the 1950s and 1960s influenced by both Pirandello and Artaud, Godard took above all a keen interest in the theory of epic theatre developed by Bertolt Brecht, whose first play in Paris in 1954, *Mother Courage*, shook up the Aristotelean principles that still dominated French theatrical practice at the time. Roland Barthes, one of the most astute commentators on Brecht, describes the principles of the 'Brechtian revolution' in a 1955 essay:

> Now comes a man whose work and thought radically contest this art so ancestral that we had the best reasons in the world for believing it to be 'natural'; who tells us, despite all tradition, that the public must be only half-committed to the spectacle so as to 'know' what is shown, instead of submitting to it; that the actor must create this consciousness by exposing not by incarnating his role; that the spectator must never identify completely with the hero but remain free to judge the causes and then the remedies of his suffering; that the action must not be imitated but narrated; that the theater must cease to be magical in order to become critical, which will still be its best way of being passionate.⁶⁶

With his distanced approach intended to break the theatrical illusion, as Barthes analyses so shrewdly, Brecht shakes audiences out of their passive viewing experience so as to encourage a critical engagement with the fictional world on stage, and, through a process of transfer, with the power structures that perpetuate social inequality. Traditionally channelled through identification with the characters of the play, illusion is shattered by means of distancing techniques such as title cards, direct address to the audience or interspersed song that constantly remind spectators that what they see is merely a representation. This rendering strange (*Verfremdung*) of the world on stage aims at triggering a process of awareness that helps audiences grasp the constructedness of a social order that the reigning powers would like to pass off as 'natural'. If Brecht thus draws on formal devices to invite a critical reflection on human alienation, he is also the first dramatist to claim the same importance for scenic language as for dramatic language, indeed the first, as stage director Roger Planchon signals, to give an equal responsibility to both:

> a movement on a stage, the choice of a colour, of decor, of a costume, etc, these things engage a total responsibility. Scenic writing is totally responsible, in the same way that writing in itself is responsible, I mean the writing of a novel or the writing of a play.[67]

It is immediately obvious why Brecht's emphasis on scenic language, his insistence on technique as a form of responsibility, and, more generally, his radical overturning of traditional staging practices would appeal to an auteur like Godard. Though still some way from the leftist militantism of his work post-1968, in Godard's films of the New Wave period the influence of Brecht's anti-illusionism is tangible, amid a broader engagement with theatrical forms. In *À bout de souffle*, as Klaus Kreimeier points out, manifold are the references to a medium from which cinema was supposed to have long emancipated itself. The use of the aside, notably in Michel's famous direct address to the spectator at the beginning of the film; employment of the iris-in that evokes both the end of a sequence in silent cinema and the falling of the curtain on stage; or the erotic 'chamber drama' in Patricia's bedroom, which allows us to look in at the couple's intimacy as though through a picture frame, all playfully rework theatrical conventions.[68] The smashing of the 'fourth wall' that traditionally separates the world of fiction and that of the audience was of course to become a trademark of Godard's anti-naturalistic style, alongside other Brechtian-inspired devices such as the fragmentation of the film narrative into theatrical tableaux, the use of intertitles to sum up the action to come, characters' intermittent breaking into song or dance, or the unveiling of the technical apparatus behind the construction of the spectacle.

Godard first adapted a theatrical work with *Les Carabiniers*, loosely based on the eponymous play by Beniamino Joppolo, one of Italy's most acclaimed twentieth-century playwrights alongside Pirandello. His casual attitude to the source text is emblematic of the emphasis on circulation and remediation in adaptation which we already observed in the previous chapter: as Roberto Rossellini was preparing a stage production of *I Carabinieri* for the Festival of Spoleto, Godard asked his scriptwriter Jean Gruault, during a trip to Rome, to record Rossellini's account of the play with a tape recorder, and, on this basis, to draft a short adaptation of some fifteen pages.[69] Godard never read the original, which was not available in French translation. In his introduction to *Les Carabiniers*, the director insists on the film's indebtedness to Brechtian principles, notably in its redefinition of realism not as a quest for mimetic, but for truthful representation:

> This film is a fable, an allegorical story in which realism serves only to reinforce the imaginary. It's in this way that the action and the events described in the film can very easily be situated anywhere, to the left, to the right, in front, at the same time a little bit everywhere and nowhere. In the same way, the few characters aren't situated psychologically, morally or still less sociologically. Everything takes place at an animal level, and still this animal is filmed from a vegetal perspective when it isn't mineral, which is to say Brechtian. [. . .] In short, everything, the set decoration, the characters, the actions, the landscapes, the adventures, the dialogue, everything is just *ideas*, and, as such, will be filmed as simply as possible, the simplest way in the world, the camera being, dare I say, in its simplest manifestation, in homage to Louis Lumière. Because it must not be forgotten that the cinema today, more than ever, must follow as a rule of conduct this observation by Berthold [sic] Brecht: 'Realism isn't real things but how things really are.'[70]

Contrary to Resnais and Rivette, theatre in *Les Carabiniers* is not enlisted as a mirroring device between staged and 'real' worlds, nor as a metalepsis to dissolve the boundaries between different diegetic levels. Rather, through a Brechtian-inspired de-dramatisation of the action and through distancing techniques such as the use of title cards, Godard encourages spectators to reflect critically on the dehumanisation and violence represented on screen. Enlisted as a means to render visible the process of human alienation, theatre also, on a meta-level – and here we are close to Resnais and Rivette again – becomes a tool to self-reflexively interrogate the nature of the cinematic image, notably in the scene of Michel-Ange's (Albert Juross) first visit to the movies. The three short films on the programme (the train entering the station, baby's breakfast, and the upper-class lady in her bath), Joachim Paech explains, trace a potted history of early cinema,[71] but the film-within-the-film also serves to pit the specificity of cinema against the properties of theatre. Mistaking the illusory presence of cinematic projection for the embodied here-and-now of theatrical performance, the naive Michel-Ange approaches the stage to be closer to the alluring figure of the woman immersed in her bathtub. Yet his grotesque endeavours to grope the elusive female form merely bring down part of the screen, leaving a gaping hole where there used to be flickering images. Cinematic desire is quite literally unveiled as being constructed around a void as the exposure of the cinematic apparatus brutally shatters the illusion of presence.[72] Their inability to distinguish between representation and reality – culminating in the protracted scene where they proudly show off their war bounty consisting of a suitcase filled with postcards – makes the *carabiniers* the perfect targets of political manipulation: easily recruited with the promise of financial gain, unquestioning of their actions, they kill, destroy and pillage in the name of their king, until, after the war has been lost, they are slaughtered themselves.

Before moving to a detailed analysis of *La Chinoise*, a film which, in the words of Jacques Rancière, shows us 'what mise-en-scène means in the cinema',[73] let us briefly examine the Vietnam protest skit in *Pierrot le fou* as an example of what Susan Sontag calls Godard's construction of 'political micro-entertainments' in the manner of Brecht.[74] Cash-strapped and drifting, Ferdinand and Marianne have decided to entertain a group of American tourists with a sketch of the Vietnam conflict. As befits an improvised street performance, the horrors of the war – which was among the main triggers for Godard's political radicalisation in the late 1960s[75] – are conjured up by the most meagre of means. A piece of cardboard and lit matches, manipulated by hand in the style of a puppet show, stand in for American air raids and napalm bombing. The actors' performance boils down to a burlesque parody of cultural stereotypes: a gun-brandishing, whisky-gulping Ferdinand in the role of an American officer yells 'Yeah, sure', 'Hollywood' or 'Communist' in a heavily French-accented voice, while the civilian victim played by Marianne – face painted yellow and dressed in a kimono and straw-hat – resists in a phonetic mimicry of the Vietnamese language. Their acting-out of imperialist warfare is intercut by shots of a soldier applauding the grotesque spectacle. The embedding of the play-within-the-film allows Godard to ironically imply two audiences: on the one hand, the intradiegetic audience of the performance, that is, the patriotic Americans relishing the spectacle of 'Uncle Sam's nephew versus Uncle Ho's niece', as signals a Brechtian intertitle; on the other, the more discerning movie spectator, who can quite literally 'see the bigger picture' (in both the sense of the medium cinema and the wider

Figure 2.4 Vietnam protest skit in *Pierrot le fou* (Jean-Luc Godard, 1965).

story), bemused by the subversive anti-war skit destined to lighten the tourists of their dollars. Where in Resnais and Rivette cinema and theatre become permeable, Godard, while drawing extensively on theatrical conventions and strategies, as is evidenced here, ultimately always brings us back to cinema. Referenced, parodied and appropriated, theatrical performance is absorbed into a 'total cinema' – it becomes a fold within the 'skin' of film.

In turning now to *La Chinoise*, Godard's prescient 'political comedy'[76] of five young people preparing a Maoist revolution, released less than a year before the events of May '68, we will see how an aesthetic explicitly borrowed from Brecht intersects with practices inspired by the contemporary avant-garde. A work 'in the making', as is announced in its subtitle, in truly Brechtian fashion the film subverts any attempts at spectator identification through a panoply of distancing effects: frontal addresses to the camera, actors stumbling over their lines, mini-plays embedded into the filmic diegesis, repeated unveilings of the cinematic apparatus in shots where the camera or the clapper become visible, as well as documentary-style interviews of the actors conducted by Godard himself who remains absent from view, but whose presence in the off-field is made palpable by his whispering voice. The centrality of Brecht for the filmic fiction is signalled in a scene where the actor Guillaume (played by Jean-Pierre Léaud, the only professional actor among the cast) erases one by one the names of great Western thinkers and writers from a blackboard until, in the middle, there remains only that of the German playwright, poet and theatre director.

Filmed for the most part within the confines of a bourgeois apartment – in fact, Godard's own flat, repainted in vivid primary colours for the shooting – *La Chinoise* plays with the 'filmed theatre' effect of works such as Cocteau's *Les Parents terribles* (1948) or Melville's *Les Enfants terribles* (1950) similarly set in a *huis clos*. Scenes filmed from the balcony through the windows give the impression that we are looking in on a stage, a conjuring of the theatrical space that is reiterated in the final scene in which the closing of the shutters evokes the falling of the curtain at the end of a play. If the film thus engages in dialogue with the theatre in its construction of the cinematic space as a stage and employment of Brechtian estrangement effects, the actors' performance – indeed the whole filmic action – is suffused with the 'excess of theatricality' which for Bazin was key to the success of filmed theatre. Transposing the classical trope of the *theatrum mundi* to the political plane, *La Chinoise* shows the idealistic youngsters – each of whom, with the exception of Guillaume, is to a certain extent a (stereo)type rather than a fully developed character – *playing* at being revolutionaries. As evidenced in their over-eagerness when they regurgitate lines from the Little Red Book, debate the virtues of Marxism-Leninism, submit to Communist-style sessions of self-criticism, or even plot the suicide of one of the members of the 'cell', the Mayakovsky-inspired painter Kirilov (Lex de Bruijn), the would-be revolutionaries have lost any critical distance towards their roles. As Michael Lommel comments in a compelling reading of the film,

> the revolution as a theatrical play in *La Chinoise* makes transparent the relation between existence and role, that is, the absurd illusory world of characters [...] who take their own roles seriously, estrange themselves in them. [...] Godard's filmed theatre is not political in a Brechtian sense, but politics itself takes a theatrical air in *La Chinoise*.⁷⁷

The characters' identification with their roles points once more to that other counter-illusionist, Pirandello, notably his tragic farce *Henry IV*, where the eponymous main character – not unlike Véronique (Anne Wiazemsky) in the film – has become one with his role to such an extent that, at the end of the play, he commits a crime.

The question of what constitutes an actor and what are the essence and purpose of theatre is broached in the first of the documentary-style interviews that punctuate the filmic narrative. To a barely audible question from Godard, Guillaume (Jean-Pierre Léaud) replies with a live demonstration of theatre in action: bandaging his face with gauze, he tells – and, at the same time, re-enacts – the story of a Chinese student purporting to have been beaten up by Russian policemen. When the student slowly removes his

Figure 2.5 Brechtian theatre in action: Guillaume (Jean-Pierre Léaud) re-enacting the Chinese student's performance in *La Chinoise* (Jean-Luc Godard, 1967).

bandage in front of the assembled Western press, revealing a perfectly intact face, the crowd treats him as an impostor. Yet his performance, Guillaume explains, is genuine theatre in the tradition of Brecht or Shakespeare, in that it invites a critical reflection on reality. In this played parable, then, theatre is quite literally considered as a process of unveiling destined to reveal the truth, albeit a truth quite different from what the spectacle-hungry media expected: in a strategy akin to what one of the most lucid critics of the society of the spectacle, Guy Debord, calls *détournement*, the actor confronts the media with its own sensationalism.

The interrogation of illusion and truth that underpins Guillaume's theatrical demonstration is transported to the sphere of cinema when a counter-shot reveals cinematographer Raoul Coutard behind his camera, reminding spectators that the young man re-enacting the performance of the Chinese student is in fact a fictional character played by an actor in a film in the making. The implied presence of a second camera, hidden from view, but necessary to unveil the presence of the cinematic apparatus that has intermittently become visible, alerts us to the impossibility to ever 'penetrate the final veil and experience cinema unmediated by cinema'.[78] The mise-en-abyme raises questions as to who speaks: is it the character Guillaume who answers Godard's question or, more likely, the actor Léaud, who, at the time of filming *La Chinoise*, was getting involved in more popular, engaged forms of theatrical representation?[79] As at the beginning of *Deux ou trois choses que je sais d'elle*, where Godard interviews Juliette Jeanson (Marina Vlady), the distinction between character and actor gets blurred in a metaleptic contamination between different narrative levels. Introducing what, in narratological terms, Brian McHale calls a 'short circuit' between the 'fictional world and the ontological level occupied by the author',[80] the metalepsis lifts the mimetic illusion. Add to this Brecht's description of the alienation effects used in Chinese theatre – notably the Chinese actor's '*mak[ing]* it clear that he knows he is being looked at' – in his 1961 article 'On Chinese Acting',[81] and we are in a loop of acting and re-enacting.

Following Guillaume's enactment of the Chinese student's performance, an insert asking 'What's the state of new theatre' alludes to the influence of contemporary avant-garde theatre on the film's 'politics as theatre' mode. As a meditation on the work of the actor and on the possibility of changing society through theatrical practices, *La Chinoise* is poised in-between a Brechtian mode and the so-called 'New theatre' of the 1960s. While the various 'plays-within-the-film' – anti-Vietnam skits directed by Guillaume and Kirilov and performed by Yvonne (Juliet Berto) – are, like the street theatre in *Pierrot*, situated in the lineage of Brecht, the filmic plot traces Guillaume's move towards participatory forms of theatre that recall the experiments of companies such as the Living Theatre or Marc'O.[82] At the beginning of the film, in the aforementioned interview, Godard asks Guillaume/Léaud: 'What is a true socialist theatre?' An extended coda at the end shows the actor's experiments with more direct forms of cultural action. In a strongly oneiric scene, Guillaume stumbles upon an improvised theatre space, *Le Théâtre zéro*, among the rubble of a house in the process of demolition. With a homeless person as the only spectator, isolated between glass walls, he is solicited by two women – one old, the other young, both in swimming costume – who insistently knock against the partition. As the camera lingers on a medium shot of the young man, the lights slowly fade, suggesting the end of a theatrical performance. Intercut with shots of Véronique's friends finding their parents' trashed flat and words that gradually form into a sentence that can be read as an intertextual model for the film – 'The theatrical vocation of Guillaume Meister and his years of apprenticeship and travels on the road of a true socialist theatre' – two further scenes document Guillaume's engagement with the new models of direct audience participation that emerged in the course of the 1960s. In the first, an open-air happening-style performance, the public is invited to throw vegetables and eggs at the actor. The second, in a variation of the 'door to door' theatre, shows the actor and a neighbour engaging in a theatrical conversation on the landing of an apartment block. Making use of the collage practice we identified in *Alphaville*,[83] Godard assembles selected verses from four Racine plays – *Iphigénie*, *Bérénice*, *Britannicus* and *Athalie* – into a stylised dialogue that ends with Guillaume extolling the virtues of the Little Red Book.

What, then, is the 'true socialist theatre' that Guillaume, a modern avatar of Goethe's Wilhelm Meister, is discovering (and putting into action) in the deconstructed *Bildungsroman* that is *La Chinoise*? It is important to bear in mind that, in the wake of the theatrical experiments of the 1950s and 1960s, Jean Vilar's *Théâtre national populaire*, aimed at educating the masses, was replaced by a more political theatre that challenged traditional staging conventions. Like his former colleagues from *Cahiers du cinéma*, Godard had long despised Vilar's *TNP* with its 'grand masses of frozen, dusty, academic popular theatre'.[84] The new socialist theatre for him, as is evidenced in *La Chinoise*, must involve a more involved audience engagement, be it through the Brechtian destruction of illusion or the new forms of audience participation that were developed by the Living Theatre, street theatre or performance. Anchored in a history that needs to be confronted – *Le Théâtre année zéro* alludes to Rossellini's iconic *Germania anno zero* (*Germany, Year* Zero, 1948), filmed in a bombed-out Berlin – political theatre quite literally here emerges from the ruins of a past it ceaselessly interrogates, revisits and reclaims. Dressed as a figure of the Great Revolution, citing Racine and following in the footsteps of Wilhelm Meister, Guillaume forges a theatrical language that nourishes itself in past centuries while being radically contemporary in its form. Inverting the logic of *Wilhelm*

Meister, Rancière explains, where the hero 'starts in love with the theatre and ends by finding certainty in collective knowledge', Godard's protagonist 'moves in the opposite direction and leads collective knowledge back to the elements of the art of the theatre'.[85] Guillaume's playful recasting of two of the classics of Western literature – Racine and Goethe – and experiments with contemporary theatrical practice echo Godard's own dismantling and re-appropriation of artistic works of diverse historical periods.

Speaking of the director's attack on cinematic tradition, Susan Sontag lucidly remarks that 'this art of demolition is executed with the élan of someone working in an art form experienced as young, on the threshold of its greatest development rather than at its end'.[86] We could say the same for Godard's summoning of film's neighbouring arts: as the youngest and, as New Wave filmmakers sought to demonstrate, most vibrant in the canon of the arts, but also, crucially, as the only one which can absorb and evoke all the others in its multimedia texture, cinema, in the hands of Godard, confidently deploys its capacity to cite and refract the other arts. Incorporating a heterogeneous array of images – paintings, photographs, newspaper clippings, posters, cartoons – quotations and performances, *La Chinoise* is one of those radically open and self-consciously hybrid works that invite, indeed compel, the spectator to be alert to its ever-shifting types of representation and combinations of image, text and sound. It is a work where politics itself, as Antoine de Baecque points out, becomes a matter of aesthetics:

> politics is a plastic as much as a poetics, a pre-68 actualisation that is always a principle of Godard: form is content, content is form. Politics takes place in the intensity of a colour, the editing of a sequence, the rhymes of a slogan, the tracking shot across a balcony, the manner of shooting a conversation as well as a face. It's above all an aesthetic material.[87]

Perhaps on the deepest level, it is in this equation between politics and aesthetics that Godard joins Brecht and the contemporary avant-garde in a shared commitment to what Barthes, with reference to Brecht, calls the 'responsibility of forms'.[88] Fundamentally, despite their evident divergences, this is also what unites our three directors' engagement with theatrical forms: the forging of an aesthetic apt at self-reflexively examining (and expanding) cinema while dissecting the *theatrum mundi* of a society stifled by conventions, but shaken up by a new generation of artists and thinkers.

Notes

1. Narboni, 'Le Temps de la critique', p. 24.
2. Sand, 'Entretien avec Alain Resnais', p. 5.

3. Bontemps, Comolli, Delahaye and Narboni, 'Lutter sur deux fronts', p. 68.
4. Bazin, 'Theater and cinema', p. 80.
5. Ibid. pp. 78–9.
6. Canudo, 'Reflections on the seventh art', pp. 297–8.
7. On cinema's syntax see Dulac, 'The expressive techniques of the cinema'.
8. Abel, *French Film Theory and Criticism*, vol. 2, p. 17. See also Bazin's critique of Pagnol's filmed theatre in 'Le cas Pagnol'.
9. Bazin, 'Theater and cinema', pp. 101–2.
10. Ibid. p. 114.
11. Ibid. p. 116–17.
12. Ibid. p. 123.
13. Corvin, 'Une Ecriture plurielle'.
14. Roloff, 'Theater und Theatralität im Film', p. 5.
15. Ibid. p. 5.
16. Ibid. p. 8.
17. Roloff mentions Rohmer, Truffaut and Chabrol, Louis Malle, as well as directors influenced by the New Wave such as Marguerite Duras and Alain Robbe-Grillet ('Theater und Theatralität', p. 7).
18. The term is borrowed from Vincent Amiel's 'cinémalité' coined itself from 'théâtralité' ('Comme au théâtre!', p. 40).
19. See Canudo, 'Reflections on the seventh art', p. 293. Resnais cited in Winter, 'Kino-Schauspiel', p. 42.
20. Winter, 'Kino-Schauspiel', p. 42.
21. It is also useful to consider that, between 1940 and 1942, Resnais studied acting at a Paris-based drama school, the Cours René Simon.
22. Libois, 'Théâtre, cinéma, l'autre-scène', p. 22.
23. Leutrat, *L'Année dernière à Marienbad*, p. 41.
24. Robbe-Grillet, *L'Année dernière à Marienbad*, p. 28.
25. Paraskeva, 'Samuel Beckett, Alain Resnais', p. 33.
26. Winter, 'Kino-Schauspiel', p. 44.
27. Paraskeva, 'Samuel Beckett, Alain Resnais', p. 35.
28. The truncated title of the play-within-the-film, *Rosmer*, alludes to Ibsen's 1886 play *Rosmersholm*.
29. Amiel, 'Comme au théâtre!', p. 40.
30. See Deschamps, *Jacques Rivette*, pp. 8–9.
31. Caratini, 'Le Fantôme du théâtre'.
32. Aumont et al., 'Le temps déborde', pp. 15–16.
33. Jacques Rivette, *Paris nous appartient*, DVD BFI, Extra 'New Filmed Introduction by Jonathan Romney on Rivette and *Paris nous appartient*'.
34. Susan Sontag makes a helpful distinction between 'improvised' cinema and 'filmmakers, notably Godard, who have become fascinated with the "look" of improvised [. . .] cinema, used for formalistic ends' ('Theatre and Film', pp. 112–13).
35. Wiles, *Jacques Rivette*, p. 27. The reading that follows is based on Wiles's extensive analysis of the film.

36. Wiles, *Jacques Rivette*, p. 29.
37. Ibid. p. 30.
38. Rivette, 'Conférence de presse', p. 34, cited in Wiles, *Jacques Rivette*, p. 30.
39. Aumont et al., 'Le temps déborde', p. 7.
40. Ibid. p. 7.
41. See Wiles, *Jacques Rivette*, pp. 12, 16 and 45.
42. Rivette had collaborated with Labarthe on a three-part television film on Jean Renoir.
43. See Wiles, *Jacques Rivette*, p. 44 and Deschamps, *Jacques Rivette*, p. 21.
44. Aumont et al., 'Le temps déborde', p. 11.
45. Wiles, *Jacques Rivette*, p. 48.
46. Ibid. p. 49.
47. Styan, 'J. L. Styan on Pirandello's Innovations', p. 81.
48. Paolucci, 'Anne Paolucci on Pirandello's Exploration', p. 56.
49. Ibid. p. 56.
50. For Pirandello's legacy see de Jomaron, 'En quête de textes', p. 787.
51. See Wiles, *Jacques Rivette*, p. 51.
52. For these two groups see articles '1962a' and '1962b' in Foster et al., *Art Since 1900*, pp. 456–69.
53. Béghin, 'Le Grand jeu', p. 70.
54. See Aumont et al., 'Le Temps déborde', p. 8.
55. See Michael Lonsdale's, Bulle Ogier's and Stéphane Tchalgadjieff's accounts of the improvisational techniques in Béghin, 'C'est comme vous voulez. Entretien avec Michael Lonsdale' and Frappat, 'L'Angle du hasard. Entretien avec Bulle Ogier et Stéphane Tchalgadjieff'.
56. For the emergence of collective creation see Dort, 'L'âge de la représentation', p. 1009.
57. Béghin, 'C'est comme vous voulez', p. 75.
58. See Béghin, 'Le Grand jeu', p. 70.
59. Dort, 'L'âge de la représentation', p. 995.
60. See Béghin, 'Le Grand jeu', p. 70.
61. Agamben, *Infancy and History*, p. 138.
62. See Dort, 'L'âge de la représentation', p. 996.
63. Letter to Pierre Braunberger, cited in de Baecque, *Godard*, p. 191.
64. De Baecque, *Godard*, p. 187.
65. Bontemps et al., 'Lutter sur deux fronts', p. 68.
66. Barthes, 'The Brechtian revolution', pp. 37–8.
67. Interview with Arthur Adamov and René Allio, April 1960, cited in Dort, 'L'âge de la représentation', p. 984.
68. Kreimeier, 'Theatralität und Filmsprache'.
69. De Baecque, *Godard*, pp. 213–14.
70. Godard, 'Introduction' aux *Carabiniers*, collection scénario, dossier 'Les Carabiniers', BiFi/ Cinémathèque française, cited in de Baecque, *Godard*, p. 216.
71. Paech, 'Das Kino als Bühne', p. 21.

72. It is worth mentioning here that the Lettrist group of the 1950s with which, as we saw in Chapter 1, Godard shares certain practices, similarly interrogated the cinematic apparatus: in Maurice Lemaître's *Le Film est déjà commencé?* (1951), for instance, actors posing as members of the audience sabotaged the viewing experience by blocking part of the screen with their bodies, eventually ripping it open with a knife.
73. Rancière, *Film Fables*, p. 143.
74. Sontag, 'Godard', p. 164. Sontag lists the Feiffer dialogue of the two radio operators in *Deux ou trois choses que je sais d'elle* and the home political theatre performance in *La Chinoise* as other examples of 'Godard Brechtianising' alongside other song and stage performances that interrupt the story such as the dance trio in the café in *Bande à part* or the singing telephone call in *Weekend*.
75. For the impact of Vietnam on Godard see McCabe, *Godard*, pp. 181–2.
76. The term is by de Baecque (*Godard*, p. 355).
77. Lommel, '68er-Reflexionen', p. 77 and p. 81.
78. Sontag, 'Godard', p. 170.
79. On Léaud's acting career at the time of *La Chinoise*, see de Baecque, *Godard*, p. 356.
80. McHale, *Postmodernist Fiction*, p. 119 and p. 213.
81. Brecht, 'On Chinese acting', p. 130 (emphasis in original).
82. De Baecque signals Godard's interest in Marc'O's 1966 play *Les Idoles* later turned into a film (*Godard*, p. 386).
83. Cf. Chapter 1.
84. Cited in de Baecque, *Godard*, p. 372.
85. Rancière, *Film Fables*, p. 152.
86. Sontag, 'Godard', p. 156.
87. De Baecque, p. 355.
88. Barthes, 'Pourquoi Brecht', p. 164.

CHAPTER THREE

Painterly Hybridisations

> I would like to believe that the two conceptions, that of the painter and that of the filmmaker, are not irreconcilable.
>
> Éric Rohmer[1]

Long considered as the *first* art – the art whose material, in Hegel's words, is 'the making visible as such'[2] – painting is harshly put to the test in Rohmer's 'Le Siècle des peintres' ('The Century of Painters'), the second essay in his 'Le Celluloïd et le marbre' series. Drawing on Malraux's theory of the evolution of the arts which also inspired Bazin, the critic pinpoints the heyday of painting as the late nineteenth and beginning of the twentieth century, when painters such as Matisse, Cézanne, Bonnard, Picasso and Klee took the art to new heights in an extraordinary flourish of creative liberty. For half a century, Rohmer admits, painting became the leading art, imposing its laws on all the others, indeed refashioning the world we inhabit with its new vision. Yet, in mid-century, he argues, painters' liquidation of figurative expression (that is, the abstract revolution spearheaded by movements such as Op Art, Informal Art or Conceptual Art that shook the art world in the course of the 1950s) is jeopardising the very essence of their art: visuality. While painting has entered a period of inevitable decline, its younger sibling, cinema, currently in the prime of a *classicism* that all other arts have lost, is about to take its place.[3]

In the double repudiation of inheritance that we already saw at work with regard to literature, Rohmer not only deposes an important rival, but, in the same breath, sweeps aside the experiments of the classical avant-garde who aligned film with painting, poetry and music in their quest for a non-narrative, 'pure' form of cinema. Lashing out against hybrid forms such as the *poème-cinématographique* or the *film d'essai*, he equally dismisses Elie Faure's concept of 'cineplastics' – defined by Faure as 'a living rhythm and its repetition in time', which he deems to be a category of painting rather than of cinema.[4] Film, Rohmer cautions, will not establish its credentials as art by imitating its siblings, as is still upheld by too many critics and even film professionals, who feel that 'cinematic imagination is the respectful daughter of pictorial or poetic invention'.⁵ Cinema's possibilities as a mechanical system of reproduction must not be reduced to making it ersatz painting: 'never will the most beautiful photograph equal the least brushstroke, the least scrap of writing. If the ambition of the new art were merely to bang out what its elders have perfected, I really wouldn't hold out much hope for it.'⁶ For Rohmer, cinema's strength lies precisely in its ability to reproduce exactly, yet, like Bazin, he does not consider this to be a hindrance to the filmmaker's creativity.

In a 1963 preface to a planned collection of essays entitled *L'Âge classique du cinéma* (*The Classic Age of the Cinema*) that remained unpublished, later recycled as the preface to the publication of *Le Celluloïd et le marbre* in book form, Rohmer nuances some of his more polemical points in the essays, especially his championing of film at the expense of contemporary art in 'Le Siècle des peintres'. If he has a tendency to glorify the former while denigrating the latter, he explains, this is to counter the still widely held view that cinema's ambition is inferior to that of the other arts. Cinema, he asserts, is free to 'pillage its rivals [. . .] as long as it doesn't relegate itself to a state of inferiority towards them'.⁷ While insisting on cinema's specificity, Rohmer concedes that there undoubtedly exists 'a more secret agreement, that blooms in the higher spheres of aesthetic contemplation, in this heaven in which all the beauties mingle and make one whole'.⁸ It is at this aesthetic level, and not on a merely structural one, he argues, that one can conceive artistic cross-fertilisation.

In a long interview of 2009 with Noël Herpe and Philippe Fauvel, returning to his reflection on cinema's relations to the other arts, developed in the 'Celluloïd et le marbre' series, Rohmer discloses to what extent his own filmic work has been continuously enriched in dialogue with other artistic forms. Citing Cézanne, Picasso, Matisse, Paul Klee and Nicolas de Staël as artists with whom he has a particular affinity – alongside numerous other painters from van Eyck to Edward Hopper testifying not only to his passion, but broad knowledge of art – he notes that if, as a matter of principle, he never references cinema, all of his films contain allusions to either literature or painting. Beyond the use of 'hidden quotations' that serve as a commentary on the affective lives of characters – such as the Mondrians in Rémi's (Tchéky Karyo) home in *Les Nuits de la pleine lune* (*Full Moon in Paris*, 1984) or a Nicolas de Staël in Blanche's (Emmanuelle Chaulet) apartment in *L'Ami de mon amie* (*Boyfriends and Girlfriends*, 1987) – the director reveals a deeper engagement with painting on the level of colour, composition and mise-en-scène: in *Le Genou de Claire* (*Claire's Knee*, 1970), for instance, the sequence by the lake draws on the colours and decorative style of Gauguin's Tahiti paintings, while in *Pauline à la plage* (*Pauline at the Beach*, 1983) the main colour scheme reworks the colours of Matisse's *La Blouse roumaine*, a reproduction of which is visible in Pauline's (Amanda Langlet) room. The costumes and décor for *La Marquise d'O* (*The Marquise of O*, 1976) were inspired by theatre sets, German neoclassical painting, as well as later Romantic painters, notably Caspar David Friedrich. Moreover, his sustained interest in painting is evidenced in his diaporamas on Titian and Raphael, commissioned for exhibitions at the Grand Palais, and the presence of painter-protagonists in several of his films: the third sketch of *Les Rendez-vous de Paris* (*Rendez-vous in Paris*, 1995), *4 aventures de Reinette et Mirabelle* (*Four Adventures of Reinette and Mirabelle*, 1987), and *Triple Agent* (2004).[9]

Rohmer's ambivalent stance on painting, marked by both a refusal to bow to a more prestigious ancestor, yet, at the same time, an interest in the fine arts as a source of inspiration and creative reworking, is to a certain extent paradigmatic of a wider paradoxical attitude towards painting among the early *Cahiers* critics. As Jacques Aumont points out, painting was at the same time a taboo object and a means of legitimising cinema as art through a process of appropriation and reworking:

> It was therefore the pursuit of a paradoxical critical tradition (that of the *Cahiers* of the yellow era, essentially), in which painting was considered *a priori* the bad object par excellence, that which mustn't be found there (there: in films), because it would stain, because it would ruin all possibility of specific artistic virtue, because it was a reactionary force, the symptom of cineastes' attachment to roots that didn't belong to them.
>
> The place of the 'belated inferior' of cinematographic art would thus have led it to encounter ideas, sometimes forms, not to say formulae, that had already been invented elsewhere, principally in painting, but which it alters in taking them up again. Now these coincidences nearly always are magnetised by an inevitability, which is that 'cinema' wants to show itself as art, and for that reason borrows, or recycles, or transforms something from an inheritance that's either real or imagined.[10]

It is once more Bazin, in an article that rehearses arguments which we have already encountered in 'For an Impure Cinema' and 'Theater and Film', who propounds an intermedial aesthetic that reconciles these conflicts. Just as he had advocated adaptation and filmed theatre as exemplars of artistic cross-fertilisation, so too in the short but dense 'Painting and Cinema', the critic makes himself the champion of post-war art films, a genre which, as Steven Jacobs notes, 'confront[s] the paradox that art objects are still while films trace movement in space and time'.[11] Bazin cites the post-war art documentaries of Luciano Emmer, Resnais's *Van Gogh* (1948), Pierre Kast's *Les Désastres de la guerre* (*Goya: The Disasters of War,* 1951), and Resnais and Robert Hessens' *Guernica* (1950) as examples of films about painting that use paintings 'to create something the structure of which is cinematic'.[12] Refuting the arguments of painters and art critics who contend that such films are not true to painting, he argues on the contrary (as with literature and theatre previously) that cinema is a privileged means to making painting accessible to wider audiences: far from compromising or betraying painting, film has the capacity to save it by bringing it to the attention of the general public.

Within the wider perspective of an impure cinema, for Bazin the postwar art films, though autonomous art works, are a crucial example of the enhanced aesthetic properties of cinematic hybridisations. He writes:

> These films are works in their own right. They are their own justification. They are not to be judged by comparing them to the paintings they make use of, rather by the anatomy or rather the histology of this newborn aesthetic creature, fruit of the union of painting and cinema. The objections I raised earlier are in reality a way of giving definition to the new laws following upon this mating. The role of cinema here is not that of servant nor is it to betray the painting. Rather it is to provide it with a new form of existence. The film of a painting is an aesthetic symbiosis of screen and painting, as is the lichen of the algae and mushroom.[13]

Where in 'For an Impure Cinema' Bazin draws on the geological metaphor of erosion and irrigation, here the botanical image of the lichen, a composite organism that lives in a symbiotic association and whose combined properties are different from those of its composing organisms, is engaged to make his plea for the mutually beneficial relationship between cinema and painting. Like his examination of filmed theatre, the interrogation of films about painting allows the critic to reflect on what is specific about the two arts, leading him to the well-known distinction between the 'centripetal' picture frame that 'polarises space inwards' and the 'centrifugal' cinema screen whose field of vision 'seems to be part of something prolonged indefinitely into the universe'.[14] If integrated into a film, he argues, '[w]ithout losing its other characteristics the painting thus takes on the spatial properties of cinema and becomes part of that "picturable" world that lies beyond it on all sides'.[15]

Disparaging the critics of art documentaries, Bazin largely makes a case for how painting can benefit from cinema. Yet how about film? How is cinema nourished and transformed by crossing over into a 'space the orientation of which is inwards'?[16] What can it gain from dialogue with painting? What new configurations, apart from the art documentaries discussed in 'Painting and Cinema', are born out of cinema's 'mating' with its older sibling? And, most importantly for us here, how are the hybridisations advocated by Bazin borne out among the New Wave's wider interrogation and dissolution of media boundaries?

Attentive to the diversity of interactions between film and painting, our approach in this chapter will be informed by Jacques Aumont's idea of artistic 'migration', itself inspired by Aby Warburg's notion of 'migration' as the subterranean passage of artistic figures and motifs across centuries, geographical space and even seemingly unconnected cultures. For Aumont, it is not so much the practice of citation that defines the relationship between painting and film, but, rather, the more complex, often diffuse ways in which a film re-actualises an art work, tradition or cultural heritage by means of its own specific language and expression. In the wake of Bazin, who insists on film's capacity to critically shed light on painting in 'Painting and Cinema',[17] Aumont conceives of film's refashioning of painting as a form of art criticism in action, as well as a practice akin to translation: 'The artist is a critic to the extent that he practises an art that reproduces in its own form the work of the past, transformed, metamorphosed. Migration is this power of translation.'[18] The question of the relationship between cinema and painting, then, cannot be reduced to the mere practice of citation, even if this practice establishes the most visible, and, arguably, the most accessible bridge between the two art forms.

Where literature and the theatre invite the cinema to reflect on its similarities and differences with regard to narrative-driven art forms, as a non-narrative, 'pure' art, painting engages the medium in a reflection on looking and seeing, on the visibility and making visible that Hegel identifies as the material essence of painting. Interrogating film as a scopic regime, painting's encounter with film encourages a wider meditation on the nature and status of the image, especially as regards its relationship to reality – an issue that is particularly ambivalent in cinema, a medium that, while offering a particularly privileged access to the real, is in no way reducible to a mere copying of life.

New Wave film, as we will see, exhibits a wealth of interactions with painting, ranging from the most literal inscriptions – the referencing of paintings, presence of painter figures and recording of the act of painting – to a plethora of more subterranean interactions: from the appropriation or playful negotiation of artistic traditions with their specific canons of beauty to the practice of *tableaux vivants*; from the espousal of painterly compositions to the choice of colour palettes inspired by individual paintings or artistic movements; from ekphrastic recreations of art works in the language of film to the refashioning of painterly techniques. Making its own a visual heritage no longer perceived as a restrictive model, but, on the contrary, as a rich repository of iconographies, motifs and techniques to be appropriated and reimagined, the New Wave reframes the visual arts with a view to enriching its own artistic language.

Our journey into the world of painting begins with a famous run across the Louvre, before zooming in on three directors – Agnès Varda, Jean-Luc Godard and Guy Gilles – whose background in and lifelong engagement with the fine arts make them particularly pertinent for our investigation, though they were by no means the only New Wave directors who drew upon the history of art and painting.[19] As the 'secret child of the New Wave', Gilles's position at the margins of the movement will need to be investigated in some depth before turning to his 'plastic' notion of the cinematic image shaped by poetry and the visual arts. But first: ready, set, go!

REVISITING THE LOUVRE: THE (IMAGINARY) MUSEUM

A shaky pan from left to right brings into view the full expanse of the Louvre, the world's largest art museum and France's former royal palace. Jump cut. We are in the Grand Gallery, in the section of French neoclassical painting. Three young people, Franz (Sami Frey), Arthur (Claude Brasseur) and Odile (Anna Karina) run towards the camera; on either side of the gallery, we perceive paintings in quick succession without being able to make out their exact subject matter. As the camera is overtaken by the runners, it lingers for a moment on a close-up of Jacques-Louis David's neoclassical *Oath of the Horatii* (1784), contemplated by a museum visitor. A second long take repeats the same composition of the runners running towards the camera and overtaking it, with the variation that, this time, it follows them from the back as they run towards the end of the gallery. Finally, a third long take follows the actors running down the monumental staircase – *The Winged Victory of Samothrace* coming briefly into view in the depth of field – and making their exit via the collection of Greek sculptures. The trio have won their bid: to beat the record of an American man, who has 'done' the Louvre in nine minutes and forty-five seconds.

Twenty-four seconds long, Godard's Louvre insert in *Bande à part*, allegedly added to compensate for the film's short running time, is itself a burlesque prank that playfully subverts the educational values traditionally associated with the museum space. An obligatory station on the 'grand tour', destined to sensitise upper-class young people of previous centuries to the aesthetic canons of classical European art, and a must for the modern tourist in Paris, the ritual visit to the Louvre is reinvented here as an improvised competition to traverse – and be done with – the venerable temple of high art in as little time as possible. The popular assault on high culture that is at the heart of the prank is all the more palpable in that neither the Louvre staff nor its visitors had been informed about the shooting. Authorised by France's Minister of Cultural Affairs, André Malraux, and filmed without the possibility of a

Figure 3.1 Arthur (Claude Brasseur), Odile (Anna Karina) and Franz's (Sami Frey) run through the Louvre in *Bande à part* (Jean-Luc Godard, 1963).

retake, the sequence takes the form of a live happening as the three actors run past visibly astonished members of the public while museum attendants try in vain to halt their joyous advance.

For spectators versed in classic French fiction, the trio's race through the Louvre instantly evokes another, literary visit, that of the wedding party in Zola's *L'Assommoir* (1877), which Godard, an avid reader of literature, seems to reimagine in the twentieth-century idiom of film. In Zola's satirical description, a working-class wedding party pays the obligatory visit to the Louvre, at first transfixed by the cultural prestige of the French gallery and the treasures of European painting, but soon fatigued by the sheer wealth of art works whose subject matter and style remain undecipherable to them. Lost in the meandering galleries and corridors of the museum, they become a bemusing spectacle for more educated visitors, not so different from our trio of marginal characters in *Bande à part*.

At the nodal points of literature, painting and film, the Louvre insert, in tune with Godard's wider positioning towards the arts, offers a demonstration of the expressive powers of the filmic medium. Pitting the vertiginous mobility of Raoul Coutard's camera against the immobility of the museum exhibits, it constitutes what Valentin Nussbaum calls 'a lesson in cinema'.[20] In the first shot in particular, the long take and the close-up – as 'two principles of cinematic grammar' – are associated with the cinema and painting respectively, the first shot of the runners advancing towards the camera being reminiscent of the Frères Lumières's frontal view compositions, whereas the close-up of the *Oath of the Horatii* 'suspends a still image in the tradition of history painting'.[21] The appearance of the neoclassical painting, Nussbaum argues,

> expresses the paradox of modernity in its reflection of novelty through a nostalgic search for classicism. In Godard's montage, the painting plays a provocative role, not mapping a definitive definition of what 'classical' or 'modern' should signify but placing the question itself at the crossroads.[22]

Godard here extends to the domain of painting an interrogation that was launched with regard to literature at the beginning of the film when the English teacher dictating Shakespeare provocatively pens the equation 'classique=moderne' on the blackboard. If for Godard the classic is modern, what he implies – in a striking similarity to Proust, who pursued a similar reflection at the beginning of the century in the essay 'Classicisme et romantisme'[23] – is that all true art is at first perceived as radically modern before acquiring the status of a classical work. Classicism thus does not refer to any timeless beauty or form, but can be measured precisely – and herein lies its paradox – in the shock caused by the genuinely modern work of art when it first meets its public. Hence Godard can state in an interview about *Bande à part*, 'I made a modern film on a classical subject. [. . .] When Corneille wrote the *Cid*, he was *nouvelle vague* at that time, when Sophocles wrote, as well.'[24] It is important to note that David's *Oath of the Horatii* on which the camera lingers in the museum sequence was itself a manifesto piece that introduced a new style of painting breaking away from rococo art and that, though painted four years before 1789, became emblematic of the revolutionary era.[25] In singling out this one particular painting, Godard aligns himself with a vanguard tradition, yet also signals how outdated the work's idealised representation of patriotism has become in the 1960s, an era of profound social mutation which requires a new revolutionary aesthetic.

Finally, as a genuine visit to the Louvre, showcasing – albeit only fleetingly – some of the masterpieces of the European canon, the museum sequence playfully engages with cinema's capacity to act, in Bazin's words, as an 'open sesame for the masses to the treasures of the world of the past'.[26] In its ironic revisiting of a museum that holds objects from all over the globe, the sequence from *Bande à part* implicitly enters into dialogue with Malraux's influential essay *Le Musée imaginaire*, in which the writer and critic extols the virtues of an imaginary museum made up of photographic reproductions of the artworks of the world thus rendered accessible to a mass audience. If the imaginary museum in no way replaces actual museums, its attraction for Malraux lies above all in its facilitation of comparison between artworks pertaining to far removed historical periods and cultures. Conceived in this way, art history becomes an exercise of putting in relation works that are devoid of any evident connection or influence, but which are united in an artistic or humanist quest that transcends temporal and geographic boundaries. Ever in flux and metamorphosis, the art of the past needs to be confronted with that of the present, which retroactively changes its interpretation, just as the artworks of a Europe long dominated by Christianity must be confronted with the art of other cultures, religions and aesthetic canons. Richly illustrated with photographic reproductions, Malraux's essay doubles up as the personal imaginary museum of an artist whose creative work was perpetually nourished by dialogue between literature, film and the visual arts. Among a privileged group of artists – Piero della Francesca, Michelangelo, Manet, to name only three – who recur in the essay, it is striking to note the *Victory of Samothrace*, reproduced twice (first in detail, later on its ship's bow) and commented at some length as an example not only of the expressiveness of Hellenistic art, but of the bringing alive of artworks of the past in our contemporary museum culture.

Though sensitive to film as a global art, as discussed earlier, Malraux does not assign it the role of 'ambassador of art'[27] that he awards photography and, by extension, the art book. Likewise, Godard in *Bande à part* refuses any merely didactic role for cinema that would reduce it to illustrating the riches of the museum. Rather, as a filmmaker he asserts a comparative intermedial method that is in itself quite close to Malraux's concept of putting artworks of different periods, genres and cultures in relation.[28] If the Louvre sequence literally and metaphorically puts painting in its place – that of the museum, but also of an ancestor surpassed by a more vibrant younger sibling – its revisiting of works of the past raises fundamental questions about the different ontologies of cinema and painting, the relation between tradition and modernity, and the renewal of aesthetic canons. And it provocatively demonstrates that, where painting in film is opened up to the exterior world outside its frame, so a film containing paintings can behold a (radically) abridged art history – hence, in its own terms, become an imaginary museum.

The Visual Artist's Gaze: Agnès Varda's Intermedial Layerings

Unlike the Young Turks, Varda – often nicknamed the 'mother of the New Wave' – had little exposure to film before taking to the camera. Trained as an art historian and a photographer, she began her career as official photographer for the Avignon festival, for which she worked between 1948 and 1960, taking portraits of actors – her photos of Gérard Philipe have become legendary – as well as being responsible for still photographs of rehearsals and production shots. In 1951, when the *Théâtre national populaire* was reborn under the direction of Jean Vilar, she also became the company's official photographer. By her own admission, aged twenty-five, Varda had seen fewer than ten films.[29] It is thus not so much an intimate knowledge of film acquired through cinephilia, but a deep understanding of and affinity with the fine arts that have shaped her moving image work, as is testified by the wealth of painterly references and re-workings in her oeuvre.[30] As Rebecca DeRoo argues in her excellent study of Varda's engagement with a range of visual traditions as a means to mediate social and political concerns, 'working in dialogue with multiple aesthetic media and traditions has always been central to her practice'.[31] Varda herself has drawn attention to the subterranean influence of German Renaissance painter and printmaker Hans Baldung Grien on her most famous film, *Cléo de 5 à 7*, explaining that his vanitas paintings of beautiful young women in the throes of death, though never explicitly referenced, 'have very quickly become the meaning of the film and its force'.[32] In an interview, the director recalls pinning postcards of Baldung's paintings on the set and shows her preparatory notebook for the film, adorned with clippings of several of his paintings developing the Renaissance Death and the Maiden motif.[33] As we will see in a selection of her lesser-known films from the 1950s and 1960s, from its inception, hers is a cinema that openly stages intermediality through its referencing of artworks, a painterly use of composition and colour, not forgetting a marked penchant for *tableaux vivants*. Drawing on a wide range of influences from Early Renaissance painting via Impressionism and Modernism to Pop Art, and invoking the visual as well as the stage arts in her work, Varda creates a hybrid media texture where different artistic traditions and representational modes intersect.

Varda made a prominent entrance onto the film scene with *La Pointe courte*, a film that not only heralds the New Wave with its shoestring budget and cast of little-known and non-professional actors, but announces many of its aesthetic tenets in its blurring between fictional and documentary registers, outdoor shooting, highly personal style and vision, as well as, most interestingly for us here, its reaching out to film's neighbouring arts. Centred on the crisis of a couple, the film welds together two apparently separate stories – the relationship crisis of a husband and wife (played by Philippe Noiret and Sylvia Monfort) whose youthful passion has withered, and the existential struggles of a fishing community (played by the local people) in the port town of Sète, where Varda spent part of her childhood. While, at first, all appears to separate the emotional woes of the couple from the economic difficulties of the villagers, as the narrative unfolds in counterpoint, the two stories intersect and to a certain extent converge: the plight of the fishing community can be seen to echo, as well as to put into perspective, the turmoil of the couple. Structured around opposites – town versus country; the tight-knitted members of the local community versus the native returning to his roots – yet subtly alluding to links and similarities between the two groups, *La Pointe courte* opens pathways between individual and collective destinies, forging a fertile contact zone where each of the stories is illuminated in the light of the other.

This bold enmeshing of modes (fiction/documentary) and thematic concerns finds visual expression in a hybrid aesthetic at the crossroads of different representational systems. Varda herself acknowledges the influence of painting, in particular the Early Renaissance master Piero della Francesca, famous for his preoccupation with form, geometrical compositions and calm, statuesque figures: 'There were references to painting, particularly to Piero della Francesca, and this is tangible for example in the very choice of Silvia Monfort, this round face with a long neck, this sharp neckline.'[34] If Monfort's features do indeed recall the stark sculptural beauty of Piero's female figures with, in Varda's words, 'their vacant expression',[35] Philippe Noiret's monk-like hairstyle and coarse facial features bring to mind some of the painter's most striking male depictions, notably his portrait of the condottiere Sigismondo Pandolfo Malatesta, housed in the Louvre. The film's repeated close-ups of the couple, shown in sharp profile gazing at one another, reference one of the most celebrated works of the Italian Renaissance, Piero's *Portraits of*

Figure 3.2 Piero della Francesca (1410/1420–92), *Portraits of the Duke and Duchess of Urbino* (1465), reproduced with the permission of Ministero per i Beni e le Attività Culturali/ Archivi Alinari, Firenze; Location: Florence, The Uffizi Gallery; photographer: Lorusso, Nicola for Alinari; credit: Nicola Lorusso/Alinari Archives.

Figure 3.3 Agnès Varda, *La Pointe courte* (1955).

the Duke and Duchess of Urbino diptych, a particularly masterful example of the painter's 'volumetric approach to form'.[36] Not only are Monfort's high forehead (accentuated, as in the painting, by her pulled-back blond hair) and elegant pallor reminiscent of the noble features of the Duchess; the mise-en-scène of the couple, placed face-to-face amidst the Mediterranean landscape, recalls Piero's figures poised against a lake surrounded by low mountains.

In its unusual combination of portraiture with landscape, DeRoo argues, the visual reference encourages us to consider 'how the filmed couple is represented by their surroundings – albeit not so much by physical resemblance, as by symbolism'.[37] Just as importantly, I would add, the panel's back, depicting the Duke and Duchess approaching each other on triumphal carriages, in its shifting from individual portraiture to a collective scene painted in miniature style which absorbs husband and wife into the surrounding environment, is paradigmatic for the alternation between portrait-type close-ups and long shots of the couple embedded into the local community that punctuate the filmic narrative. Thus, if cinema, according to Pascal Bonitzer, is a direct inheritor to the code of perspective of the *Quattrocento*,[38] just like Renaissance portraiture is itself indebted to the representations in profile on Roman coins, so in turn Varda can be seen to reactivate the compositional techniques of Renaissance painting in her carefully composed shots. Echoing the powerful vertical and horizontal lines that structure Piero's geometrical compositions – for instance, his recurrent dividing of a scene in two by the presence of a column in works such as *The Annunciation to Mary*, *The Dream of Constantine* or *The Flagellation of Christ* – Varda often arranges the couple on either side of a material object, be it a pole or a pier, 'defining', in the words of Steven Ungar, 'a spatial perspective and concomitant horizon point that recalls Italian Renaissance paintings in which represented space was understood as both real and symbolic'.[39]

As is characteristic of the director's practice more widely, in *La Pointe courte* different artistic references and aesthetic canons intermingle, making it impossible to align the film with any one particular artistic movement or single representational model. Indebted, as we have seen, to the geometrical compositions and spatial perspective of Renaissance painting, Varda also revisits seventeenth-century genre painting in the style of Murillo in her depiction of everyday scenes (especially the portrayal of children), while the eighteenth-century *vedute* of Canaletto and Guardi find a contemporary incarnation in the colourful water-jousting spectacle. Cinema's own origins are self-reflexive summoned in the startling shot of the train advancing directly towards the camera – a cinephile nod to the Lumière brothers' 1896 projection of *L'Arrivée d'un train en gare de la Ciotat* (*The Arrival of a Train at La Ciotat Station*), which is said to have left spectators terrified by the illusionistic powers of the new medium.[40]

The frontal view shot in this scene is emblematic of a wider penchant for what Michael Fried terms 'facingness',[41] manifest in the numerous compositions where husband and wife – together or individually – are framed facing the camera, most strikingly so in a head-and-shoulders portrait of Noiret set against a blank white wall. We are no longer in the aesthetic context of the Italian *Quattrocento* here – though frontal portraits did of course exist in Renaissance painting – but, rather, in the realm of modern painting spearheaded by Manet, a revolution in style that was itself propelled by the advent of photography. Fried credits Manet for having initiated modernism by prioritising a radical frontality that acknowledges the presence of the spectator, combined with a new flatness in the construction of pictorial space.[42] The 'facingness' that emerges in French painting of the 1860s, in marked contrast to eighteenth-century painting, where the depicted scenes and the space of the spectator are kept strictly separate, Brigitte Peucker explains, 'facilitates spectatorial awareness of the painting *as* painting'.[43] Referenced in *Cléo de 5 à 7*, where the protagonist Cléo (Corinne Marchand) is framed against a poster of Manet's *Berthe Morisot au bouquet de violettes* in the Café du Dôme, in *La Pointe courte* Manet-style frontal compositions hover between the photographic mode in which Varda was trained and the painterly register which she acknowledges to be a continuous source of reflection and reverie.[44] Add to this the marked theatricality of Monfort's and Noiret's dialogues (both were members of Vilar's *Théâtre national populaire*), spoken in a deliberately flat, non-naturalistic tone – Varda calls their fabricated way of speaking a 'theatre of the couple'[45] – and we get a fuller picture of the intermedial layering at work in this first feature, permeated by the director's rich knowledge of art history, as well as her experience as a photographer for the theatre.

After this crucial New Wave predecessor, let us now turn to two of her features of the 1960s, *Le Bonheur* (1965) and *Lions Love (. . . and Lies)* (1969), as examples of her painterly concern with colour and light, and her invocation of an intermedial figuration *par excellence*, the *tableau vivant*. Varda has repeatedly stressed the influence of Impressionist painting on her first film shot entirely in colour, *Le Bonheur*, her 'most misunderstood film, often criticized for its seemingly anti-feminist themes and opacity', as DeRoo notes.[46] Suffused with disturbingly beautiful images, the film dissects the triangular relationship between a happily married man, François, his wife Thérèse (played by Jean-Claude and Claire Drouot, who were husband and wife in real life) and lover Émilie (Marie-France Boyer). While making the film, Varda remembers, she was thinking about 'the palettes of the Impressionists, of their landscapes, of their discoveries of complementary colours',[47] but also the melancholy that emanates from Impressionist painting.[48] *Le Bonheur*'s sumptuous colour scheme dominated by green, yellow and orange, its open air scenes shot in lush woodland, flowery meadows and gardens (especially the family picnics reminiscent of Monet and Berthe Morisot that punctuate the narrative), the popular ball at Fontenay-aux-Roses evoking Renoir's celebrated *Bal du moulin de la Galette*, Thérèse's dresses with their ubiquitous flower motifs – all tacitly pay homage to the Impressionists. They engage a movement credited – not unlike the New Wave – with having liberated nineteenth-century art from stale academic conventions in their choice of simple, everyday scenes and their concern with perception rather than photographic precision. In visual terms, the repeated use of shallow and selective focus (for instance, the bringing in and out of focus of one particular character in the shot) translates into cinematic language the characteristically blurry texture of Impressionist painting obtained by means of dissolving contours into vibrant shimmers of light and colour.

If Varda engages Impressionist tropes and techniques, she nonetheless insists on the difference between painting and cinema, the former, in her view, being defined by unchangeability, the latter by impermanence:

> What pleasure I had playing with colours without pretention nor amalgam with painting which proposes itself as immutable. In cinema, one fixed colour comes to life, another is just passing, one apprehends a coloured effect at the same time as the music or a moment of conversation. Then the effect is undone.[49]

Though establishing a clear distinction between the two arts, Varda's emphasis on cinema as a fluid medium where visual effects come into life before being undone again is not without recalling Impressionism's preoccupation with the fleeting nature of the moment: the changes to surface appearances brought about by different light conditions and the effect of the passage of time. Without losing sight of cinema's distinctiveness, then, her painterly aesthetic in *Le Bonheur* appears like a continuation in different medial form of some of Impressionism's most prominent concerns.

Yet, here also, as in her oeuvre more widely, a seminal art historical influence is conjugated with more modern references. In visual terms, the film's central conflict between the illusory happiness of traditional family life and the more liberated mores of 1960s France embodied by Émilie takes the form of a clash between two aesthetic traditions, one associated with nature and the country, the other with urban life as a site of adventure and temptation. In stark contrast to the family's picturesque, turn-of-the-century house surrounded by a flower garden, the minimalist functionality of the lover's flat in a modern apartment block signals the new lifestyle of the 'modern woman',[50] whose career outside the house offers greater financial and personal independence. Her more sexually liberated attitude, reflected in her words to François at the beginning of their affair ('Don't worry. I'm free and you're not the first one'), is emphasised visually through the rapid editing and fragmentation of the bodies in close-up when the couple make love. As the 'modern woman', in the figure of Émilie, encroaches on the traditional space of happiness embodied by the nuclear family, the film's aesthetic shifts from the painterly style inspired by Impressionism to a perspicuously modernist film language recalling Godard in the repeated use of starkly coloured backgrounds, colour filters, dissolves in red and blue, and intercalated monochromatic shots. As if to acknowledge her source, Varda explicitly references Godard's *Le Mépris* (released two years before *Le Bonheur*), which similarly touches on questions of marital life and adultery, albeit with inverted gender roles. In the ball scene, it is difficult not to see the systematic tracking forward and backward between the dancing couples as a remake of Godard's famous lateral tracking shot of the arguing couple in their apartment. In both, the different planes of the shot (and thus, on either side, its protagonists) are divided by a vertical object that comes periodically into view: in Godard an oversized lamp, in Varda a tree trunk.

In Varda's female interrogation of domestic life and adultery, in a cruelly ironic turn at the end of the film, the disruptive force of the 'modern woman' is in its turn absorbed into a traditional relationship when Émilie agrees to become François's second wife after Thérèse's tragic death by drowning – most likely (though the scene preserves a certain ambiguity) an act of suicide triggered by her husband's casual admission of his affair. The family idyll resumes in a chilling replication of the characters' earlier domestic life, culminating, in the final scene, in another of their ritual excursions to the country that is constructed as a precise mirror image of the opening scene, with the sole difference that an autumnal palette in the manner of Monet has replaced the bright colours of summer and that the characters are moving away from rather than towards the camera. While the recomposed family are about to disappear in the woods, a colour fade blurs the human figures and their natural surroundings before morphing into an abstract yellow screen. As an art concerned with the fleetingness of time, Impressionist painting, invoked once more here, is a perfect vehicle for making visible the changing passions of the heart, caught in a cycle of birth, death and rebirth like the natural seasons. But this final colour fade to a monochromatic image also brings home an art historical lesson that tacitly underpins the whole film: Impressionism has paved the way for modernity in art – including cinematic modernism.

Very different is Varda's take on the love triangle in *Lions Love (. . . and Lies)*, one of her least discussed films, shot during an extended stay in the US with her husband Jacques Demy at the end of the 1960s. Enmeshing the love life of a threesome with the electoral campaign and subsequent murder of Robert F. Kennedy, this counterculture film captures the spirit of the hippy era in the vivid colours of pop art. In casting Andy Warhol 'superstar' Viva in tandem with James Rado and Gerome Ragni, known for having created and starred in the rock musical *Hair*, Varda pits the old stars of Hollywood, lovingly evoked throughout the film, against a new breed of underground actors on their way to stardom. Exhibiting an 'aesthetic of multiplicity', J. Brandon Colvin notes, the film combines an eclectic array of formal strategies, ranging from 'Warholian static long takes of conversations, re-photographed television footage, narrated documentary segments about old Hollywood, surreal interludes, fourth-wall breaking interviews, and filmed performances of Michael McClure's (1967) comic play *The Beard*'.[51]

As part of the film's wider invocation of the other arts, Varda stages selected etchings from Picasso's Vollard Suite (a series of 100 neoclassical etchings considered to be the artist's most important group of prints) into cinematic *tableaux vivants*.[52] Produced between 1930 and 1937, the Vollard Suite is itself part of a period in Picasso's oeuvre that initiates a new 'dialogue between painting, drawing, engraving and sculpture'.[53] In works of this artistic phase, themes migrate across different media, notably the trope of the sculptor's studio, which is central to the Vollard Suite and which also often figures in paintings and drawings.[54]

Before examining the *tableaux vivants* in *Lions Love* in more detail it is useful to note that the cinematic restaging of visual artworks is not entirely new in Varda's oeuvre at this point. Already in *La Pointe courte*, her portraits of husband and wife, immobilised for a few moments to be undone again as the actors resume their movement, gesture towards this intermedial trope. In the short *L'Opéra-Mouffe* (*Diary of a Pregnant Woman*, 1958), the static shot of a reclining female nude holding a mirror imitates Velázquez's famous *Venus at her Mirror* (aka *Rokeby Venus*), albeit inverting the composition of the painting as if to signal its refashioning through the mirror of cinema. Looking ahead some thirty years, two other reclining nudes, Titian's *Venus of Urbino* and Goya's *Naked Maja*, provide the material for a series of *tableaux vivants* in *Jane B. par Agnès V.* (*Jane B. by Agnès V.*, 1987), a film infused more widely by art history.[55] If Varda's fascination with the *tableau vivant* can be traced from her first feature, the practice of staging actors to embody famous paintings goes back to medieval pageants, becoming, as Steven Jacobs shows, a veritable fashion in early nineteenth-century European culture, when *tableaux vivants* were developed in the domestic setting of the drawing room.[56] On the theatre stage, the performance of *poses plastiques* – that is, the arrangements of nude or partially dressed actresses in the manner of classical sculptures – provided erotic titillation at a time of strict stage censorship. The practice of *tableaux vivants* is also traceable in nineteenth-century stage photography, filtering into film in the 1890s when cinematic stagings of *tableaux vivants* were shown next to living pictures performed on stage and copies of the originals, inviting spectators to compare the source and its reproduction in different media.[57] Prominent in early film, *tableaux vivants* virtually disappeared from classic cinema, but resurface in European modernist cinema of the 1960s, 70s and 80s, where they have a paradoxical status. Jacobs explains:

> By including tableaux vivants in their films, modernist filmmakers attempted to determine the specificity of their medium – movement was juxtaposed with stasis, pictorial or sculptural space with cinematic space, iconic immediacy with filmic duration and so forth. On the other hand, because of their hybrid and heterogeneous nature, both cinema and tableaux vivants were difficult to reconcile with a modernist aesthetic of self-investigation based on the idea of essence and purity of a specific medium. At the nodal point that joins painting, sculpture and theatre, tableaux vivants are impure by definition. When they are evoked in a film, they create, in the words of Brigitte Peucker, 'a moment of intensified intermediality'.[58]

In a sequence in *Lions Love* presented as the wakeful dream of experimental filmmaker Shirley Clarke (played by herself), Varda arranges her three lead actors in the manner of two etchings from the Vollard Suite, 'Sculpteur au repos avec son modèle, anémones et petit torse' and 'Sculpteur, modèle couché et sculpture'. Produced in 1933, the two plates appear like mirror images. In both, a reclining model is cradled in the arms of the sculptor while he contemplates a sculpture, doubtless one of his creations: in the former plate, a small torso on a plinth; in the latter, a classical male nude with a club positioned on a pedestal. Like the rest of the Sculptor's Studio grouping, the plates are autobiographical in inspiration, reflecting the relationship between Picasso and his muse and lover Marie-Thérèse Walter, and showcasing his intensive preoccupation with sculpture during this period (in 1930, Picasso set up a large sculpture studio at the Château de Boisgeloup, where he produced several plaster sculptures of Marie-Thérèse).[59] In her *tableaux vivants*, Varda minutely reconstructs the composition of the two etchings in terms of the bodies' arrangement in space, their posture and surrounding decor, but not without introducing some playful variations. In her reworking of 'Sculpteur au repos avec son modèle, anémones et petit torse', the torso on a plinth is substituted with the half-hidden body of Gerome Ragni, whose position behind the replica of a classical column gives the impression of a living sculpture, a *pose plastique* in the tradition of eighteenth and nineteenth-century entertainment. On the other hand, in 'Sculpteur, modèle couché et sculpture', the classical male sculpture is replaced by James Rado. The constellation of

Figure 3.4 Pablo Picasso, 'Sculptor at Rest with His Model, Anemones and Small Torso' (Sculpteur au repos avec son modèle, anémones et petit torse) from the 'Vollard Suite' (Suite Vollard), 1933, published 1939. Etching, plate: 19.4 x 26.7 cm; sheet: 33 x 44.5 cm. Location: Museum of Modern Art (MoMA), New York © 2018. Digital image, The Museum of Modern Art, New York/Scala, Florence © Succession Picasso/DACS, London 2018.

Figure 3.5 Agnès Varda, *Lions Love (... and Lies)* (1969).

creator, muse and artwork in the two plates – echoing the Pygmalion myth of the sculptor falling in love with his own creation – thus gives way to another triangular constellation, that of the threesome,[60] among a wider updating of Picasso's etchings to the cultural values and tastes of the hippy era, tangible also in the *tableaux vivants*' flowery backdrop.

With their nudity and focus on an illicit love (Picasso was still married when he started a relationship with the seventeen-year-old Marie-Thérèse), the two etchings of the Vollard Suite provide an ideal means for expressing the more liberal attitudes towards the body, sex and relationships in the wake of the 1960s sexual revolution. Yet, more importantly, in tune with Picasso's own self-reflexive gaze in the Sculptor's Studio grouping, they also serve as a catalyst for interrogating the nature of artistic representation, as becomes evident when Varda and Clarke (who appears as an alter ego of Varda, just as the sculptor is a double of Picasso in the etchings) in turn enter the frame, circling around the *tableau vivant* with a fake camera cut out of cardboard. Varda comments:

> nudity being one of the demands of the era, the three actors have accepted with pleasure to pose to imitate a drawing of Picasso (of the Vollard suite). I have always sought the support and inspiration of painters. Picasso, with whom I've never spoken, has been for me a virtual master. We were shooting. I entered into the frame with a fake camera. I circulated in a tableau vivant of false pretences. Sometimes, it was Shirley Clarke, a true experimental filmmaker, who pretended to film. A real camera was recording this little allegorical film.[61]

What, then, is the function of thus giving visibility to the cinematic apparatus in a *tableau vivant* that joins together cinema, painting, sculpture and theatre? As Brigitte Peucker points out, 'those moments in films that evoke tableaux vivants are moments especially focused on film's heterogeneity'.[62] In making visible the filming of the *tableau vivant* (albeit by means of a fake camera), Varda highlights the overlaying of representational modes in *Lions Love*, playfully alerting us to the fact that cinema is no less fabricated than the living paintings: it is a copy of a copy, what Barthes terms a 'secondary mimesis'.[63] As a 'lens that focuses hybridity',[64] the *tableau vivant* posits cinema *as* cinema (that is, as a system of representation), while at the same time drawing attention to the medium's inherent impurity. Moreover, in its juxtaposition of older and newer artistic practices, cinema's self-reflexive posturing here makes tangible a chain of artistic reworkings, whereby Picasso's etchings drawing upon the neoclassical painter Ingres (who, in turn, had revitalised the style and spirit of classical antiquity) are reimagined in the iconography of the late 1960s. As Godard put it in *Bande à part*: 'classique=moderne'.

WHAT IS ART, JEAN-LUC GODARD?

Nicknamed 'God-art' by cinema historian Georges Sadoul as early as 1964, Godard is without doubt the New Wave auteur whose work is most symbiotically linked to the fine arts. Hailed as a successor of Cubist collage by the poet Louis Aragon, who, in 1965, devoted a seminal essay to the painterly use of colour in *Pierrot le fou*,[65] self-stylised as the inheritor in technoscope of Renoir and Sisley,[66] and oft associated with the iconography and aesthetic of pop art,[67] Godard has taken art out of the museum into film, where it is ceaselessly cited, de-assembled and re-assembled, refashioned and remediated. As Didi-Huberman remarks, 'the reassembly of images, words and sounds is evidently the beating heart of Jean-Luc Godard's work'.[68] Already Godard's pieces of film criticism and first interviews as a filmmaker in the 1960s, Aumont reminds us, intermittently use the metaphor of the filmmaker as painter,[69] an association developed in later writings, most importantly *Histoire(s) du cinéma*, in which references to painting abound. It is not insignificant that, before taking to the camera, Godard contemplated a career in painting. Three portraits painted when he was seventeen or eighteen years of age, reproduced in Antoine de Baecque's biography, testify to a strong sense of colour and a distinctly expressionist style. Godard himself, in an interview in 1992, linked his work as a filmmaker to his passion for painting:

> I did a bit of painting when I was very young. And above all, since then, I have seen a lot of it. So, in a way, cinema is a return. A return not to childhood

but to this childhood terrain that for me was painting. Cinema still has a very great power because it is the inheritor of painting, as a vision of the world.[70]

In his oeuvre, painting, on the most literal level of citation, is ubiquitous, be it in the Renoir posters that adorn the walls of Patricia's room in *À bout de souffle*, the numerous postcards, reproductions and full screen inserts of Picasso, Matisse, Chagall and other painters in *Pierrot le fou*, the Klee reproductions Véronica and Angela contemplate in *Le Petit Soldat* and *Une femme est une femme*, the book of ancient erotic art Prokosch shows Camille in *Le Mépris*, not forgetting the numerous references to a particular artist, artwork or piece of art criticism in filmic dialogues. To these selective examples, we need to add the staging of *tableaux vivants* in *Passion* (1982) and, of course, the monumental *Histoire(s) du cinéma* project which is conceived of as an imaginary museum in the tradition of Malraux.[71] 'Godard's cinema', Jacobs comments, 'presents itself as an all-encompassing image archive producing new meanings by the juxtapositions of artworks of divergent styles, periods and cultures.'[72] Unlike Varda, who, as we have seen, draws on a wide range of artistic traditions from Renaissance painting to neoclassical etchings, Godard in the late 1950s and 1960s firmly situates himself within the modern canon, from the omnipresent references to Auguste Renoir (who, as the father of one of the New Wave's most admired directors, Jean Renoir, points to a privileged nexus between painting and the cinema), via Picasso and Nicolas de Staël to Warhol and Lichtenstein, two artists who were instrumental in shaping the pop-art aesthetic of *Pierrot le fou* and *Made in U.S.A.*

In the discussion that follows, rather than focusing on Godard's citational mania (which, as we saw with regard to literature and the theatre, is not confined to any one medium) or returning to his collage aesthetic and painterly use of colour that have been brilliantly analysed by critics such as Dalle Vacche and Jean-Louis Leutrat,[73] I will explore intermedial figurations that go beyond citation in two seminal films from the 1960s: the diptych *Vivre sa vie* and *Une femme mariée*. Elaborating on the idea of media rivalry that we already saw at work in the museum sequence in *Bande à part*, this section will examine further how Godard invokes painting, but also persistently pits the pictorial arts against cinema. As will be shown, Godard repeatedly engages in instances of what Jay David Bolter and Richard Grusin term 'remediation', that is, a 'particular kind of intermedial relationships in which, through processes of medial refashioning, "both newer and older [media] forms are involved in a struggle for culture recognition"'.[74] A highly ambivalent practice, Bolter and Grusin explain, remediation pays homage to, but also competes with, other media 'by appropriating and refashioning the representational practices of these older forms'.

With its subtitle 'film in twelve pictures' ('tableaux'), *Vivre sa vie* instantly aligns itself with painting, a connection that is reinforced by the opening shots of Nana (Anna Karina), framed first in sharp profile, then a fully frontal shot, followed by another profile facing the opposite direction. The multiple close-ups of the actress's face that punctuate the film, some of them displaying a striking facingness that defies the convention of the fourth wall, insert the film in the tradition of the nineteenth-century portrait. Moreover, the numerous café and bar scenes where the conspicuously named Nana – referencing Manet's 1877 eponymous picture of a prostitute as well as Zola's novel about a courtesan, published three years later – is either framed against or reflected in a mirror recall one of Manet's most celebrated paintings, *A Bar at the Folies-Bergères*, with its striking composition of a young woman seen in radical frontality, reflected in a mirror. In *Histoire(s) du cinéma* Godard refers to the painting in a well-known passage that posits Manet as the direct ancestor of cinema: 'because finally the world / the interior world / has rejoined the cosmos / and with Edouard Manet / begins / modern painting / that's to say / the cinematograph'.[75]

Godard's ambivalent engagement with the genre of portrait painting in *Vivre sa vie* is played out in tableau 12, announced as 'The Oval Portrait' in the intertitles. The scene opens with a shot of Nana's friend (Peter Kassovitz), absorbed in reading Edgar Allan Poe. On alternating shots of the young man and Nana, the words of the two lovers' inaudible dialogue appear in the manner of subtitles, aligning the film with the silent tradition. A fade visually introduces a voice-over reading of extracts from Poe's short story 'The Oval Portrait', passed as the voice of the young man, but in fact spoken by Godard in his characteristically Swiss-inflected accent. As the voice-over moves to the literary Narrator's description of the portrait, the camera cuts to a close-up of Karina standing against a window. Framed like a portrait by the window panel, the actress substitutes for the painting in the literary text: it is her features that the voice-over seems to describe. Yet, the spoken text – an example of literary ekphrasis, that is, the verbal description of a visual work of art – also evokes 'real' painting through a reference to the vignette style of nineteenth-century American portrait painter Thomas Sully. Set now against a blank wall, Karina's face is offered to scrutiny as the voice ponders the reasons for his enthralment with the portrait; finally, the actress is framed against a photo of Elizabeth Taylor – another mirroring double – while the voice explains that it is the lifelike execution of the painting that so moved him. If, thus far, the voice-over merely read Poe's text, at this point, an authorial interjection links the story of 'The Oval Portrait' to Godard's and Karina's personal life, breaking the illusion of a diegetic voice-over spoken by the young man: 'It's our story: a painter making a portrait of his wife.' As

Karina paints her lips in a mirror – a device traditionally signalling mise-en-abyme – the voice conveys the chilling ending of the story: so entranced by his lifelike creation was the painter that he failed to notice that his wife has died during the sitting.

Ágnes Pethő offers a coruscating reading of this scene as an example of what Joachim Paech terms 'cinematic ekphrasis'. She writes:

> Godard's film foregrounds cinema's 'ekphrastic impulse' that aims at rivalling the other arts by remediating traditional forms of portraiture both in the visual arts and in literature. The embedded representations flaunt cinema's multiple mediality, but they also result in an endless process of signification, an endless attempt at 'figurating' the 'infigurable' identity and beauty of Nana/Anna Karina (through a vertigo of media embedded within media: Poe's literary text, the painting described by his text, Godard's personally voiced narration, the cinematic intertexts, the photography on the wall, the earlier painterly analogies, etc.). The ultimate image of Nana/Anna Karina that we get is placed (or displaced) somewhere in an impossible space between art and reality, between sensual presence and imagination, between one medium and another.[76]

Conjoining literature and painting, the Oval Portrait scene hints at the permeability of different artforms, but also, crucially, draws attention to the transformational processes inherent when moving from one representational mode to another. It is important in this context that the extracts from the story delivered in French are themselves a translation of a text originally written in English (the young man reads Baudelaire's translation of Poe's *Complete Works*). Significantly, in Godard's own recasting, parts of the source text remain unspoken, notably the narrator's comment on the conflict between the painter's passion for his art and his devotion to his wife: he 'having already a bride in his Art', her 'hating only the Art which was her rival'.[77]

It is tempting to read this omission as a further instance of authorial comment (albeit, here, precisely through what is *not* said), especially in light of the crisis Godard's own marriage was undergoing at the time of *Vivre sa vie*: according to his biographer, Karina, who had for some time felt neglected by her artist husband, always absorbed in his work, attempted to commit suicide during the shooting.[78] Intriguing though such a tacit biographical subtext may be, for our concerns here it is more pertinent to unravel another artistic connection in this dense intermedial web. Interestingly, before being embedded in Godard's *Vivre sa vie*, the storyline of 'The Oval Portrait' was interpolated by Jean Epstein in his 1928 silent film adaptation of *The Fall of the House of Usher*, in which Poe's Gothic tale merges with the story of the painter obsessed with painting the portrait of his wife, who dies during the execution of the work.[79] While we can only assume that Godard would have been familiar with this particular avant-garde film, his indebtedness to Epstein as both a pioneering filmmaker and theorist is well established.[80] In the wake of Louis Delluc, who linked the notion to painting and poetry, Epstein became the leading proponent of the concept of 'photogénie' that was instrumental for the early avant-garde's championing of film as art. He defines as photogenic 'any aspect of things, beings, or souls whose moral character is enhanced by filmic reproduction'.[81] For Epstein, if *photogénie* solicits an emotional response from the viewer, the close-up – in its elevation of parts of the human body (or objects) to almost divine status – is particularly apt for such an affective experience. 'Disruptive of space and time, story and spectacle', Abel explains, '*photogénie* contained the potential for a modernist aesthetic'.[82]

Godard explicitly connects to the era of silent film with its predilection for expressive close-ups in the film-within-the-film scene in which Nana is moved to tears by Falconetti's emotive face in Dreyer's *La Passion de Jeanne d'Arc* (*The Passion of Joan of Arc*, 1928). It seems more than a coincidence that Henri Langlois, in a long article on Epstein, published in a 1953 issue of *Cahiers du cinéma* (that is, at a time when Godard wrote for the journal), appraises Epstein's *La Chute de la Maison Usher* as the counterpart of Dreyer's *Jeanne d'Arc*, explicitly referring to Epstein's amalgamation of Poe's eponymous story and 'The Oval Portrait'.[83] Thus, from an intermedial perspective, *Vivre sa vie* should be considered within two artistic traditions, which, as Godard suggests in the reference to Manet cited above, directly derive from one another: while aligned with nineteenth-century portrait painting, the film also reactivates the first avant-garde's fascination with the human face in its expressive close-ups of Karina. Godard himself has described *Vivre sa vie* as 'a film on prostitution that tells how a young and pretty Parisian salesgirl gives her body but keeps her soul'[84] – a soulfulness made visible by the continued magic of *photogénie*.

With its luminous black and white, intermittent use of intertitles and inner monologue imprinted over the image, as well as its concern with the role of women in male-dominated society, *Une femme mariée* is the exact counterpart to *Vivre sa vie*, developing the theme of marriage as a form of prostitution that runs through many of Godard's films. Where, in the earlier film, Zola's *Nana* subtly underpins the narrative, here Flaubert's *Madame Bovary* provides a tacit intertext for Godard's ironic anatomy of a marriage involving the bored young wife Charlotte (Macha Méril), her possessive husband Pierre (Philippe Leroy) and equally proprietorial lover Robert (Bernard Noël). Musing in voice-over about the discrepancy between dream and reality, Charlotte is easily recognisable as a modern-day Emma Bovary, seeking solace from the banality of her existence in an extramarital affair. Yet just as her predecessor 'found again in adultery all the platitudes of marriage',[85] so to does the repetition of almost identical gestures and exchanges between her and the two men (playfully inverted when she asks her husband about his flaws, her lover about his qualities) translate into cinematic terms the circularity of her predicament.

The literary intertext – expanded in references to Balzac's *Illusions perdues*, Apollinaire's poem 'La Rousse' and, most explicitly, the maid's ribald account of lovemaking with her husband derived from Céline's *Mort à crédit* – intersects with the pictorial and stage arts, invoked, on a literal level, through paintings in the domestic interiors and Robert's profession as a stage actor. In sociological terms, the decor of the family's modern home, where photos of planes and of Pierre in his pilot's uniform hang next to framed reproductions of Klee, a Picasso *Pierrot*, a classical etching, and, most strikingly, a Cocteau mural, designate them as a well-to-do middle-class couple flirting with modernity, but with no affirmed taste of their own. A portrait of Molière and photos of actors in Robert's Parisian flat, by contrast, like the sinuous interior space with its improvised roof access, emphasise the lover's more artistic *habitus*.

From the outset, *Une femme mariée* is aligned with the art of painting through the opening shot of a white screen – a projection surface to be populated with moving images, but also the blank canvas of a picture not yet painted. A female hand slowly glides towards the centre of the image, soon to be joined by a male hand interlocking its wrist, the two arms cutting out a triangle. Held for a few seconds, the shot resembles an almost abstract, geometrical composition. Repeated throughout the film in manifold variations, these close-ups of the human anatomy, decomposed into fragments by a static camera and edited into tableaux by punctuating fades, designate the film as an experiment in visual form akin to the work of a painter. Godard's arrangements of the human body, laid out on the canvas of a bed sheet or framed against a blank wall, in their manifest preoccupation with lines and shapes, evacuate traditional narrative at the expense of a formal exercise in 'pure' art. The lines of Macha Méril's face cut out by her bob-styled hair, her bent knees drawing an M-shaped figure, head forming a triangle with her bent forearm, the rounded line of her belly shot in profile or the softly hollow curve of her back gliding into the gentle protuberance of her buttocks – each of these shot compositions seems to vie for the status of an artwork to be appreciated above all for its formal beauty. Extreme close-ups of Charlotte and her lover emphasising the grainy, dimply texture of the human skin covered in beauty spots, goose pimples or beard stubbles abstract the body into a rugged painterly landscape to be explored by the spectator's wandering eye. The scopophilic pleasures to be gained from such crossings into the art of painting – with its slowed-down regime of looking and its spatial (static) rather than temporal (sequential)

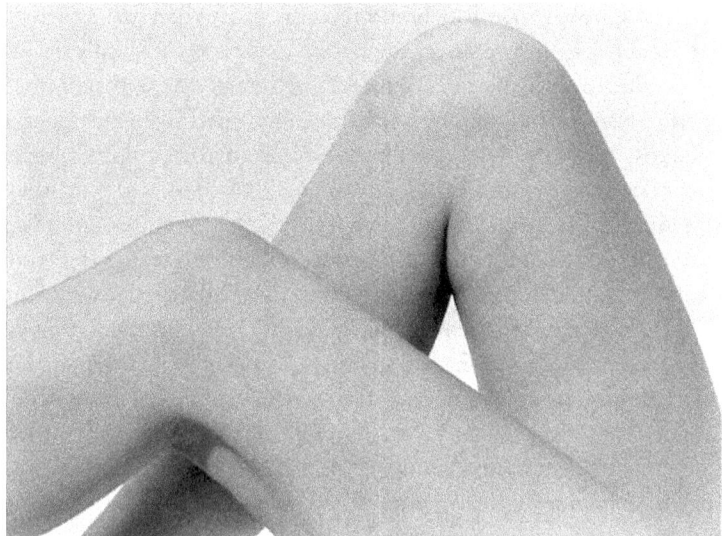

Figure 3.6 Abstracting the body into pure form in *Une femme mariée* (Jean-Luc Godard, 1964).

organisation – are hinted at in Charlotte's question to her husband, 'What does "look at" really mean'?', to which he replies, 'To look at…, I don't know. It means taking in with your eyes.' Looking in a painterly way implies a different manner of beholding, observing at close distance and repeatedly – a contemplative practice seemingly counter to the fast-moving pace of cinema.

If the blank canvas and the fades reminiscent of brushstrokes associate Godard's endeavour in *Une femme mariée* with painting, his artistic arrangements of the female form also interface with sculpture by way of three brief inserts of iconic pieces by early twentieth-century sculptor Maillol as the lovers drive past the Tuileries Gardens. The furtive images of a dramatically poised reclining nude (*La Rivière*), a pensive seated (*La Méditerranée*) and a gracefully standing female figure (*Ile de France*), presented like flashbacks, refer back to the arrangements of Méril's body in the opening sequence. The second sculpted figure in particular, folding in on herself in interlocking triangles, appears as a double, albeit inverted as if reflected in a mirror (the mise-en-abyme of intermediality) of one of the actress's earlier poses. With her round limbs and sculptural body – in stark contrast to the elfin silhouettes of a Karina or Seberg – Méril resembles the classical ideal embodied in Maillol's monumental female nudes, characterised by their calm strength and earthen solidity. In an interview, the actress reveals that Godard was fascinated above all by the plasticity of her body: 'he treated me like a statue, a block of marble he was going to sculpt'.[86]

With their emphasis on touch and tactility, more than just a visualisation of the sensuality of physical love, the haptic close-ups of Méril's naked body become an allegory for the fashioning of the female form in sculpture, as is evidenced in a shot of the young woman's belly, vigorously massaged by her lover's hands, recalling the modelling gestures of the sculptor. Just as the voice-over spoken by himself in *Vivre sa vie* aligned Godard with the writer Poe, so here the close-ups of the female form associate the filmmaker with the figure of the sculptor, an identification all the more telling if we consider that Maillol's relationship to his muse and model Dina Vierny contributed to a renewal in the sculptor's creation, particularly evident in the daring composition of *La Rivière*. In his assimilation and refashioning of an artistic heritage, Godard mobilises what Pethő calls the 'sensual mode' of intermediality, a mode that 'invites the viewer to literally get in touch with the world portrayed not at a distance but at the proximity of entangled synesthetic sensations, and resulting in a cinema that can be perceived in the terms of music, painting, architectural forms or haptic textures'.[87]

In *Une femme mariée*, the cinematic image – placed in the tradition of painting and sculpture – is opposed to photography, notably in the fashion shoot scene, shot in negative, where we see the professional photographer click away mechanically. As the inheritor of photography's technological apparatus, Godard seems to caution, cinema needs to distance itself from the all too facile, quasi automatic practice of pointing a camera at life if it wants to affirm itself as art, and a fortiori from commercial photography's instrumentalisation as a means to sell capitalism's false dreams. Omnipresent in the inserts of fashion magazine pages and advertising billboards scrutinised by the camera, the deceptive lure of photography is embodied by Charlotte, whose work for a fashion magazine echoes Méril's role (before her debut in cinema) as an assistant and muse to American fashion photographer Richard Avedon. Art critic Benjamin Buchloh aptly sums up what was at stake in the work of photographers such as Avedon, who revolutionised fashion photography in the course of the 1950s and 1960s with their glamorous shots of 'modern women': 'Functioning as a conduit between the mirage of the subject and the commodity object, photography would compel the mass subject to acquire the substitutions that compensate for the loss of subjective experience.'[88]

By way of the double process of de-authorisation and re-authorisation that, according to Didi-Huberman, characterises his citational practice,[89] Godard absorbs these hollow images of consumer culture into the texture of his film, where they are elevated to the status of art. In a contemporary review of *Une femme mariée*, Georges Sadoul analyses this artistic valorisation of popular visual culture as being akin to the practices of pop art:

> There is for me a relationship between Pop Art and God-Art. This pun, concerning an author who likes bad plays on words, can be understood as the observation that certain modes of expression are in the air, and that if around 1895 the filmmaker Louis Lumière could make impressionism without knowing it, it's normal that the avant-garde of the seventh art can today meet the avant-gardes of other arts.[90]

In a press conference at the 1990 Cannes festival where he made a triumphant return with *Nouvelle Vague,* Godard presents himself not as the author, but as the 'organising consciousness' of his film. His citations across a range of media, he insists, are nothing but an act of putting cinema in relation with the cultural heritage of humanity: 'For me, all quotation – whether it's pictorial or musical – belongs to humanity. [. . .] I am simply someone who puts together Raymond Chandler and Fyodor Dostoevsky in a restaurant one day with minor actors and major actors. That's all.'[91] If putting heterogeneous entities into relation with one another, with a view to creating new significations, is at the heart of Godard's dialectical method,[92] his intermedial practice of bringing different art forms into dialogue, as we have seen here with regard to painting, sculpture and, to a lesser extent, photography, allows the director to extend the boundaries of film. As a director who, as Deleuze has argued, marks thresholds and claims the in-between,[93] Godard mobilises artworks and artistic practices as a means of pushing the frontiers of cinema and, in so doing, enhancing its formal properties. Godard's practice of impure cinema places him firmly in opposition to medium specificity arguments that span from Lessing's classical injunction against a confusion between the arts developed in his *Laocoon,* to Rudolf Arnheim's critique of the talkies on grounds of cinematic purity and Clement Greenberg's modernist call for a 'willing acceptance of the limitations of the medium of the specific art' that still exerted influence on avant-garde filmmakers of the 1960s and 1970s.[94] Indeed, in their voracious absorption of an artistic heritage, Godard's films epitomise the hegemonic struggle that Greenberg considers to be the reason for a confusion between the arts.[95] Unlike Varda, who accommodates the pictorial arts in a gesture that, with Derrida, one may term hospitality, Godard – as Jean-Louis Leutrat remarks with regard to *Passion* – 'makes use of painting to foreground cinema's specific capabilities'.[96] Intermediality is the motor of an artistic practice destined to firmly establish film as the dominant artform of the twentieth-century.

GUY GILLES: THE SENSITIVE IMAGE

Among the vagaries of canon formation, the quasi-oblivion of Guy Gilles in discussions of the New Wave and film studies more widely urgently demands to be rectified. Unlike Jacques Demy, Jacques Rozier or even Jean-Daniel Pollet, who have all been recognised as part of the New Wave constellation, 'the youngest of the New Wave', as he is called by Noël Simsolo, remains an unknown entity, especially outside France.[97] A fortiori, his status as 'one of the greatest gay filmmakers', noted by gay magazine *Têtu* in 2005, is blatantly disregarded.[98] Following an uncompromisingly personal path, this prodigiously gifted, prolific director – his legacy includes eight features, more than a dozen shorts, plus an extensive and varied output for television – remained in the margins of French film until his death from AIDS in 1996. Absent from most film histories, at best furtively mentioned in specialist works on French post-war cinema, Gilles is virtually unknown to a larger public, in spite of belated homages at several film festivals,[99] and a full retrospective at the Paris Cinémathèque in 2014. Rarely screened outside festival circuits, his films have gradually become more accessible thanks to the untiring efforts of his brother Luc Bernard, his cousin Jean-Pierre Stora (who composed the music for most of his films) and fellow director Gaël Lépingle. A good selection of his features are now available on DVD alongside several documentaries about his life and work, a richly documented website, and an excellent collective volume.[100] In light of his continued absence from film studies in the anglophone world and of the more inclusive mappings of the New Wave that have emerged in recent scholarship, it is high time to claim Gilles's position in the New Wave canon and to appraise his intermedial aesthetic.

Born in Algiers in 1938, Gilles studied at the Beaux-Arts and directed two poetic shorts before leaving for Paris in 1960, at the height of the Algerian War. There, he almost instantly came into the orbit of the New Wave through legendary producer Pierre Braunberger, who produced his first short *Soleil éteint* (1958), an assistant's job on the shooting of Jacques Demy's *La Luxure* (1961), and a small role in *Tire-au-flanc 62* (*The Army Game*, 1961), co-directed by Truffaut. In 1962, he embarked on a melancholic first feature, *L'Amour à la mer* (*Love at Sea*, 1964), that sketches out a fragile love story between a Parisian office worker (Geneviève Thénier) and a taciturn sailor (Daniel Moosmann). Remarkably assured for the work of a twenty-six-year-old director without official training, the film was awarded the critic's prize at the Locarno festival, but failed to obtain a general release.[101] In the course of the 1960s, Gilles directed two further features of a great visual splendour, *Au pan coupé* (*Wall Engravings*, 1967) and *Le Clair de terre* (*Earth Light*, 1970; Grand prix at the Hyères Festival for Young Cinema), which crystallise the poetic, yet rigorously formal style that characterises all of his work. These films also mark the collaboration with his 'modèle' (in the Bressonian sense) and partner Patrick Jouané, who came to embody the fragile, drifting characters that populate Gilles's filmic worlds. A documentary on the Cannes and Hyères film festivals he made for French television, *Festivals 1966, Cinéma 1967* (1967), brought Gilles into closer contact with Godard, Truffaut, Rivette and the *Cahiers* critics.

All, then, seemed ready for this original young filmmaker to join the ranks of the New Wave and to assert his place alongside the more established directors of the movement he so ardently admired.[102] Yet his somewhat delayed advent on the film scene in comparison with the Young Turks and the Left Bank group proved to be too late already, his public and critical reception fraught with conflict. With their intimate portrayals of characters in the throes of existential anguish and their propensity for nostalgia, Gilles's films were out of kilter with the 1968 generation's belief in direct action as a means to propel change. Not unrelated, his editor Noun Serra blames the blatant homophobia of the contemporary film industry and the *Cahiers* group's reservation against a director perceived as somewhat sentimental, not to say kitsch, for his lack of artistic recognition.[103] As Lépingle explains, the New Wave had little place for 'a homosexual sentimentality that didn't make political use of its singularity (in the manner of a Pasolini), and that could recall the old guard that had to be unbolted (L'Herbier, Carné and the like – Cocteau being the exception)'.[104] Add to this the director's difficulties in securing funding and, consequently, his highly precarious working conditions, which, in the eyes of some, discredited him as an amateur, and we begin to grasp the numerous obstacles that impeded his success.[105] An outsider in the profession, Gilles was to remain at the margins of the New Wave, failing to gain the vital support of *Cahiers du cinéma*. It was only after his death that the journal published a homage to this 'messenger of a cinema of poetry', 'one of those figures incomprehensibly excluded from film history'.[106]

Just how eager the young director was to reach out to the New Wave is tangible in many a reference and nod in his early films. The cameo roles of two of the movement's fetish actors, Jean-Claude Brialy and Jean-Pierre Léaud, in *L'Amour à la mer*; the casting of the female New Wave triad Macha Méril (*Au pan coupé*), Delphine Seyrig and Jeanne Moreau (*Le Jardin qui bascule*, 1974); indeed even the choice of Emmanuelle Riva as the voice-over for *Proust, l'art et la douleur* (1971), inscribe his works in a New Wave genealogy. A string of citations – notably, the world of sailors and their love interests in *Au pan coupé* echoing Demy's imaginary or, in *Le Clair de terre*, the scene of the children miming an execution reminiscent of Truffaut's *Les Mistons* – consolidate the visual construction of a cinematic lineage.[107] With their self-reflexive cinephilia (emblematised in the film-within-the film scene in *L'Amour à la mer* starring Juliette Greco and Alain Delon), focus on youthful love and portrayal of students, artists and rebellious outsiders, Gilles's early films share some of the New Wave's key thematic features, with a particular affinity for two better known 'satellites' of the movement, Demy and Rozier.[108]

Yet, despite his desire to be part of the *bande* (as the core New Wave directors were often called), Gilles was never a mere epigone. Quite the contrary, he played *bande à part* in his own way, unflinchingly faithful to his personal vision, and remarkably resistant – especially in the light of continued setbacks – to dominant fashions or trends. If Astruc famously compared the filmmaker to the writer of an essay or novel, for Gilles directing was above all akin to poetry and painting: 'I make films as one writes verse, as one uses paintbrushes'.[109] His training in drawing and painting at the Beaux-Arts, he reveals, was undertaken with a view to making films.[110] Thanks to the excellent website dedicated to his life and work,[111] we discover a talented painter of watercolours, some inflected with the landscapes and physiognomies of his native Algeria, others evoking the world of the circus or the commedia dell'arte, exquisitely beautiful in their delicate lines and vibrant palette. If the young Gilles admired Modigliani, Chagall, Soutine and the decorative artist Jean-Denis Malclès,[112] painting was to remain a lifelong inspiration, informing his approach to framing, colour, lighting and composition. For this filmmaker who, in the tradition of Proust and Malraux, considers form not as a stylistic exercise, but an expression of sensitivity, 'with a camera, you also paint'.[113]

Less interested in referencing paintings than Varda or Godard, Gilles strives for a cinematic poetry conveyed by way of the image and 'plasticity' – revealingly, he recalls Henri Langlois's insistence that cinema is 'above all a plastic art', in a 1967 text on the cinema that reads like a personal manifesto.[114] Misunderstood by contemporary critics, who accused him of a futile aestheticism,[115] he detested 'beautiful images', aspiring instead to 'a good image', that is, 'an image that has meaning, that contains an idea, that seeks to express a feeling, a thought through form'.[116] His preoccupation with form, therefore, contrary to aestheticism's self-sufficiency, is a means of conveying thought and affect, not so far from Godard's idea of cinema as 'a form that thinks'. Wistful and diaphanous, his sentient portraits of people, places and things probe the relationship between physical and mental spaces, inside and outside. Often infused with a dreamlike atmosphere, his films apprehend the physical world as a mirror of interiority, a landscape of the soul externalising the emotional states of characters who struggle to anchor themselves in reality.

Seemingly out of touch with the prevalent mood of youthful rebellion, Gilles's works of the 1960s and early 1970s are permeated by an anguished consciousness of the transience of life, rendered palpable through recurrent visual motifs: 'photos of stars hanging on the walls, neighbourhoods being demolished and weathered stones, local cinemas, old postcards or photo albums, end up creating a melancholy network of signs'.[117] On a formal level, this concern for the transitory and fugitive is given expression in rapid montage sequences that syncopate temporal duration into a series of flashes. As Safia Benhaïm states, 'barely apprehended, the perception of time becomes the perception of a lost, immemorial time; every filmed object seems to slide into the past, becomes immediately anachronistic'.[118] In Gilles's expressive use of montage, the fast editing produces aesthetic shocks, endowing faces, bodies and objects with an aura that Walter Benjamin famously denied the media of mechanical reproduction, but which is reclaimed here for a practice of cinematic poetry.[119] Resolutely one of those directors 'who put their faith in the image', rather than 'those who put their faith in reality', to use Bazin's distinction,[120] Gilles draws on the plastic qualities of the image to convey his subjective vision: 'I think it's [. . .] impossible to translate by other means but that of the image and plasticity, the cinematographic poetry in the Wellesian sense of the word: "the camera is an eye in the head of a poet".'[121]

For this poet of cinema, the filmmaker is above all a passionate spectator of the everyday in the wake of Baudelaire's *flâneur*, that restless urban wanderer in search of 'the multiplicity of life and the flickering grace of all the elements of life'.[122] In a moving auto-portrait inserted into *L'Amour à la mer* in the form of an extended flashback, Gilles presents himself as a *cinéaste-flâneur* through the character Guy (played by himself), freshly arrived in Paris. With a suitcase in one hand and the portrait of his late mother in the other, the young man is visually constructed as a nomadic figure, a solitary walker who roams the streets, indulging in the joys of looking. The camera aligns with Guy's point of view as he discovers the manifold pleasures of the capital with the enchanted eyes of a child not yet blunted by habit. Cafés, parks and funfairs, the view of the Eiffel Tower as he climbs down the stairs from his garret, shop windows and billboards, faces glimpsed in the crowd: they all partake in the atmospheric spectacle afforded to the newcomer. In *Le Clair de terre*, too, the protagonist Pierre (another alter ego of the director) is defined by his scopic relationship to the world. By way of point-of-view shots and eyeline matches, we discover the textures of the urban fabric with its sinuous streets, curious architectural details and diverse human crowd through his agile gaze. Apprehending the real through Pierre's (Patrick Jouané) eyes, we learn to find poetry in the seemingly banal, to embrace the manifold forms and shapes of the visible, to touch the plasticity of life itself.

A twentieth-century 'Painter of Modern Life', Gilles reclaims the magic of material things, infusing them with a tantalising charm and grace. Not afraid of the sentimentality of popular taste, he lovingly films bibelots and bric-a-brac, vases, shop mannequins, tacky souvenirs, even an outmoded cash register, arranging objects that would traditionally be considered as everyday into painterly compositions. Shot with a fixed camera, thanks to careful framing, atmospheric lighting and luminous colours, they take on a still life-like quality, every picture like a world unto itself. The scene in *L'Amour à la mer* in which Geneviève, her friend Josette (an aspiring decorator) and a young man (Bernard Verley) stumble upon an antiques courtyard is witness to this painterly elevation of the world of things. A rapid montage sequence affords poetic value to a motley collection of objects: neoclassical busts and religious paintings, Italianate vases and mouldings, an early twentieth-century tricycle – messengers of an era where beauty was still valued above utility and travel had none of the frenzy of the modern age. In their capacity to connect us to the past, objects such as these, the young man muses, constitute a memory trace: 'I also like objects because of the memories, the traces of time they contain. They also frighten me a bit. I feel like I've seen them before.'

It is useful to briefly compare the role of objects in Gilles's work with the Surrealist obsession with the mysterious world of things that resonates in this remark. As is well known, Surrealism – by taking everyday objects out of their habitual contexts – profoundly altered the ways in which we perceive the concrete world. At the heart of the Surrealist project, the banal or ritual object – Duchamp's *ready-mades*, but also the mannequins, masks and costumes, as well as the manifold natural and scientific objects showcased in Surrealist photography or exhibited in the 1936 *Exposition surréaliste d'objets* – is enlisted to unsettle spectators' habitual vision, alerting them to the marvellous and the uncanny that permeate human existence. Walter Benjamin, the most ingenious analyst of Parisian material culture and an astute commentator of Surrealism, calls attention to the movement's preoccupation with obsolescent objects:

> [André Breton] was the first to perceive the revolutionary energies that appear in the 'outmoded' – in the first iron constructions, the first factory buildings, the earliest photos, objects that have begun to be extinct, grand pianos, the dresses of five years ago, fashionable restaurants when the vogue has begun to ebb from them.[123]

Gilles visibly shares with Surrealism this fascination for the strange, but nonetheless familiar world of things. Yet, though attentive to the inherent uncanniness of everyday objects (highlighted through close-ups and unusual camera angles), his interest lies less in their disturbing strangeness than their incarnation of a past that continues to permeate our present. Ultimately, in its concern with the material world as a trace, his vision is closer to Proust – an author to whom he is often compared – than to the Surrealist aesthetic. Like the author of *In Search of Lost Time*, for whom objects have the ability to capture the souls of the departed,[124] Gilles endows what are habitually considered soulless things with a presence of their own. In an interview of 1973, insisting on his stylistic proximity with Proust, he likens his own affinity for close-ups to the author's famously detailed descriptions, both offering a profounder portrayal of external realities:

> if I do a close-up of a certain light, on a neck, a hand, a part of a face, a body part, I make it appear more precisely than in a long shot, it's impossible to deny. [. . .] And I believe that this deepening by means of description also exists in the Proustian sentence.[125]

If *L'Amour à la mer* introduces Gilles as a nostalgic gleaner of images in the poetic and visual tradition that stretches from Baudelaire via Proust to the Surrealists, it is in his following feature, *Au pan coupé*, that his painterly approach to the filmic medium finds its most sustained expression. At the heart of this slow-paced, lyrical second feature, Jeanne (Macha Méril) remembers her love for Jean (Patrick Jouané), a tormented former runaway who one day hits the road with a group of beatniks, true to his ideal of personal freedom until death. Poignant and intimate, the film explores the emotional world of the lovers less through dialogue than by means of minutely recorded gestures, bodily poses and the delicate expressiveness of the human face. Marguerite Duras, one of the film's early advocates, notes Gilles's attention to the female face, offered in close-up like an inner, spiritual landscape:

> Here, finally, love isn't shown from an embrace-in-a-hotel-bed. Its evocation by the face – the face of a woman fifty times repeated, but for a shadow, a glance, a contraction under the stress of the wound – is quite simply admirable.[126]

Emblematic of a painterly concern with frames and framing that traverses all the director's work, the couple are frequently shown next to pictures in Jeanne's flat (including the portrait of Gilles's mother first shown in *L'Amour à la mer* whose reappearance here and in the later *Le Clair de terre* weaves a visual thread across the three films) or framed against windows and doorways.

The filmic plot explicitly engages painting through the contrasting (but, as suggested by their names, also complementary) figures of Jeanne, a painter who makes a living from illustrating books, and Jean, a manual worker who paints the facades of buildings. As part of a wider reflection on social class, education and creativity, the work of the trained artist who anchors herself in an established artistic tradition is pitted against the natural 'paintings' found in the urban fabric. Receptive to the raw beauty of architectural surfaces, Jean urges Jeanne to paint the textures of walls: 'You ought to paint canvases that represent the walls exactly as they are. [. . .] Traces, fundamentally it's perhaps not discovery that is important, but to find again.' In Gilles's own painterly vision of the city, fissured walls covered in peeling paint, arrested in close-up, take on the appearance of an abstract painting, infinitely more modern than Jeanne's drawing of a human figure perceived earlier. A series of wall graffiti extracted from the urban fabric by the camera recall the experiments of Surrealist photographer Brassaï, who began taking pictures of wall carvings and markings in the early 1930s, and the initiator of *Art Brut*, Jean Dubuffet, who, in 1945, produced a series of lithographs entitled *Les Murs*, inspired by Parisian graffiti as well as Eugène Guillevic's eponymous poem. The artistic tradition in which Gilles inserts himself with his own ciné-paintings of walls is duly referenced by Jeanne, who comments, 'That already exists, not only paintings, but also photos'. On one level, what is at stake here is a meditation on elite versus popular forms of image-making, embedded into a broader interrogation of the human desire to leave traces that is central to Gilles's thought. On another, more abstract level, Gilles – as a filmmaker who straddles the visual arts and poetry – hints at possible migrations between artistic practices. It is not, Jean insists, because poetry is carved into the urban fabric that one should not also write it on paper. Or, one is compelled to add, paint it with a camera. In their linking of poetry, photography, painting and film, the wall graffiti point to pathways between the arts, dialogues that were embraced by avant-garde artists such as Brassaï and Dubuffet who worked across a range of media, and which are revitalised in Gilles's intermedial work.

In 1964, during the shooting of *Au pan coupé*, Gilles made a short about the figurative painter Francis Savel (whose style has been likened to the better

Figure 3.7 Wall graffiti in *Au pan coupé* (Guy Gilles, 1967).

known Bernard Buffet). Filmed in the painter's Montmartre studio, *Journal d'un combat* documents the genesis of a painting, from the blank canvas via first charcoal sketches to the application of colour. In the feature, this filmic record of the painter at work is reiterated in miniature in the sequence where Savel (fictionalised as the painter Michel) paints a portrait of Jean. At first, the sitter and canvas are framed frontally in one shot, allowing us to compare the model with the artistic representation that is beginning to take shape. But, rapidly, as the contours of the portrait become more detailed, the camera cuts to (selectively): shots of Jean in profile, Jeanne framed against a doorway and, subsequently, against a flower painting, Jeanne in shallow focus behind the portrait, and, finally, her face half-covered by the painting, forming a new animate-inanimate hybrid. If film affirms itself as a plastic medium analogous to painting here in these pictorial compositions, the cut from the portrait and its sitter to the surrounding studio environment also affords a comparison between what Bazin has termed the 'centripetal' art of painting and the 'centrifugal' art of cinema. While the painting remains closed in upon itself, the cinema screen evokes an off-screen, a wider reality which, as is shown here, it can at any moment bring into view.

Our analysis would not be complete without considering Gilles's use of colour, inflected, like his attention to framing, surface textures and compositions, by a painterly sensitivity. In *Au pan coupé*, flashbacks to the couple's happy days together are suffused by a warm palette of shimmering colours, whereas the scenes during and after their breakup are shot in an overexposed black and white (intermittently tainted with a ghostly bluish hue) that dissolves contours and flattens the image. In the sequence of their trip to the south of France, Jean's changing mood – the onslaught of the black sun of depression – is mirrored in the muted pastels of the Mediterranean in autumn, a landscape drained of its vibrancy. More than an aesthetic fad or a mere narrative device, the shifts between black and white and colour in four of his features (*L'Amour à la mer*, *Au pan coupé*, *Absences répétées* (*Repeated Absences*, 1972) and *Nuit docile* (1987)), Marcos Uzal states, give visual expression to the insurmountable sadness of Gilles's characters: 'it's about inscribing in the very image the melancholy that afflicts them by making feel visually the ruptures between time and space that regrets, nostalgia or despair have definitively detached'.[127] In the flashback sequences in *Au pan coupé*, colour 'bleeds into' the mournful black and white, furtively energising the image as the visual trace of past happiness. Jeanne's own artistic work, reflecting the demise of the couple and her regret at not having been able to instill a love of life in Jean, moves from oil painting to black and white drawing. While, in Provence, she dreamt of painting Paris in the warm colours of the south and found fresh inspiration in the rich shades of nature, after Jean's disappearance she doubts ever being able to paint again. A close-up of her hands idly doodling on a piece of paper visualises her predicament.

Inversely, in *Le Clair de terre* painting is endowed with a therapeutic role. Pierre's friend Maria (Annie Girardot) recounts how an exhibition of Bonnard's paintings helped her rekindle an interest in life after her husband's death. Whereas her words cannot quite capture the painting *Méditerranée* (*c*.1941), which made a particular impression on her – 'all blue, all white, impossible to tell' – its radiant colours seem to have migrated into the close-ups of the Mediterranean as Pierre sets off on his journey of self-discovery. 'Pierre travels in colour', Bernard Benoliel comments, likening the painterly quality of the sea ('the blue-painting') in this scene to Godard's non-naturalistic, artistic treatment of colour.[128] Moving and splattering, the seascape reveals itself to be sensually richer than its counterpart fixed on canvas evoked earlier: thanks to cinema's multiple tracks, it engages the acoustic as well as the visual sensorium. It is an animated painting.

But as in the wall graffiti scene in *Au pan coupé* – and herein lies a fundamental difference from Godard – though inviting us to compare and contrast the arts of painting and cinema, Gilles appears less preoccupied with 'showing off' the expressive possibilities of film than with mapping possible migrations between the arts within the wider poetics of traces that is central to his work. Just as past and present are inseparably enmeshed in his films, fusing into a syncopated time of emotion, so Gilles bridges the arts of painting, poetry and film in his quest for a sensitive image.

Notes

1. Rohmer, *The Taste for Beauty*, p. 70.
2. Hegel, *Aesthetics*, I, p. 87.
3. Rohmer, 'Le Siècle des peintres', p. 45 (emphasis in original).
4. Rohmer 'Le Siècle des peintres', p. 37 and 'Avant-propos', p. 17. For cineplastics see Faure, 'The Art of Cineplastics', p. 260.
5. Rohmer 'Le Siècle des peintres', p. 37.
6. Rohmer 'Le Siècle des peintres', p. 38.
7. Rohmer, 'Avant-propos', p. 14.
8. Rohmer, 'Avant-propos', p. 15.
9. Rohmer, 'Deuxième entretien', pp. 120–3.
10. Aumont, *L'Œil interminable*, pp. 324–5.
11. Jacobs, *Framing Pictures*, p. 1. For an extensive discussion of post-war art documentaries, including Resnais's *Van Gogh*, *Guernica* and *Gauguin*, see ch. 1: 'Camera and canvas: Emmer, Storck, Resnais and the post-war art film'.
12. Bazin, 'Painting and cinema', p. 164.
13. Ibid. p. 168.

14. Ibid. p. 166.
15. Ibid. p. 166.
16. Ibid. p. 166.
17. Ibid. p. 169.
18. Aumont, *Matière d'images*, p. 56. On the question of migration, in particular in relation to Warburg, see also Aumont, *L'Œil interminable*, p. 16.
19. To give a few examples, one only needs to think of the thirteen Picasso paintings that punctuate the filmic narrative in Truffaut's *Jules et Jim*, Philip Kaufman's *art brut* inspired drawings and the Modigliani postcards in Rivette's *Paris nous appartient*, the triangle between painter Daniel (Daniel Pommereulle), art dealer Adrien (Patrick Bauchau) and 'collector' (albeit of men) Haydée (Haydée Politoff) in Rohmer's *La Collectionneuse* (1967), the amateur painter Jeanne in Demy's *Lola*, not forgetting Demy's painterly approach to colour in films like *Les Parapluies de Cherbourg* (*The Umbrellas of Cherbourg*, 1964) and *Les Demoiselles de Rochefort* (*The Young Girls of Rochefort*, 1967).
20. See Nussbaum, 'Classic=modern', p. 296.
21. Ibid. p. 294 and p. 295.
22. Nussbaum, 'Classic=modern', p. 299. See this article for a more detailed discussion of Godard's undermining of the division between classicism and modernity.
23. See Proust, 'Classicisme et romantisme', pp. 313–14.
24. Nussbaum, 'Classic=modern', p. 299.
25. See Schapper, *Jacques-Louis David*, pp. 162–7.
26. Bazin, 'Painting and cinema', p. 167.
27. Malraux, *Le Musée imaginaire*, p. 122.
28. On Malraux's wider influence on Godard see Didi-Huberman, *Passés cités par JLG*, pp. 136–53.
29. Varda, *Varda par Agnès*, p. 22.
30. For a succinct reading of painterly references and reworkings in Varda's oeuvre see Smith, *Agnès Varda*, pp. 32–42.
31. DeRoo, *Agnès Varda*, p. 1.
32. Varda, *Varda par Agnès*, p. 48.
33. DVD *Cléo de 5 à 7*, Bonus 'Memories and Anecdotes', Artificial Eye, 2010.
34. Fieschi and Ollier, 'La Grâce laïque', p. 45.
35. Varda, *Varda par Agnès*, p. 44.
36. Beck, *Italian Renaissance Painting*, p. 163.
37. DeRoo, *Agnès Varda*, p. 35.
38. Bonitzer, *Décadrages*, p. 8.
39. Ungar, *Cléo de 5 à 7*, p. 24.
40. See Giraud, 'La Picturalité dans le cinéma d'Agnès Varda', pp. 49–50. I would like to acknowledge my indebtedness to this piece of research, which the author has kindly made available to me and which has greatly enriched my understanding of the role of the visual arts in Varda.
41. Fried, *Manet's Modernism*, p. 307 *et passim*. I am indebted to Brigitte Peucker for her compelling reading of Fried in her book *The Material Image*.

42. Fried, *Manet's Modernism*.
43. Peucker, *The Material Image*, p. 89.
44. See Varda, *Album d'Agnès V. images et notes latérales* (booklet included in DVD box set *Tout(e) Varda*, Ciné-Tamaris and Arte Editions, 2012), p. 8.
45. Jacques Ledoux, 'Interview with Agnès Varda', *Cinémathèque Royale de Belgique, Radio-Télévision-Belge* (1961–2), cited in DeRoo, *Agnès Varda*, p. 31.
46. DeRoo, *Agnès Varda*, p. 49.
47. Varda, *Varda par Agnès*, p. 62.
48. Bonus DVD *Le Bonheur*, 'Agnès Varda parle du *Bonheur*', in box set *Tout(e) Varda* (2012).
49. Varda, *Varda par Agnès*, p. 62.
50. For Varda's interrogation of contemporary representations of domestic harmony see DeRoo, *Agnès Varda*, ch. 3.
51. Colvin, 'Explaining Varda's *Lions Love*', p. 20. On intermediality in *Lions Love* see also Giraud, 'Intermediality and gesture'.
52. For Varda taking inspiration in Warhol and pop art, but also Picasso's neoclassical etchings in *Lions Love*, see Giraud, 'Intermediality and gesture'. For the Picasso etchings, see also Giraud, 'La Picturalité dans le cinéma d'Agnès Varda', pp. 13–14.
53. Léal, Piot and Bernadac, *The Ultimate Picasso*, p. 297.
54. See Léal, Piot and Bernadac, *The Ultimate Picasso*, p. 262.
55. For a discussion of the *tableaux vivants* in *Jane B. par Agnès V.*, see Smith, *Agnès Varda*, pp. 38–42.
56. Jacobs, *Framing Pictures*, p. 90.
57. Ibid. p. 91.
58. Ibid. p. 94.
59. On Picasso's sculptor's studio see Léal, Piot and Bernadac, *The Ultimate Picasso*, p. 259.
60. It is intriguing to note that in paintings and drawings of the studio, Picasso himself had substituted 'the family trio (father, mother, and child, or Picasso, Olga, and Paolo), with another trio that concerned him more deeply: the creator, his muse, and art, or Picasso, Marie-Thérèse, and the work' (Léal, Piot and Bernadac, *The Ultimate Picasso*, p. 262).
61. Varda, *Album d'Agnès V.*, p. 26.
62. Peucker, *The Material Image*, p. 31.
63. Barthes, *S/Z*, p. 55.
64. Peucker, *The Material Image*, p. 31.
65. Aragon, 'Qu'est-ce que l'art, Jean-Luc Godard?'.
66. See de Baecque, *Godard*, p. 298.
67. See for instance Dalle Vacche's seminal 'Jean-Luc Godard's *Pierrot le Fou*'.
68. Didi-Huberman, *Passés cités*, p. 33.
69. Aumont, *L'Œil interminable*, p. 281.
70. Cited in de Baecque, *Godard*, p. 29.
71. On *Passion* see Jacobs, *Framing Pictures*, ch. 4: 'Tableaux vivants 1: painting, film,

death and Passion plays in Pasolini and Godard'; for an intermedial reading of *Histoire(s) du cinéma* see Pethő, *Cinema and Intermediality*, ch. 8: 'Post-cinema as pre-cinema and media archeology in Jean-Luc Godard's *Histoire(s) du Cinéma*'.
72. Jacobs, *Framing Pictures*, pp. 116–17.
73. See Dalle Vacche, 'Jean-Luc Godard's *Pierrot le Fou*' and Leutrat, 'Godard's Tricolor'.
74. Bolter 'Transference and transparency', p. 14 (cited in Rajewsky, 'Intermediality, intertextuality and remediation', p. 60).
75. Godard, *Histoire(s) du cinéma*, vol. 3, *La Monnaie de l'absolu, Une Nouvelle Vague*, p. 54.
76. Pethő, *Cinema and Intermediality*, p. 298. See also Maureen Turim's unpicking of the film's manifold cultural references in 'Three way mirroring'.
77. Poe, 'The Oval Portrait', p. 252.
78. De Baecque, *Godard*, pp. 180–1 and p. 209.
79. See Wall-Romana, *Jean Epstein*, p. 37.
80. See ibid. pp. 4, 177 and 184.
81. Epstein, 'On certain characteristics of *Photogénie*', p. 314.
82. Abel, *French Film Theory and Criticism,* vol. 1, p. 111.
83. Langlois, 'Jean Epstein', pp. 22–3.
84. Cited in Turim, 'Three way mirroring', p. 98.
85. Flaubert, *Madame Bovary*, p. 371.
86. DVD *Une femme mariée*, in *Jean-Luc Godard – Fiction* – box set (Gaumont, 2010), Annexe JLG/MM.
87. Pethő, *Cinema and Intermediality*, p. 99.
88. Buchloh, '1959d Richard Avedon's *Observations* and Robert Frank's *The Americans* establish the dialectical parameters of New York School photography' in Foster et al., *Art Since 1900*, p. 428.
89. Didi-Huberman, *Passés cités*, p. 30.
90. Cited in de Baecque, *Godard*, pp. 270–1.
91. Godard, 'Conférence de presse', p. 11.
92. On Godard's dialectical montage see, among others, Didi-Huberman, *Passés cités*, pp. 31–54.
93. Deleuze, 'Three questions on *Six Times Two*', p. 45.
94. Lessing, *Laocoon*; Arnheim, 'A new Laocoön'; Greenberg, 'Towards a newer Laocoon', p. 32.
95. Greenberg, 'Towards a newer Laocoon', pp. 24–5.
96. Derrida, *Of Hospitality*; Leutrat, *Des traces qui nous ressemblent*, p. 23.
97. Simsolo, *Dictionnaire de la Nouvelle Vague*, p. 215.
98. Gonzalez, 'Les Cicatrices intérieures'.
99. La Rochelle International Film Festival (2003), Lussas Documentary Film Festival (2004 and 2005), Pantin Short Film Festival (2005).
100. See http://www.guygilles.com; Lépingle and Uzal (eds), *Guy Gilles*; and a dossier of articles dedicated to the filmmaker in *Vertigo*, 27 (2005).
101. Lépingle, 'Une Filmographie', p. 19.

102. For his admiration of New Wave directors, see Lépingle and Uzal, 'Montage d'entretiens avec Guy Gilles', p. 42 and p. 45.
103. Lépingle, 'Entretien avec Noun Serra', pp. 93–5. For the reasons for Gilles's non-recognition see also in more detail Lépingle, 'Une Filmographie', pp. 24–5.
104. Lépingle, 'Une Filmographie', p. 24.
105. In a questionnaire for *Cahiers du cinéma*, 164 (1965), Gilles offered a good-humoured account of his artisanal working methods. See Lépingle and Uzal, 'Montage d'entretiens avec Guy Gilles', pp. 44–6.
106. Guiguet, 'Hommage à Guy Gilles', p. 19.
107. Gilles's hommage to Demy in *L'Amour à la mer* is signalled through the tellingly named singer and cabaret dancer Lola Lamour (Lili Bontemps), who alludes to Demy's *Lola* (1961).
108. See Lépingle, 'Une Filmographie', p. 17.
109. See Lépingle and Uzal, 'Montage d'entretiens avec Guy Gilles', p. 48.
110. Ibid. p. 41.
111. http://www.guygilles.com
112. Lépingle, 'Une Filmographie', p. 13.
113. See Lépingle and Uzal, 'Montage d'entretiens avec Guy Gilles', p. 54.
114. http://www.guygilles.com – Section 'Ecrits personnels': 'Sur le cinéma'.
115. See for instance Luc Moullet's scathing review of *L'Amour à la mer* in 'Contingent 65 1 A', p. 59.
116. See Lépingle and Uzal, 'Montage d'entretiens avec Guy Gilles', p. 49.
117. Lépingle, 'Arrêts sur images', p. 132.
118. Benhaïm, 'Le flâneur', p. 86.
119. For expressive montage see Aumont et al., *Aesthetics of Film*, p. 47; on aura see Benjamin, *The Work of Art*.
120. Bazin, 'The evolution of the language of cinema', p. 24.
121. Gilles, 'Ecrits personnels', 'Sur le cinéma'.
122. Baudelaire, 'The painter of modern life', p. 9. On the figure of the *flâneur* in Gilles's films see also Benhaïm, 'Le Flâneur'.
123. Benjamin, 'Surrealism', p. 210.
124. 'I find the Celtic belief very reasonable, that the souls of those we have lost are held captive in some inferior creature, in an animal, in a plant, in some inanimate thing, effectively lost to us until the day, which for many never comes, when we happen to pass close to the tree, come into possession of the object that is their prison. Then they quiver, they call out to us, and as soon as we have recognized them, the spell is broken. Delivered by us, they have overcome death and they return to live with us.' (Proust, *In Search of Lost Time*, vol. 1, *The Way by Swann's*, trans. Lydia Davis, p. 47).
125. Lépingle and Uzal, 'Montage d'entretiens avec Guy Gilles', p. 53.
126. Cited by Forret, 'Trois films du cinéaste Guy Gilles'.
127. Uzal, 'Les Couleurs du temps', p. 186. See this article for a more sustained discussion of colour in Gilles's films.
128. Benoliel, 'Le Temps d'un raccord', p. 100.

CHAPTER FOUR

Architecture of Apocalypse, City of Lights

> The form of a city changes faster, alas, than the human heart.
>
> Baudelaire[1]

> What does Mr Le Corbusier know of humanity's needs?
>
> Guy Debord[2]

Celebrated as the film camera's 'undoubted ancestor' by Sergei Eisenstein, the oldest of the arts, architecture, is arguably also the one that is closest to cinema.[3] Not only do the sites of film exhibition – from the 'palaces' and 'nickelodeons' of the early twentieth century to modern multiplexes – make the motion picture an 'architectural affair';[4] architecture, and by extension the city with its rich urban layers, buzzing life and diverse inhabitants, is the stuff that (most) movies are made of. Conjoined together from the first commercial movie, the Lumière brothers' *La sortie de l'usine Lumière à Lyon* (*Workers Leaving the Lumière Factory in Lyon*, 1895), the manifold textures and rhythms of the city afford cinema a raw material to be investigated, recorded, and reinvented by the camera eye.

Emerging at a time when architecture and the built environment were undergoing drastic changes due to the appearance of new materials (glass, iron and, soon, reinforced concrete), cinema quickly asserted its place as a medium perfectly in sync with modernity. Cinema's moving image technology, shortly to be enriched by sound, made it uniquely equipped to capture the dazzling intensity and multi-sensory fabric of the modern city. Indeed so inextricably enmeshed are the two, that the art critic Elie Faure describes cinema as 'an architecture in movement that should be in constant accord, dynamically balanced with the setting and the landscapes within which it rises and falls'.[5] Reigniting the voyeuristic curiosity of the nineteenth-century *flâneur*, whose quest for scopic pleasures has been likened to that of the modern spectator, the modern city quickly became the preferred locus of film. Post-1945, as many great European cities lay in ruins, cinema's intrinsic potential as an archive of spaces and social practices took on a new urgency: for contemporary and later generations, film became an important memory trace of cities laid to waste in the fury of war or subsequently erased in processes of reconstruction and modernisation.[6]

While it remains controversial to what extent the New Wave constitutes a genuine rupture in representations of the city,[7] there can be no doubt that it affords a refreshingly new look at Paris – the favourite setting of the majority of New Wave films and one that is inseparably bound up with the movement's allure and mythology. 'To film Paris, to film the real Paris, to film Paris "differently", formed an integral part of the New Wave project, at least for its central engine, the group issuing from the *Cahiers du cinéma*', Joël Magny explains.[8] 'To film Paris differently' first of all meant to break free from the poeticised depictions of the city that had dominated in films of the previous generation and which the *Cahiers* critics still saw at work in Albert Lamorisse's *Le Ballon rouge* (*The Red Balloon*), awarded the *Palme d'or* for short film in 1956.[9] No less important, and connected to their desire for a more truthful, realistic portrait of the city anchored in contemporary reality, New Wave directors rejected the predominantly studio-based approach of the so-called 'Poetic Realism' of the 1930s and 1940s and its inheritor, the maligned Tradition of Quality. While iconic films like René Clair's *Sous les toits de Paris* (*Under the Roofs of Paris*, 1930) and Marcel Carné's *Les Enfants du Paradis* (*Children of Paradise*, 1945) were based on elaborate reconstructions of Paris tenements, thus, in essence, reducing the capital to a set, the New Wave famously takes to the streets. In the wake of Renoir, Melville and Jacques Becker, who had paved the way for filming on location, but inspired in particular by Italian neorealism and French *cinema vérité*, the young generation of filmmakers engage in a new, more intimate, relationship with the city and its inhabitants. Unburdened by heavy equipment and large film crews, less concerned with technical mastery and freer in their approach to the medium, they are able to catch urban life in all its vibrancy, vitality and social diversity.

From the café terraces of Saint-Germain teeming with students and artists to the bars of Montparnasse glittering with neon signs, from the banks of the Seine – preferred terrain of lovers and abode for the homeless – to the colourful market stalls of the popular rue Mouffetard, from the sleazy hotels of the rue Saint-Denis to the chic business district around the Arc de Triomphe, New Wave films draw a new cartography of the city. Immersed in the concrete reality of the urban space and the daily rites of its inhabitants, feature film becomes permeable to real life. There is no better example of the quasi-unmediated, seemingly unstaged take on the real than the celebrated scene in *À bout de souffle* in which Jean-Paul Belmondo and Jean Seberg walk down the Champs-Élysées, flirting and bantering, with the surrounding crowd seemingly unaware of the shooting: a 'reality effect' obtained thanks to cameraman Raoul Coutard being hidden away in a postman's cart pulled by Godard.[10]

If the photogenic city with its easily recognisable monuments, winding old streets and modern boulevards becomes one of the most fascinating protagonists of New Wave fictions, its inhabitants, unwittingly captured in their daily routines, add to the lifelike feel of a cinema in which documentary and fictional modes have fused. 'Real streets, real passers-by, real apartments, the New Wave palpates Paris with an intimacy bursting with authenticity', writes Sonia Bruneau. 'Viewers are plunged into a spectacle that has all the aspects of their contemporary experience.'[11]

So prominent is the capital in films of the New Wave and so richly diverse are its depictions in the works of individual directors that most discussions of urban space in New Wave cinema focus on representations of Paris, risking obscuring the movement's wider preoccupation with architecture and the built environment, in particular its positioning towards architectural modernity. Alain Brassart is representative of a broader tendency to exclude modern architecture from discourses of the New Wave when he notes:

> Architectural modernity is almost absent from the New Wave and you have to wait for the short films of the ethnographer Jean Rouch or mass-market films like *Mélodie en sous-sol* (Henri Verneuil, 1962) for burning questions like neighbourhood renovation and, more widely, the housing crisis, to be treated.[12]

Such a statement seems at least surprising given the movement's contemporaneity with a period of extensive architectural modernisation and its eagerness to give a more authentic picture of modern life. While it is true that New Wave films tend to foreground the picturesque historic quarters of Paris, the challenges posed by modern urbanism went neither unnoticed nor uncommented by their directors. On the contrary, as I intend to show in this chapter, architecture is at the centre of the New Wave's grappling with modernity, compelling it to rethink canonical notions of beauty while engaging it in an extensive meditation on the relationship of the built environment to affect, memory and belonging. Moreover – and particularly pertinent to our questions here – the New Wave's confrontation with the architectural forms of modernity prompted directors to become particularly attentive to the textures, surfaces and volumes of the built environment, helping them define a cinematic language that captures the fabric of modern life. Uncovering little-known films such as Rohmer's documentaries for French state television and Guy Gilles's features, but also revisiting seminal works such as Marker's *Le Joli Mai* (*The Lovely Month of May*, 1963), Resnais's *Muriel, ou le temps d'un retour* (*Muriel*, 1963) and Godard's *Deux ou trois choses que je sais d'elle* (*Two or Three Things I Know About Her*, 1967) from an intermedial point of view, this chapter takes us on a journey where 'architecture in

Caution: Modernity!

Intimately tied up with the profound socio-cultural changes France underwent in the course of the 1950s and 1960s, the New Wave also, as tends to be less acknowledged in criticism, coincides with one of the most radical periods of urban modernisation in the history of modern France. Faced with numerous urban pressures – endemic overcrowding and insalubrity, a decaying housing stock that no longer met modern standards, the large-scale move from rural areas into urban agglomerations, rapid population growth compounded by an influx of migrants and, in the aftermath of the Algerian War, by the repatriation of nearly a million *pieds-noirs* – the central government under the leadership of de Gaulle developed 'a new planning regime for Paris and its region'.[13] In 1959–60, Colin Jones explains, '[a] new planning agency, the *Service d'aménagement de la région parisienne* (SARP), produced the *Plan d'aménagement et d'organisation générale* (PADOG)', an ambitious rehabilitation plan which allowed for the creation of major housing schemes, and, under its revised version, the so-called *Schéma directeur*, for the construction of new cities in the Paris region.[14] In the capital, urban renewal schemes were concentrated predominantly in the peripheral *arrondissements* (that is, the 10th to the 20th district), historically composed of mixed industrial and residential areas.[15] While, up to the 1950s, the height of buildings in Paris was tightly regulated, major urbanisation projects such as the *Italie 13*, *Front de Seine* and *Maine-Montparnasse* schemes saw numerous, strategically regrouped towers appear on the city's skyline, the most prominent among them – the Montparnasse tower – reaching a height of over 200 metres. Elsewhere in the outer and, to a lesser extent, the inner *arrondissements*, pockets of the old Paris deemed to be of poor architectural quality or outright unsanitary were demolished to make place for office complexes and tower blocks. Even the Marais, one of the city's oldest districts and the home of some of its finest architectural heritage, only narrowly escaped destruction thanks to André Malraux's 1962 conservation law. While *intra muros* rampant modernisation accentuated the divide between the so-called 'beautiful neighbourhoods' and the less privileged districts, the Paris suburbs saw the development of the much maligned *grands ensembles*, that is, the rectilinear, geometrical housing estates in the functional style of Le Corbusier, whose modernist principles first laid out in the 1920s saw a revival among post-war architects.[16] Strongly contested at the time, notably by the Situationist International founded by Guy Debord, as well as by leading sociologists such as Henri Lefebvre,[17] the radical urbanisation projects of the

Gaullist era threw up numerous problems that still haunt France today: from the social exclusion of some of the most vulnerable communities (notably immigrant workers) herded together in brutalist 'machines for living',[18] to the rapid degradation of the urban tissue leading to desolation and violence (and, in turn, a stigmatisation of the *banlieue*), not forgetting the fragmentation of the suburban space with its disorientating effects on residents. Urban geographer Philippe Pinchemel comments:

> Even when you put things into perspective, it is important to acknowledge the disorder manifest in the current composition of the regional fabric. It is made of pieces of urban or outer-urban fabric, in too many shapes and sizes, with purposes that don't match and are poorly articulated [. . .]. In this urbanisation one seeks in vain an urban composition, a urbanist goal of small and medium scale: the urbanised space has ceased to be legible.[19]

Famously satirised in Tati's *Mon Oncle* (1958), which laments the gradual substitution of ramshackle, convivial old districts by a nightmarish world of aseptic efficiency, as well as the focus of Carné and Maurice Pialat, who examine love and life in France's post-war urban developments in *Terrain vague* (*Wasteland*, 1960) and *L'Amour existe* (*Love Exists*, 1960), the modernising projects of the 1950s and 1960s also strongly resonate in works of the New Wave. If, as Jean-Sébastien Chauvin has argued, the movement's visualisation of the city is organised around a dialectics between room and street, the self and other,[20] it also revolves around a less acknowledged opposition between traditional and modern architecture. Indeed, in the narrative construction of many New Wave films, while the historic urban fabric offers a picturesque backdrop for amorous encounters, *flânerie* and the pleasurable distractions of city life, architectural modernity, on the contrary, tends to be associated with danger, deceit or disruption. Already in Louis Malle's *Ascenseur pour l'échafaud*, acknowledged as one of the predecessors of the movement, the modern office building is the site of a coldblooded murder, but also the trap in which the murderer is caught when he gets stuck in one of the quintessential machines of modernity: the elevator. The film's second murder likewise occurs in an archetype of modern (mainly North American) architecture, the motel – soon to become the site of a famous screen murder in Hitchcock's 1960 *Psycho*. Instrumental to the filmic plot, modern architecture, as Malle himself states, distances *Ascenseur pour l'échafaud* from the works of contemporary French cinema, operating an aesthetic rupture and introducing a more dystopian vision of contemporary modernity:

> Traditionally it was always the Paris of René Clair that one saw in French films, and I undertook to show one of Paris's first modern buildings. [. . .] I

showed a Paris, not of the future, but at least a modern city, a universe already dehumanised.[21]

In the similarly film noir-inflected *À bout de souffle*, Michel makes contact with a shady accomplice in the glass-fronted modernist lobby of an international travel agency, while the police are hot on his heels. Though all of Paris becomes hostile to Pierre in *Le Signe du lion* (*The Sign of Leo*, 1959) when his inheritance fails to materialise, even in his destitution he cannot fathom crossing the city's boundaries: 'You think I'll go to that godforsaken place? You're nuts', he contemptuously replies to a friend who suggests a possible lifeline in Nanterre. A shot of the CNIT, one of the first buildings built in the new La Défense district, visually distances the historic Paris *intra muros* from the modern *banlieue* as the protagonist eventually makes his way to the suburbs where he hopes to make contact with a smuggler.

Not surprisingly, in another facet of this negative coding of architectural modernity, the modern house or building site is enmeshed with the crisis of the modern couple. In Godard's *Le Mépris*, the couple's costly modern flat at the outskirts of Rome is the main reason why Paul agrees to work for the brash producer Prokosch, an act of (self-)betrayal that compromises his artistic integrity and provokes his wife's eponymous contempt. It is in one of the most striking masterpieces of architectural modernity, Adalberto Libera's Casa Malaparte, a modernist red cube vertiginously perched over the Mediterranean on the isle of Capri, that the breakdown of their marriage will be precipitated. Intriguingly for a film which dramatises the conflict between the American studio system and European art house cinema, architectural modernism serves as a signifier of menace, thus ironically aligning representational codes with one of the stereotypes of classical Hollywood whereby, as Steven Jacobs explains, the modernist interior is 'practically always associated with cruelty, control and vanity'.[22] Focusing on a less privileged social milieu, Jean Rouch, in the sketch 'Gare du Nord' for the New Wave anthology film *Paris vu par . . .* (*Six in Paris*, 1965), makes the construction of a modern building depriving the couple of their views over one of Paris's most beloved monuments, the Sacré Coeur, the catalyst of a quarrel that ends in their separation. In Godard's *Deux ou trois choses que je sais d'elle*, as we will see in more detail later, the cost of modern housing in the suburbs is shown to drive young women into casual prostitution.

Threatening, divisive and corrupting, architectural modernity – in an extension of this trope – becomes the perfect metaphor for totalitarian oppression in two works of science fiction which we have already encountered in a different context: in *Alphaville*, the architectural modernity of 1960s Paris and its suburbs, collaged into a fictive geography that uses the present to visually evoke the city of the future, comes to embody the emotionless world of the technocratic regime. Filmed 'in the studios of French national radio, in the vast computer research complex of Bull [. . .], in the new modern office and residential complex of La Défense',[23] the modernist interiors with their glass-fronted, travertine-covered lobbies, interminable corridors with strictly symmetrical doors, and lack of ornamentation become an ideal setting for Godard's dystopian allegory of surveillance and indoctrination. The camera frequently lingers on architectural details, such as the helix-shaped staircase of the *Institut de Sémantique générale*, after characters have already made their exit, as if it were taking the functionalist architectural forms to task for the portrayed dehumanisation. Similarly, in Truffaut's *Fahrenheit 451*, rows of identical post-war houses and concrete tower blocks – the film features, among other council estates, the Alton Estate in southwest London – are the aseptic dwelling places where citizens are conditioned into unquestioning consumerism by the totalitarian government. Enhancing the value-laden architectural connotations, in both films pockets of resistance are nestled in historical buildings, ironically in *Alphaville* an insalubrious hotel near the Place d'Italie already earmarked for destruction by the Paris municipality.[24]

So enshrined is the tension between historic and modern architecture in works of the New Wave that *Cahiers du cinéma* critic Luc Moullet – like Gilles and Pollet one of the peripheral figures of the movement – conjugates the old versus modern binary as part of a burlesque pastiche of New Wave topoi in his first film *Brigitte et Brigitte* (*Brigitte and Brigitte*, 1966). Freshly arrived in Paris from provincial France, the two naive protagonists begin their studies at the new university of Nanterre, a campus still under construction. Though their classes are constantly interrupted by the noise of jackhammers, the two young women relish the atmosphere of modernity, in stark contrast to their native villages which, as they deplore, have been left untouched by the 'sixième plan d'aménagement'. In a comic evaluation of key monuments and Paris tourist sites, they give poor marks to historical landmarks such as Notre Dame, while giving a staggering 18/20 to Nanterre university – further evidence, in the film's satirical plot, of their lack of critical judgement. Beyond our temporal frame of reference here, but in keeping with the negative or, at least, satirical representations of architectural modernity, Jean Rouch's *Petit à petit* (1971) follows an African businessman on his peregrinations through Paris in search of an architect who will realise his dream of a 'tall building'. Revealing the absurdities of contemporary urban living in a *Lettres persanes*-style approach, the film also satirises the delusions of grandeur of recently de-colonised countries prey to a corrupt leadership. Modern architecture, then, far from being absent in films of the New Wave as Brassart claims, is instrumental in a wider critique of functionalist modernity, even if, as we shall see in more detail now, the new architectural language of modernity exercises a certain degree of fascination on New Wave filmmakers.

A Difficult Kind of Beauty

Among all the New Wave directors, it is without doubt Éric Rohmer who has engaged the city and its architecture most extensively in both his critical and artistic work. From his first feature, *Le Signe du lion*, which charts the wanderings of a bohemian artist in an increasingly hostile city space via two films set in France's 'new towns', *Les Nuits de la pleine lune* and *L'Ami de mon amie*, to his critique of context-insensitive modern architecture in the satirical *L'Arbre, le maire et la médiathèque* (*The Tree, the Major, and the Mediatheque*, 1993), Rohmer evinces a profound preoccupation with the ways in which human beings are impacted by architectural space, both as regards their physical conditions of living, but also, no less important, in the relationships they build with others and in their affective lives.[25] The last art to be examined in his 'Le Celluloïd et le marbre' series, Rohmer takes modern architecture to task in an article ominously entitled 'Architecture d'Apocalypse'. To what extent, the critic asks in this polemical piece, has modern architecture fulfilled its promise of creating a neat new world 'worthy of our pleasure, our quest for freedom'?[26] Or, on the contrary, is modern urbanism – which he considers to be inseparable from the question of architecture – responsible for the widespread sense of isolation and the loss of genuine experience that is the plight of modern city dwellers? If questions of urbanism and architecture will inform his fictional work of the following decades, they are first aired in a series of documentaries Rohmer directed for French television after stepping down as the main editor of *Cahiers du cinéma* in 1963: an architectural portrait of European capitals, *Paysages urbains* (1963); a lyrical documentary on the refashioning of the built environment in the wake of the industrial revolution, *Métamorphoses du paysage* (1964); a film dedicated to Victor Hugo's drawings, *Victor Hugo, architecte* (1969); an enquiry into the architectural use of concrete based on interviews with the architect Claude Parent and the cultural theorist-cum-urbanist Paul Virilio, *Entretien sur le béton* (1969); and, finally, a series of four television documentaries on France's *villes nouvelles* (1975). My focus here will be on *Métamorphoses du paysage* and *Entretien sur le béton* as two films that are emblematic for Rohmer's ambivalent attitude to architectural modernity, an attitude which, as we shall see later in this chapter, is shared by the New Wave more widely.

What kind of beauty is there to be found in industrial landscapes or, rather, how can an alert and curious gaze re-inject poetry into rural and urban sites ravaged by industrialisation? This is the topic Rohmer investigates in one of his first pedagogical films for the French educational channel RTS, intended, in his own words, not as an argument for or against the past or the present; nor indeed as a material trace of the profound changes our built environment has undergone in the course of the last 150 years or so; but, rather, as an invitation 'to find in this metamorphosis an opportunity for meditation and poetic reverie'.[27] For a director who hitherto had exercised his art predominantly in the feature genre the commission presented an opportunity to explore the poetic and philosophical capacities of the filmic medium in a particularly challenging context: the viscous, grimy underbelly of modernity. To appreciate Rohmer's strategy in this little-known filmic gem, it is useful to refer to the third essay of the 'Le Celluloïd et le marbre' series, 'De la métaphore', which compares modern poetry (understood in the traditional sense of both poetry and prose) and the cinema. In a world governed by cause and effect relations where results are valued higher than processes of becoming, Rohmer argues, poetry has abdicated the use of figurative language – in particular metaphor – that once was its privileged domain. If modern poetry, increasingly turned towards abstraction, can no longer reveal the universal laws that are enshrined in metaphoric expression, by contrast, the cinema, last-born among the arts, has become the sole refuge of the poetic.[28] It is this double premise of the poetic potential of cinematic form and its singular capacity to capture the real that Rohmer takes as his starting point in *Métamorphoses du paysage*.

The filmic voice-over (spoken by Pierre Gavarry) sets out on a simple observation: what we habitually consider as bucolic or poetic is not intrinsic to an object, but the result of cultural conditioning. The windmill, poetic companion of our childhood fables, is no less a functional machine than the modern excavator. Nature and machines are not opposed in any ontological sense: man-made, the machine is shaped in our image; human and non-human in equal measure, it has become an integral part of nature. Confronting traditional notions of the natural and the artificial, beauty and ugliness, *Métamorphoses du paysage* challenges spectators' aesthetic sensibility, opening their eyes to the paradoxical beauty of industrial landscapes, which, at first view, may appear formless, unfinished or chaotic. Taking us from the mining towns and industrial ports of the north to the Parisian *banlieue*, and, eventually, the capital's northern and eastern quarters with their rich industrial patrimony, the camera tracks the manifold traces and imprints left by the industrial age. In the course of the film, two semantic fields – one revolving around monstrosity, the amorphous, malady and internment; the other dwelling on idealist notions such as grace, harmony and order – intersect in a sustained exercise of trans-valuation. The maligned eyesores and waste products of modernity, as is suggested by repeated shot compositions where the sight of traditional buildings is obstructed by fences, barbed wire or telegraph poles, appear to strangle our environment; yet industrial architecture and machinery, valorised by close-ups, rhythmical editing and unusual camera angles, also reveal their inherent beauty and lyricism, in stark tension with the compromised landscapes they inhabit.[29]

'All poetry is metaphor', the voice-over declares about halfway through the film, naming the trope that henceforth is called upon to poeticise a world 'that bears the mark [. . .] less of man's creative joy than of his sweat and labour, which [. . .] evokes more easily the ruin of the past than the edification of the future'.[30] Rohmer does not use parallel editing, which, in the tradition of the Russian montageurs, remains a privileged means of translating metaphor into cinematic language. Instead, voice-over, sound, and above all, an expressive use of framing, lighting and composition perform the spell whereby the ordinary and the ugly are metamorphosed into curious sites of beauty. Touched by the magic wand of the cinema, cement mixers morph into towers, and flour mills into enchanted palaces, in an increasingly fantastical sequence on the *Porte de Pantin* building site. Seen through the eyes of a filmmaker sensitive to the lines, textures, and rhythms of industrial modernity, the shafts of cranes and telegraph poles take on a weightless elegance. The oxymoronic welding of opposites effected by the voice-over accompanied by

Figure 4.1 The paradoxical beauty of industrial landscapes in *Métamorphoses du paysage* (Éric Rohmer, 1964).

aestheticising camera angles, soft lighting and rhythmical editing reconcile nature and culture, the industrial and the artisanal, pre-modernity and modernity, into one common project of human labour. From the origins of our civic communities, Rohmer reminds us, our environment has been subject to perpetual change, a transformation that is merely accelerated – albeit leaving more visible traces – by industrialisation. Rather than a threatening rupture in the history of humanity, the industrial age and its aftermath thus constitute a continuum in human evolution, just as industrial architecture develops and recycles the language of forms of its civic and domestic predecessors.

Were it not for its aestheticising style and the overtly humanist approach that characterises Rohmer's thinking about cinema and the other arts, it would be tempting to align *Métamorphoses du paysage* with the work of the German photographers Bernd and Hilla Becher who, from the late 1950s, embarked on a project to record Europe's industrial architecture, threatened by decay.[31] Rohmer's nostalgia for an architectural patrimony about to disappear – articulated in the last sequences of the film – in a different medium recalls the melancholic gaze the two photographers cast on industrial sites slated for demolition. Yet, where the Bechers – committed to a de-historicising approach which puts the architectural object at the centre of their art – cut out human presence altogether, architecture for Rohmer can have no aesthetic status except in its intrinsic relationship to the human. As he reiterates in 'Architecture d'Apocalypse' and in a follow-up interview with Noël Herpe and Philippe Fauvel of 2009, if architecture qualifies as an art form inasmuch as it satisfies our love for beauty, contrary to painting, sculpture or music, it is above all an applied art in the service of humanity. Insofar as their creations change the world we inhabit, architects are faced with greater moral obligations and constraints than, for instance, painters who can give free rein to their creativity.

For all its lyricism, Rohmer's poeticisation of the ugly in *Métamorphoses du paysage* is not devoid of irony,[32] which is tangible in the hyperbolic tone, clashes between sound and image tracks, and, not least, this cautioning reference to Plato's cave – commonly seen as a prefiguration of film – alerting spectators to cinema's illusory powers:

> We are our own shadow theatre players, turning our back on the real, stuck in the cavern of our imaginations. What objects have we not, at the same time that we learn to name them, endowed with the most mysterious powers, adorned almost without our knowledge, of the highest poetical dignity.[33]

If the poetic valorisation of France's industrial heritage is thus steeped in ambivalence, current processes of modernisation are apprehended with equal scepticism. Resonating with Baudelaire's famous requiem for the old Paris, demolished by Baron Haussmann's urbanisation projects of the Second Empire, in the poem 'The Swan', the film's final sequences lament the impending destruction of the city's nineteenth- and early twentieth-century industrial structures. The last shots of identical tower blocks symmetrically aligned behind one another belie the guarded optimism of the voice-over. Despite its griminess, these monotonous images suggest, the architecture of the industrial period – fashioned in the image of humanity – engages our imagination, unlike the rationalist habitations of the nuclear age, which are little conducive to reverie. Given the constraints of his commission, Rohmer's critique of functionalist architecture remains subtly implied in this documentary. Some forty years on, in the already mentioned interview with Herpe and Fauvel, the director expresses a more candid opinion: 'I don't think we'll ever manage to find poetry in these big buildings we called HLMs and which we now call "estates".'[34]

In 'Architecture d'Apocalypse', Rohmer had proclaimed his faith in the new building materials of architectural modernity, while also admitting that, contrary to the dressed stones and wood of earlier periods, the cement, glass, and panoply of plastic materials used in twentieth-century construction afford a more 'difficult' kind of beauty.[35] A second television film on the theme of modern architecture, *Entretien sur le béton* (1969), allowed him to dwell further on the aesthetic potential, but also the possible shortcomings of the most widely used material of modernity: concrete. In an extended interview (conducted by Louis Paul Letonturier and François Loyer) with two of its most fervent advocates, Claude Parent and Paul Virilio, the film evaluates the expressive possibilities of reinforced concrete against the backdrop of widespread public hostility towards brutalist architecture. At first, this traditional expository documentary seems far removed from the poetic mode of *Métamorphoses du paysage*, yet the alleged beauty of a material commonly associated with aseptic, soulless buildings is no less exalted by the two practitioners than were the charms of industrial architecture by the voice-over in the earlier offering. With hindsight, even for the most passionate defender of modern architecture, it is difficult not to detect a degree of *mauvaise foi* in Parent and Virilio's insistence on the plasticity and tactility of concrete structures, which they deem superior to the light, transparent aesthetic of a Mies van der Rohe. Whilst for most of the film, the image track remains neutral, showing the fabrication of concrete structures or showcasing some iconic concrete buildings, the forbidding final images of the Normandy bunkers that have inspired Parent and Virilio, combined with the former's own admission of the public's widespread hostility to the material, put a question mark over the type of functionalist architecture the two practitioners present as a solution for postwar overcrowding. As in the previous documentary, the authorial stance is steeped in ambiguity: the sombre images of Second World War bunkers, rendered even more hostile by a zoom that reveals their rugged surface, belie the vision of a tactile architecture in the service of human experience drawn up by the two urbanists. Delivering a commission, here also Rohmer's scope for criticising the functionalist urbanism that rapidly changed the face of cities in the course of the 1950s and 1960s was of necessity limited. It is to the works of Marker, Resnais, Gilles and Godard that we need to turn now to gain a better understanding of the New Wave's complex positioning with regard to modern architecture.

METAMORPHOSES OF THE CITY

Chris Marker's *Le Joli Mai* opens on an arresting architectural image: a woman, dwarf-like in proportion to the sculptural mass of concrete and iron, slowly ascends the roof of a modern building. Shot from an elevated height, the fixed-frame images of Paris that follow implicitly embrace her perspective, reminiscent of the famous gaze that Eugène de Rastignac casts over the French capital from the height of the Père Lachaise cemetery in Balzac's *Le Père Goriot*. Shrouded in the mist of dawn, the city's celebrated skyline with its iconic monuments and graceful historic buildings appears strangely immaterial, even fragile. 'Is this the most beautiful city in the world?', the voice-over (spoken by Yves Montand) asks, inviting us to discover the urban space by the sole means that are available to the detectives of novels: a telescope and a microphone. This lyrical incipit connects Marker with a double inheritance: first of all literature, evoked in the film's dedication 'To the Happy Many' which ironically reworks Stendhal's famous 'To the Happy Few' from *Le Rouge et le noir*, as well as in references to Apollinaire, whose poem 'Le Joli Mai' inspired the film's title, and to Giraudoux, whose work *La Prière sur la Tour Eiffel* inspired the title of the first part and is cited at length while the camera scrutinises the Paris cityscape. But also a dual filmic tradition: on the one hand, with its use of lightweight, hand-held cameras and interviewing technique, *Le Joli Mai* continues the project opened up by Jean Rouch and Edgar Morin's *Chronique d'un été* (*Chronicle of a Summer*, 1961), which offered an unprecedented sociological portrait of Paris and its inhabitants; on the other, it reinvents the city symphony films of the 1920s, evoked by the dawn to night structure and the preoccupation with the rhythms and textures of the city. Two traditions which are implicitly linked, Rouch's notion of *cinéma-vérité* being the literal translation of Vertov's *Kino Pravda*. A barometer of French society during the first spring of peace (that is, after the Évian Accords signed in March 1962, which brought an end to the Algerian War), *Le Joli Mai* is also a poetic portrait of Paris.

Embedded in a wider interrogation of the conditions of living at a time of rapid modernisation, the film asks incisive questions about the radical transformation of the city's architectural fabric inflicted by contemporary urbanism. From the outset, shots of the 'Point du Jour' housing complex in Boulogne-Billancourt and of the CNIT Congress Center at La Défense with its iconic concrete shell, pit the historical Paris against the modern developments at the periphery of the city. Yet even Paris *intra muros* is threatened by an anarchic urbanism that has little regard for the affective needs of city dwellers, Marker cautions in an extended sequence on the city's urban renewal schemes. Like Rohmer in *Métamorphoses du paysage*, the director leaves little doubt as to what he thinks of the housing estates that are gradually replacing Paris's inner-city slums: the latter, the voice-over asserts, at least left a space for happiness, while, with the former 'we're not sure'. In stark contrast to the hand-held camera work in depictions of the rue Mouffetard – one of Paris's oldest neighbourhoods also featured in Rohmer's *Le Signe du lion* and Varda's *L'Opéra mouffe*, and much cherished by the Situationist International[36] – faced with the geometrical forms of modern architecture, the cinematic language rigidifies: a frontal tracking shot of a row of identical tower blocks followed by a lateral tracking of what earlier was referred to as the 'solitude of a thousand windows' underline the monotony of a serialised architecture governed by principles of rationality, functionality and order. Modern architects like Fernand Pouillon (who designed several housing complexes, including the allegorically named *Point du jour*), the voice-over suggests, are direct successors of Baron Haussmann who, in the second half of the nineteenth century, tore down parts of the medieval Paris to make place for mass-fabricated apartment buildings.

Figure 4.2 'There is a menace hovering over Paris': modern architecture in *Le Joli Mai* (Chris Marker, 1963).

Marker also gives voice to urban planners and Parisians directly affected by the modernisation programmes. Poised against a high-rise development under construction, two architects dream of alternative models for social housing, unconstrained by commercial imperatives. As they sketch out their idea of dwellings nestling among the treetops, the camera dances around the wasteland yet to be filled, visibly elated by their vision of a 'heavenly city' where ecology rhymes with creativity and social diversity. Yet the subsequent images of the Aubervilliers slums with their insalubrious, crammed habitations leave no doubt about the urgency of providing alternative housing to deprived communities. Pointing at walls blackened by pollution or infiltrated with humidity, gliding along narrow alleys and into overcrowded rooms, the camera uncovers the material signs of destitution. In a particularly moving sequence, an interviewer accompanies a family with nine children, who have been rehoused in a modern tower block, into their new flat. The mother and children express their joy at having more space to themselves, but the pensive look of the elder daughter gazing out at a soulless square framed by identical buildings implicitly raises questions as to what happiness can be found in habitations that are little conducive to social interaction.

POST-WAR RECONSTRUCTION: WOUNDING, TRAUMA, MEMORY

Unlike many French provincial cities, Paris emerged from the war relatively intact. Marker alludes to localised bomb damage in the capital in *Le Joli Mai*, but we need to turn to two other New Wave films, Resnais's *Muriel, ou Le temps d'un retour* and Gilles's *Au pan coupé*, for a fuller engagement with the reconstruction programmes after the Second World War. Reminiscent of the interwoven structure of *Hiroshima mon amour*, Resnais's *Muriel* conjures up the memories of two seemingly unconnected, yet intimately related traumatisms. Interlacing the stories of Hélène (Delphine Seyrig), a widow who tries to rekindle her relationship with a former lover, Alphonse (Jean-Pierre Kérien), of whom she lost sight during the Second World War, and that of her stepson Bernard (Jean-Baptiste Thierrée), recently returned from military service in Algeria, this oneiric, angst-ridden film lays bare the mental and physical wounds left by two wars that have shattered France within barely the passing of a generation. The 'time of a return' of the title alludes to a collective unspoken – the French military's use of torture during the Algerian War – that the French nation is seeking to erase, but which is coming to haunt it in a resurfacing of repressed memories. Based on a script by Jean Cayrol divided into five acts, the theatrical, visually fragmented narrative charts Bernard's coming to terms with the torture and subsequent death of an Algerian woman: the eponymous Muriel. Confronting a collective crime that both the perpetrators and the French government seek to conceal, the young man gathers documentary evidence in the form of photos, letters, a tape recording as well as a filmic record of soldiers' lives in Algeria. Yet, while the centrally positioned screening of the footage he has assembled points to cinema's imperative to witness, as Emma Wilson points out, 'the film itself is more doubtful about the possibilities of testifying, of bringing grief and guilt into the open'.[37] Ultimately, Muriel's suffering can neither be fully represented – the voice-over gives a gruelling account of torture, but the film withholds any images of bodily harm – nor shared, and even less atoned. Bernard's killing of his former comrade Robert merely perpetuates the chain of violence without him taking responsibility for his own participation in Muriel's torture.

As in *Hiroshima mon amour*, where the reconstructed city of Hiroshima becomes the site of excavation for two intertwined memories, here also the characters' confrontation with a traumatic past is set in a city that has been partly rebuilt. Cayrol explains:

> I situated the story in Boulogne, despite Resnais's doubts, because Boulogne is also a town after a drama. There are two towns, the old one spared by the war and the reconstructed town, the topography of which the old inhabitants cannot recognise.[38]

A former resistance stronghold brutally crushed by Nazi Germany and severely damaged by Allied bombings, Boulogne doubly embodies the epithet 'martyr city' given to it by Alphonse. Partly rebuilt in the 1950s and 1960s in the brutalist, functionalist style that Marker deplores in *Le Joli Mai*, the town exhibits an anarchic mixture of historical and modern architecture, referenced early on in the film in a quick montage sequence where images of the old Boulogne collide with shots of modernist-type constructions – including, ominously (for we learn later that Hélène is a compulsive gambler), the Casino – in a dizzying collage juxtaposing day and night in seemingly random fashion. Architecture first erupts into the film as a series of cuts, an incision that disrupts the flow of the narrative. The stark architectural forms are apprehended in cinema's most elementary grammar: a series of fixed-angle shots followed by a sweeping pan of the symbol of Boulogne's architecture of reconstruction, Pierre Vivien's four monumental tower blocks facing the harbour, commonly known as 'les buildings'. The city space, Wilson observes, 'is barely tracked by Resnais's moving camera; instead the urban location is known through a kaleidoscopic series of images'.[39] Accentuated by Hans Werner Henze's elegiac soundtrack, here and in later such sequences, the modern is set against the old in rapidly flashing images, evoking the famous montage sequence that conjoins Nevers and Hiroshima, even if *Muriel* refuses the visual pleasures afforded in *Hiroshima mon amour*.[40]

Monotonous and grey, marred by sterile tower blocks or context-insensitive modernist showcase pieces, Resnais's Boulogne is visualised as a disorientating architectural hotchpotch seemingly devoid of any urbanistic planning. Revealingly, at several points in the film, characters lose their bearings in the chaotic urban space: the visitor asking for the city centre is startled to hear that the modern boulevards *are* the heart of Boulogne. Locals recall the city that is no more beneath its present-day appearance: one of Hélène's friends is convinced that the attic of his house used to be at the site of her current apartment; a group of men reminiscing the location of their former homes insist that 'just because bombs fell doesn't mean that you can't remember your street'. Palimpsestic and spectral, parts of the old Boulogne, though no longer visible, remain tangible under the modernist architecture that has replaced it, buried like the traumatic memories the characters try to keep at bay, but which gradually seep back into their consciousness. Partly erased, yet continuing to live on in people's minds, the sinuous, fragmented cityscape becomes a metaphor for the process of remembering. The urban geography charts a mental space, as well as being a visual signifier, indeed a symptom, of suffering and grief. Just like the experience of war has left the characters emotionally scarred, just like Muriel's flesh has been mutilated by the hands of her torturers, so the architectural skin of the city bears the physical marks of wounding.

Inseparably tied up with the film's wider preoccupation with memory and trauma, Naomi Greene writes, Boulogne's 'modern buildings and new neighbourhoods, as well as half-glimpsed ruins serve as constant reminders of the extensive damage inflicted by bombing raids of World War II'.[41] Yet, just as importantly, in the context of 1960s radical modernisation programmes, the filmic city serves as a warning against the architectural – and human – damage caused by a careless, profit-driven reconstruction policy. It is not so much the Allies, whose bombing campaigns were after all aimed at France's liberation, the film suggests, but greedy property developers who are responsible for Boulogne's disfigured cityscape. Cayrol and Resnais broach the question of who really benefited from the rapid reconstruction after the war – local residents in need of housing or shady businessmen – through the fittingly named Roland de Smoke (Claude Sainval), an entrepreneur in charge of completing the demolition of the old Boulogne after 1945. Semiotically linked to the vapours billowing from beneath street level in the ominous first architectural montage, in Resnais's uncanny mise-en-scène the shifty de Smoke is endowed with a devilish air, inseparable from the 'architecture of apocalypse' (to use the term coined by Rohmer) for which he has cleared the way. That the modernist estates that mar the city centre and tower over the harbour were not intended for durability is brought home by the entrepreneur's sinister story of a subsiding building destined to collapse before it was even inhabited: 'it's new, it's empty, and we're waiting for it to fall down. It won't make a pretty ruin.' His ironic lament 'not one espagnolette to salvage, not one espagnolette for me' exposes the vested interests of the businessman, brought into the open in the conversation that follows where he boasts of possessing (and reselling) countless objects – windows, fireplaces, even the marble staircase of a former hotel – recuperated from demolished buildings. Architectural salvage, pillaged from the ruins of the martyred city, fuels a business all the more lucrative that, as one of Hélène's clients remarks, in a town like Boulogne – that is, a city robbed of its architectural patrimony – antique objects carry an important affective charge.

Modern architecture in *Muriel*, then, more than merely a memory trace as the film's commentators tend to argue,[42] plays an intrinsic part in the web of deception in which the characters are entangled. Menacing and anthropomorphic, the modernist architecture of reconstruction is established as a character in its own right, nowhere more so than in the dramatic unveiling sequence where Adolphe's construct of lies (he obfuscated his marriage and bankruptcy behind an invented *pied-noir* identity) is brutally torn down by his brother-in-law in front of the dismayed Hélène and her assembled friends. Intercut between Ernest's tirade, images of Vivien's *buildings*, rendered uncannily alive through the use of different camera angles, varying shot distances and *décadrage* effects, appear to partake in this public trial. Devoid of any human presence, first captured in their entirety, then in a series of close-ups, their windows reminiscent of gaping eyes and mouths, the tower blocks seem to join the accuser; yet, as the symbol of the city's reconstruction policy, they also stand accused. Conjoined with Adolphe's nauseous betrayal through the parallel montage, the brutalist *buildings* raise questions about modernist architecture's consideration for people's sensitivities and affective needs, challenging, as did Rohmer in the 'Architecture d'Apocalypse' article, post-war architecture's promise of collective happiness.

Very different in tone, yet as we will see in many ways a counterpart to *Muriel*, Gilles's *L'Amour à la mer* draws the portrait of another city that was almost entirely destroyed during the war: the Brittany port of Brest, razed to the ground during the historic 'battle for Brest' in 1944. Like Boulogne, the town was rebuilt in the course of the 1950s in the dominant functionalist style. Moving forwards and backwards between Paris and Brest, the film contrasts the picturesque historic areas of the capital ideal for promenades with the sterile uniformity of a reconstructed city offering little in terms of ocular pleasures or distractions. Visualised as a *non-lieu* that one traverses,

Figure 4.3 Architecture of reconstruction: Pierre Vivien's *buildings* in *Muriel* (Alain Resnais, 1963).

but which invites neither strolling nor dwelling,[43] Brest is initially not even delineated as a distinct space. The first images of city lights reflecting on a rain-soaked tarmac are almost abstract: this could be any street, in any location. Gilles's Brest is an epistolary city, narrated by the sailor Daniel in letters to his girlfriend Geneviève. Before becoming image, Brest is doubly text: the first letter cites a tourist brochure destined at Navy personnel duly captured by the camera, as if the city's architectural shapes did not warrant visual representation. When it finally coalesces into material form, the montage sequence of Brest, as in *Muriel*, offers a kaleidoscopic vision of the city, where the grey tower blocks of reconstruction alternate with a few remaining historic buildings. Here also, the rebuilt town is visualised as a place without a centre, a disorientating urban sprawl lacking in readability.

If Gilles's Brest seems strangely close to Resnais's Boulogne this is not only because the two towns are linked by a common traumautic history, nor, as we saw in the previous chapter, because Gilles frequently pays homage to his more established New Wave colleagues. As the editor for *L'Amour à la mer*, Noun Serra, reveals, the two films are welded together by a common materiality: the soundtrack for the Brest sequences was constructed with location sound from *Muriel* recuperated from Resnais's sound engineer Antoine Bonfanti.[44] Thus the soundscape of the earlier film lives on in parts of the later one, in the aural atmosphere of a city battered by wind and rain. Moreover, *L'Amour à la mer* counterpoints and complements Resnais's engagement with the Algerian War in *Muriel*. In both films, the male protagonists have recently returned from military service in Algeria. But where Resnais's Bernard seeks to uncover the atrocities committed by the French military against Algerian civilians suspected of collaborating with the FLN, Gilles's Daniel, charged with repatriating the French *pieds-noirs* population,[45] evokes the terrorist attacks by the FLN against French civilians. If, in *Muriel*, the only *pied-noir* character is revealed to be a fraud who has constructed himself a false identity, *L'Amour à la mer* invites spectators to feel compassion for the nearly 1 million *pieds-noirs* forced to leave their native Algeria and start a new life in France. Such emphasis on a community that tended to be associated with colonial exploitation would have been uncomfortable in the contemporary political climate, but in no way did it blind Gilles to the injustices of French colonial rule in Algeria.

In his portrait of Brest, the director does not fail to include those whom history has forgotten amongst the flurry of post-war reconstruction: the bombed-out inhabitants who were to temporarily find shelter in makeshift barracks, but who, some twenty years after the battle for Brest, continue to be crammed into precarious shanty-towns. 'People will die there. Children were born there and live there', Daniel comments in voice-over over documentary-style images of men, women and children in front of their precarious habitations. In Moullet's New Wave pastiche *Brigitte et Brigitte*, released two years after *L'Amour à la mer*, the two students stumble upon a shanty town adjacent to the Nanterre campus in their search for affordable housing. Faced with the ramshackle wooden shacks, they for the first time apprehend the destitution of France's social and cultural Other: poor migrant workers originating predominantly from the Maghreb. Inversely, for Gilles, the shanty towns of Brest become a cue to condemn the deeply ingrained social inequalities under French rule in Algeria and the indifference of certain French-Algerians towards the poverty of indigenous people. Comparing the poor districts of the city with what he has seen in Algeria, Daniel castigates: 'there it was shameful, the poverty was so well established that some people ended up not seeing it and confusing it with the picturesque.' Close-ups of a window covered in graffiti, from which the anguished eye of a child framed by the smoky glass is looking outwards, capture the material textures of modern poverty. Seen through Gilles's own eyes, architectural space opens a fold, a privileged access to the real that allows him to stretch out to the most vulnerable – on either side of the Mediterranean, past and present – in a gesture of empathy. 'Architexture', to use a term coined by Giuliana Bruno,[46] in the film's attentiveness to the effect of spaces of dwelling on forms of living and feeling, becomes the tissue of life itself.

PATHOLOGY OF THE HOUSING ESTATE

In his monumental history of French cinema from the New Wave to the present, Jean-Michel Frodon makes a crucial distinction between cinema as a mere imprint of social reality and film as a form of enquiry that uses the specific properties of the medium to interrogate the conditions of living at a specific moment in time. While what he terms 'youth cinema' merely registers the societal transformations France underwent in the course of the 1960s, using changes in lifestyle, language, clothing or housing above all for decorative purposes, 'modern cinema' invents 'a new cinematic language apt to make the world better seen and better understood'.[47] For Frodon, two directors in particular embody this project of interrogating the conditions of modern living via the medium of cinema in the run-up to May '68: Jacques Tati and Godard. Tati's *Playtime* (1967), shot on a purpose-built, futuristic set nicknamed 'Tativille', denounces the sterile uniformity of modern living in a series of sketches relying largely on visual comedy. Godard, in *Deux ou trois choses que je sais d'elle*, released the same year, true to the New Wave principle of location shooting, takes the 'cité des 4000' at La Courneuve as his test case for what was to become the most sustained filmic enquiry into life in the so-called *grands ensembles*. Designed by architects Clément Tambuté and Henry-Charles Delacroix, both of whom were involved in the reconstruction of bomb-damaged French cities after the Second World War, the 'cité des 4000' (named after its capacity for 4,000 apartments) became one of the prototypes of industrial-type, serialised housing estates in the outskirts of Paris. Commissioned by the city of Paris to alleviate demographic pressure, it promised middle-class comfort in the form of bathrooms, toilets and central heating to a diverse group of residents, many of them working-class and of immigrant background. Yet the *cité des 4000* soon became a symbol of the failures of post-war suburban housing schemes.

As is well known, Godard drew on two articles from the magazine *Le Nouvel Observateur* that called attention to the financial difficulties faced by residents of the *grands ensembles*, asserting that women turned to casual prostitution to pay utility bills or buy coveted consumer goods.[48] More generally, he was inspired by French philosopher Raymond Aron's *Dix-huit leçons sur la société industrielle* (1963), whose cover punctuates the narrative in several inserts. In the wake of Rouch and Morin's *Chronique d'un été* and Marker's *Le Joli Mai*, the film is set up as a sociological enquiry, as is reflected in the interview-style conversations to which the director (who remains invisible, but communicates with his actors via a microphone and earpiece) intermittently subjects his actors, as well as in a series of testimonies delivered in direct address to the camera. In one of the voice-over commentaries spoken by Godard, the director likens himself to an evolutionary biologist tackling the problems of social pathology in the hope of shaping a 'real new town'.

Ravi Hensman notes that Godard seems to have borrowed some elements, including the character of the *grand ensemble* housewife, from Pialat's documentary *L'Amour existe*.[49] Intriguingly, given the connections between films we traced in the previous section, the director also explicitly places himself in the lineage of *Muriel*, which, three minutes into the film, is referenced through a poster in the living room of the Janson family. 'The inclusion in *2 ou 3 choses* of the poster showing the partly torn-away image of a woman', Alfred Guzzetti argues, 'suggests that knowing something about "elle" is like remembering Muriel – that is, it is a task that involves assembling pieces and that has a political meaning.'[50] But who or what is the mysterious 'elle' of the title? The filmic trailer offers a puzzling array of assignations:

> the cruelty of neo-capitalism, prostitution, the Paris region, the bathroom 70% of the French don't have, the dreadful law of the housing high-rises, the physics of love, modern living, the Vietnam War, the modern call girl, the death of human beauty, the circulation of ideas, the structure gestapo.

The opening titles home in on one of these significations, identifying 'elle' with 'the Paris region', an equation that is affirmed in the ensuing shots of construction sites overlaid by Godard's whispered voice-over commentary on the new governance of the Paris region. Yet, as the camera cuts from this documentary footage to images of Marina Vlady framed against the tower blocks of the 'cité des 4000', in a Brechtian turn highlighted in her monologue, the 'elle' is reassigned to both the actress and the female protagonist she embodies. The double signifier 'elle' – referring to both the Paris region undergoing a radical modernisation programme and a young woman living in

Figure 4.4   Juliette (Marina Vlady) and the 'cité des 4000' in *Deux ou trois choses que je sais d'elle* (Jean-Luc Godard, 1967).

the *grand ensemble* – informs the hybrid texture of the film where documentary-type shots of building sites punctuate a loose fictional narrative itself grounded in a documentary source. The character Juliette Janson, Hensman points out, becomes 'a personification of "Sarcellite", a media-coined term for the social pathology of *grand ensemble* living'.[51]

Brought into dialogue throughout the film, the two 'elles' collide in two montage sequences with strong formal and thematic resonances. Following Juliette's first transaction with a client, the testimony of a secretary unable to find work who, we gather, may similarly turn to prostitution, intercuts views of construction sites and inhospitable tower blocks. The mise-en-scène of the female figure framed next to a partly visible old print is echoed in the composition of the architectural images with their pronounced vertical and horizontal lines. 'This interlocking of forms between the master shot and the cutaways, along with the intercutting itself', Guzzetti explains, 'asserts [. . .] a causal relation between the woman's experience and the new Paris.'[52] A similar formal strategy is at work in the sequence where Juliette and her friend Marianne (Anny Duperey) prostitute themselves to an American war correspondent freshly returned from Vietnam (played by producer Raoul Lévy). Juliette's framing against an engraving of a seascape while she delivers a monologue directly facing the camera, with little variation replicates the mise-en-scène of the earlier scene. Here also the fictional sequence is intercut with shots of construction sites, inviting a comparison between the movements of the two women executing the orders of their voyeuristic client and those of the cranes in the documentary footage:

> Besides restating the equivalence 'prostitute/*grue*,' the cut makes it seem that Faubus, whose voice continues over the shot ('Turn around . . . Show me your back'), commands this action as well. In other words, behind the prostitution and the building of the new Paris lie American commands and American money.[53]

Creating a visual link between the two scenes as well as between functionalist urbanism and prostitution, Godard's rapid intercutting of architectural shots also alludes to the montage sequence from *Muriel*, where, as we saw earlier, Vivien's *buildings*, juxtaposed to the unveiling of Adolphe's false identity, become a metaphor for the moral bankruptcy of a society unwilling to confront its past. Godard himself described *Deux ou trois choses* as a 'continuation of the movement begun by Resnais's *Muriel*: an attempt at a description of a phenomenon known in mathematics and sociology as a "complex."'[54] In its telescoping of the personal and the social, the housing complex as a microcosm of society becomes a prism through which to understand the wider ills of 1960s consumer society. Just how entangled these questions are for Godard can be gathered from the preface to the script of *Deux ou trois choses*, where he links the Gaullist modernisation projects to the American intervention in Vietnam in a sinuous argument, suggesting that an aggressive form of capitalism is the driving motor behind both:

> While the Americans pursue an immoral and unjust war in Vietnam, the French government, whose connections with big capital are common knowledge, sees to the construction in and around Paris of apartment complexes whose inhabitants, either through boredom, or through an anguish which this architecture cultivates or through economic necessity, are led to prostitute themselves, notably (incidentally) to Americans returned from Vietnam.[55]

Perceived as a crucial trigger in what social philosopher André Gorz calls 'the dictatorship over needs',[56] the suburban apartment complex is apprehended as a source of alienation that estranges people from themselves and others, reducing them to a dehumanised, robotic existence. At several instances in *Deux ou trois choses*, the filmic apparatus probes the vast expanse of the estate. Some eight minutes into the film, the camera carries out a sweeping pan from left to right, bringing into view rows of straight-lined tower blocks broken up by a vast concrete esplanade eerily devoid of human presence. The camera lingers on one of the high-rise blocks before returning to its starting point. How to capture a site of such gigantic dimensions, this marked use of a camera movement habitually designed to give an expansive view of off-screen space seems to ask? How can a camera, let alone a human being, apprehend forms that far surpass human scale? Monumental in both width and height, the *grand ensemble* cannot be fully grasped by the camera eye. Here, the truncated top floors of the tower blocks, in the later scene when the couple drive home a striking *décadrage* effect as their high-rise dwelling comes into view, visualise the difficulty of finding anchorage in an urban landscape that defies our desire for belonging. That the *grand ensemble* is little conducive to forging communities, let alone to play, is brought home in a wide-angle shot of children behind a window dwarfed by the giant facade composed of prefabricated, exactly identical panels.

Throughout the film, Godard showcases bridges, highways or other infrastructure developments under construction. Yet these views of urban arteries destined for motorised traffic, alongside Juliette's musings about modern forms of communication such as television and radio, only more sharply bring into relief the danger of isolation in urban spaces designed according to the double principle of 'le tout voiture' ('the all by car') and domestic seclusion. It is interesting to note that the Situationist movement had similarly cautioned against the desertification of urban space in their journal, pointing out that 'traffic is the organisation of everyone's isolation'.[57] Juliette's disenchanted prognosis that some of the city of tomorrow's 'past semantic richness will be lost, undoubtedly' echoes the concerns of architects and sociologists looking for alternative models of town planning, notably Henri Lefebvre (who was linked with the Situationist International), who writes in a 1960 article, 'Notes on the New Town': 'Here [in the New Town] I cannot read the centuries, not time, nor the past, nor what is possible.'[58] Some fifteen years later, a similar concern about the reduced readability of the New Town will be raised in one of Rohmer's television documentaries, *La Diversité du paysage urbain* (1975). As an architect from the *Atelier de recherches et d'études d'aménagement* (AREA), interviewed by Rohmer and his colleague Jean-Paul Pigeat, points out, the traditional city with its palimpsest of architectonic and historical layers contains time. The new city, by contrast, is not diachronic, but synchronic, its lack of memory resulting in a paucity of signification.

By pointing to the nexus between *grand ensemble* and *grand capital*, Douglas Morrey explains, Godard formulates a wider critique of consumer capitalism, 'showing how the market economy creates a never-ending stream of merchandise whose rate of production always outstrips the average consumer's ability to pay for it'.[59] The director's voice-over commentary aptly sums up modern citizens' entrapment in a chain of desires stoked by consumer culture: 'It's the same old story: either no money for rent or no TV, or else a TV, but no car, or else a washer, but no vacation. In other words, in any case, no normal life.' Yet *Deux ou trois choses* is more than just a repudiation of the capitalist system that, in the run-up to 1968, had come under widespread attack. Like Marker in *Le Joli Mai*, to which the voice-over commentary cited above and its accompanying images allude,[60] Godard imagines the possibility of alternative forms of living outwith the logic of consumption. In one of the film's most creative sequences, that of the service station, the director sketches out his vision of a new world where 'men and things can live in harmony'. His goal, he states, is 'as political as it is poetic'. Over a quasi-abstract close-up of the Jansons' Mini, Godard explains his 'rage of expression' as a means to this goal, designating himself as a 'writer and painter'. If earlier in the sequence, a reference to *The Wild Palms* aligns him with Faulkner's modernist writing, here the shot of the car's red roof reflecting changing shades of light likens the filmmaker to a modernist painter experimenting with monochromatic colour. While praising the service station sequence as 'one of the richest and most beautiful in the cinema', Guzzetti criticises Godard for adopting the pose of an artist, arguing that such a self-representation exempts him from any kind of fully assumed political analysis.[61] Godard's displacement of the figure of the filmmaker to that of the writer and painter, the critic cautions, 'cuts off the root of a *politique*, in particular a *politique* that could include or subsume a *poétique*'.[62]

It is understandable why Guzzetti should deplore Godard's alleged sidestepping of the political here. Yet we should not forget that for Godard ideas are inseparable from form, as he posits himself in the conjunction of the political and the poetic. What is so novel about Godard, Nathalie Heinich points out, is precisely 'the conjunction, in cinema, of thinker and creator, of intellectual and artist, [. . .] of political struggle and aesthetic combat'.[63] In light of the wider permeability of his films to the other arts, Godard's self-designation as a 'writer and painter', therefore, should be considered as more than just an analogy. An identification with other artist figures is recurrent in Godard's reflections on the expressive means of cinema, a medium with which he wants to make 'a novel and a painting at the same time [. . .] Cézanne with Malraux's means'.[64] Indeed, as is suggested in this scene, crossing over into the other arts is the very basis of his poetics – a poetics that, in continuation of poet Francis Ponge, whose book *La Rage de l'expression* (1976) is implicitly referenced, is interested in the inherent expressivity of trivial, everyday things. In such a poetics, the extreme close-up of a car roof can become a painting, or that of sugar dissolving in a coffee cup can trigger a philosophical meditation on the limits of language and the advent of consciousness.[65]

With its typically Godard-esque narrative fragmentation, often disjunctive sound and image tracks, and dialogues crippled with non sequiturs, *Deux ou trois choses* gives visual and aural expression to the fragmentation of experience under the onslaught of consumer capitalism. Yet this radical style reminiscent of modernist writing, matched by a painterly use of colour, also affirms the film's status as an artwork akin to that of a writer or a painter. Just how inseparable the political and the intermedial are in Godard's project is brought home in the last shot of consumer goods assembled into a model of the *grand ensemble* which, besides making a political point, is 'calling attention to the unseen but nonetheless real agency of the arranger, the director'.[66] Ultimately, it is Godard the filmmaker, playing with architecture as one of the building blocks of cinema, who asserts himself as the true architect of modernity.

Urban *Flânerie* and the *Lichtspiel*

New Wave film, as we have seen throughout this chapter, defines and positions itself with regard to the new forms of architectural modernity that emerged in the course of the 1950s and 1960s. However controversial the mass housing schemes that marred historic city centres and sprawled along their suburbs may have been, they were an integral part of the fabric of modern life. Giving visibility to the metamorphoses of the urban landscape, finding a cinematic language that captures the radical transformation of urban space that France underwent as part of the wider drive towards modernisation under the leadership of de Gaulle, became a proof of the movement's own modernity. Just how intimately linked the question of architectural change was to that of cinematic modernity can be measured in Marcel Carné's attempt to reinvent himself from a director associated with the Tradition of Quality to a trendy filmmaker in touch with contemporary reality in *Terrain vague* (1960), one of the first films to address the pathologies of modern housing estates – albeit in direct continuation of Tradition of Quality practices, filmed in the Billancourt studios with only intermittent views of a real suburban building site. If modern architecture and urbanism allowed the New Wave to comment on the altered conditions of modern existence, thus joining a broader reflection (among town planners, sociologists, philosophers and intellectuals) about the effects of mass-housing on human affect and consciousness, the movement also – and this will be the focus of our last section – evinces a profound fascination with the tactile textures and surfaces of the city that, since cinema's silent beginnings, connect the filmic medium with urban modernity.

As Siegfried Kracauer, an architect by training and one of the most eloquent commentators of modern city life, has argued, film and urban space are conjoined in the same adventure of modernity. As a moving image medium, film is singularly well equipped to capture the 'flow of life' of the modern metropolis with its anonymous crowds, 'incessant flow of possibilities and near-intangible meanings'.[67] For Kracauer, the fundamental substance of modernity is revealed through surface-level phenomena, be it fashion or sports competitions, the 'mass ornament' formed by dancing chorus girls, travel and dance, or, indeed, 'the representational practices that display an elective affinity with the surface – namely, photography and film'.[68] In the tradition of Baudelaire, the critic likens the modern film spectator to the nineteenth-century *flâneur* who roams the streets in search of visual and other pleasures. With its 'fearful uncertainties and alluring excitements',[69] its potential for unforeseen encounters and quasi-infinite possibilities, the street is the arena where the furtive adventure of modernity – what Kracauer's contemporary, friend and fellow cultural critic Walter Benjamin terms *Erlebnis* as opposed to the transformative *Erfahrung* – is played out. For Kracauer, the flow of life not only enchants and intrigues, it *creates* the *flâneur*.[70] As a quintessentially ocular sensitivity, nineteenth-century *flânerie* anticipates modern spectators' fascination with the city space recorded and revealed through the filmic medium. If the city symphony films of the 1920s and early cinema more generally had a particular affinity with *flânerie*, modernist cinema of the 1950s and 1960s, Ágnes Pethő points out, similarly indulges in the spectacle afforded by the street.[71]

Cinematic *flânerie*, and, more broadly, a sensitivity towards the surfaces and textures of the city, can be traced across the broad spectrum of New Wave film: one only needs to consider the notable shift in style in Chabrol's otherwise formally quite conservative *Les Cousins*, when the exuberant Paul (Jean-Paul Brialy) takes his newly arrived cousin (Gérard Blain) on a ride through Paris. As their car zigzags down the Champs-Élysées, the camera all of a sudden rises from street level, dancing along tree crowns and roof tops while the cityscape whizzes past at great speed. *Décadrage* effects and a heterogeneous soundtrack intermingling jazz tunes with an ironic military march as the obelisk of the Place de la Concorde comes into sight, imbue the scene with a sense of drunken exaltation, reflective of the passengers' joyful immersion in the city space. Or think of Antoine in *Les Quatre cents coups* who, far from the privileges of bourgeois student life, lets himself be engrossed in the manifold pleasures of Paris's 'cinema of the street'. On one of his peregrinations across the city, he enjoys a rare moment of solace from a difficult family environment in the spinning drum of an urban fairground attraction. The emphasis on the process of looking, as the camera cross-cuts between the adolescent's view of spectators on the observer deck and their views of him in the drum, combined with the blurred, rotating images, not forgetting the cylindrical shape of the device, implicitly connect the fairground ride to one of cinema's predecessors: the zoetrope. Self-reflexively inscribed as a form of authorial signature – reinforced by the furtive appearance of Truffaut alongside his alter ego Antoine in the rotor – the cinematic apparatus symbolically partakes in the character's '*emotive*' absorption in the architectural fabric.[72] In Jean Rouch's little-known *La Punition* (1962), the high school student Nadine (Nadine Ballot) aimlessly wanders across Paris after having been expelled from her philosophy class. In tune with *flânerie*'s promise of unforeseen encounters, she meets three men with each of whom she strikes up a lengthy conversation. As in the documentary *Chronique d'un été* and *Le Joli Mai*, the narrative takes the form of an ethnographic inquiry as Nadine, an aspiring ethnographer, questions her socially diverse acquaintances about their habits, values and aspirations. As we follow her around town, lingering shots of some iconic landmarks such as the Luxembourg Gardens, the Eiffel Tower and the modernist Unesco building, imbue the film with a strong sense of urban reality.

For the fellow *flâneuse* Cléo (Corinne Marchand), her wanderings through Paris on foot, in public transport or chauffeured by a friend, likewise are part of a seminal moment of female emancipation. Hitherto the object of the male gaze, Cléo learns to look rather than passively being looked at. We follow her gaze as she discovers the alluring spectacle of the street, captured in quasi-documentary style by Varda, yet also share her anxiety and alert consciousness to the passing of time as she awaits the outcome of a medical examination. Here *flânerie*, though still pregnant with the possibility of adventure and unforeseen encounter, is tainted by a sense of disquiet, even terror, metonymically linked to France's embroilment in a colonial war – the cancer at the heart of the nation – whose unspoken horror seeps through the filmic narrative.[73] Time and urban space are similarly yoked in a menacing conundrum in *Le Signe du lion*, as Pierre, evicted from his flat and too impoverished to pay for a hotel room, embarks on a roaming journey through the city, reduced to aimlessly walking the streets and banks of the Seine. A gruelling account of utmost solitude amidst a buzzing summer crowd, the film depicts the protagonist's vagrancy as a cartographic wandering along an inhospitable urban map. As Pierre is crouching on the river banks, the camera sweeps up to the surrounding streets before zooming out into a bird's eye view of the vast expanse of the city – a geographical pattern of lines seemingly devoid of human presence. If *flânerie* and drifting are thus ubiquitous in New Wave cinema, the immersion into the urban space is often tainted with anguish or a sense of disquiet.

Situated at the interface between the cinema and architectural space, cinematic *flânerie* is a privileged terrain for intermediality. The filmed world of the *flâneur*, as Pethő points out, is not merely an ocular experience; it involves 'cross-sensory, synesthetic experiences that can be considered as sensual "gateways" to intermediality: it is through these synesthetic occurrences that the image gives way to "overtones" characteristic to other media, and thus spotlight[s] its own "fabric"'.[74] Pethő mentions the early city symphony films of Ruttmann and Vertov, with their characteristic rhythmical montage, bird's eye perspectives, and accelerated images broken down into tiny fragments as typical examples of what she calls a 'musical reading' of the street. She also traces a genealogy of modern film, based on examples taken from Antonioni, Scorsese and Coppola, where such a crossing-over into the domain of the other arts – in particular music, painting or photography – is at work.[75] What links these divergent directors is cinema's long-standing fascination with what Pethő, drawing on Scott McQuire, terms the 'liquid city' or the 'electropolis',[76] that is, the pulsating energy of the nightly metropolis glittering in a million lights.

In their celebration of nocturnal life with its bars, cafés and quasi-infinite possibilities for entertainment, the New Wave has played an important role in shaping the image of the proverbial 'city of lights' as well as of other metropolises, distant or close. From the shimmering facades of nighttime Montparnasse in *À bout de souffle* to the music halls and nightclubs of Chabrol's *Les Bonnes femmes* (1960), from Elle's (Emmanuelle Riva) nocturnal wanderings through Tokyo in *Hiroshima mon amour* to Bruno's (Michel Subor) drive through Geneva at dusk in *Le Petit Soldat* – both cities scintillating with illuminated advertising – New Wave films exhibit a passion for the glittering surfaces of the city at night. Dissolving the heaviness of material architecture into a weightless outward appearance, they render palpable the incessant flow and bristling excitement of city life through a wealth of cinematic techniques, including time-lapse photography – most notably so at the end of *Le Joli Mai* – rhythmical montage, blur effects or sharp contrasts between light and darkness.

If a fascination with architectural surfaces is widespread in New Wave cinema, it is once more to Guy Gilles, the most *flâneur* of New Wave directors, that we need to turn to fully capture the intermedial dimension – and function – of this multi-sensory spectacle of the city. Both the autobiographically inflected *L'Amour à la mer* and *Le Clair de terre* are punctuated by scenes of nightly *flânerie* that echo one another as in a mirror image: the first staging a return to Paris, the second an adieu to the city. In *L'Amour à la mer*, the sailor Daniel, back in the capital after completing his military service, lets himself be absorbed in its nightly pleasures. A lateral tracking shot shows his head silhouetted against the window of a taxi while the outside world, perceived across the milky glass, surges past in blurred images. Passers-by and architectural facades dissolve into a spectacle of lights and shadows, forming an almost abstract moving image dotted by coloured spots of light. As the camera cuts to a forward tracking movement, we embrace the young man's vision in a point-of-view shot of the Arc de Triomphe and Champs-Élysées at night, lit by symmetrical chains of light, weightless and ethereal like an Impressionist painting. In *Le Clair de terre*, the protagonist similarly begins his immersion into the city at night behind the window of a car.

In modern cinema, Pethő explains, the urban *flâneur* is often replaced by the driver 'who has his own personal "photographic surface" in the car window'.[77] This substitution, she argues, mediates cinema's crossing-over into other artistic terrains, first and foremost the photographic as cinema's direct ancestor, but also painting which is evoked through the splashes of light reflected in the windshield reminiscent of colour spread over a canvas. With reference to Nelson Goodman, Pethő reads such intermedial images of the city by night as an '"autographic gesture" of the cinema artist [...] who inscribes these photographic traces over the transparent image, and who makes the cinematic cross-over into the painterly as a result of these actions'.[78] In *L'Amour à la mer* the initial perception of the city through the mobile windscreen gives way to a more traditional *flânerie* on foot across the capital's famed entertainment districts. The cafés and restaurants of Saint-Germain rendered transparent by their interior lighting, multi-coloured neon signs of Pigalle's cabarets promising erotic titillation, backlit stained-glass windows of a traditional *brasserie* or

Architecture of Apocalypse, City of Lights 157

Figure 4.5 Play of lights over Paris in *L'Amour à la mer* (Guy Gilles, 1963).

the see-through glass top of a flipper game become so many outward projections of the city captured on the surface of the screen. Alternating between shots of Daniel contemplating the scenery and images of the city at night, and inserting furtive close-ups of eyes and faces, Gilles constructs what, with Deleuze, one may call a 'cinema of the seer'.[79] The tactility and luminous, painterly quality of the images, accentuated by the intermittent surges of Jean-Pierre Stora's emotive musical score, immerse the viewer in a multi-sensory experience. Characteristic of the intertextual dynamics of Gilles's oeuvre and the New Wave's predilection for citing other films, Daniel's communion with night-time Paris takes the form of a homage to New Wave filmmaking, summoned in a movie poster promoting *Le Mépris*, as well as his encounter with two of the movement's fetish actors, Jean-Pierre Léaud and Jean-Paul Brialy, appearing in short cameo roles. Connecting with his screen persona from *Les Quatre cents coups*, Léaud plays a youthful urban stroller given to the pleasures of looking: 'I go a little everywhere, I look at people, I observe, it interests me.' Brialy, in continuation of his extravagant persona from *Les Cousins*, exalts the intoxicating powers of the night: 'I love life at night.'

In the pendant sequence from *Le Clair de terre*, the protagonist Pierre throws himself into the Paris nightlife one last time before leaving the capital. As he roams the city's bars and streets, we encounter a diverse community of nocturnal revellers: junkies, sailors, rent boys and melancholy loners of all ages and walks of life. While already *L'Amour à la mer* was suffused with the erotic promise of nightly encounters, here a new sensibility for the marginal and even the grotesque – reminiscent of Baudelaire's evocations of the 'cursed' capital and Proust's daring portrayal of Baron Charlus's transgressive nocturnal pleasures in *Time Regained* – permeates the image. Intercut between shots of glittering facades, a series of extreme close-ups of a transvestite with garishly made-up lips, false eyelashes, and what appears to be a glass eye or other optical device – another allegory of the 'seer' – point to a realm of alternative, non-heteronormative desires. Like the batting of an eyelid, images so fast that they are barely decodable open a fold in the filmic tissue where the unspoken pleasures of the Parisian night can be furtively glimpsed. Exuberant and baroque, the film stages a *Schauspiel* (literally a 'game of looking'), where the nocturnal city and its inhabitants uninhibitedly give themselves to seeing and being seen. As announced in the large neon signs on one of the entertainment palaces, this is a world of images, flittering over architectural facades, reflected in fountains, and endlessly multiplied on television screens. We are reminded of photographer Moholy-Nagy's passion for the immaterial aspects of the city, to be captured in images of 'pure light', or of Erwin Blumenfeld's photographs of Times Square dematerialised into scintillating patches of colour.[80] Present in many of Gilles's later features and shorts, the poetic charge of the 'electric city' was the subject of a film on which the director was working for the last twenty years of his life, but which unfortunately remained unfinished, evocatively entitled *Poèmes électriques*. Stripped of any narrative, this experimental work, according to the testimony of one of Gilles's closest collaborators, Jérôme Pescayré, was to capture the lights of the nocturnal city, reflections of shop windows and luminous signs of bars, especially in the Pigalle district: 'The film's conception was quite loose, it rested only on the neon lights of Paris and people met by chance at night.'[81]

What, then, lies behind this cinematic fascination with the 'electropolis'? In one of his most beautiful essays on the city space, dedicated to Paris by night, Kracauer describes the strange, oneiric atmosphere created by illuminated advertising:

> In this swarming, one may still distinguish words and signs, but these words and signs are here detached from their practical ends, their entry into colourful diversity has broken them into brilliant fragments that come together according to laws that aren't the usual ones. The drizzle of adverts poured out by capitalism turns into constellations in a foreign sky.[82]

Liberated from their merely commercial imperatives, the scintillating neon signs of the city become one of those 'mass ornaments' that, for the critic, capture the essence of modernity. Furtive and inconsistent, they are an emblem of the capital's pulsating rhythms, a sign 'trembling with venal sensuality', an affirmation of the 'fragmentary nature of the urge to adventure'.[83] In one of his astute observations where the cultural commentator dialogues with the film critic, Kracauer likens the glittering city lights – reflective of the incessant flow of time – to a cinematic projection: 'There or below, watches are ticking; above, circles are undone and the light effects over evening dresses are a film under the rain'.[84] The *Lichtspiel* ('play of light') of the city is presented as akin to the immaterial images of cinema – *Licht-Spiel*, as Nia Perivolaropoulou reminds us, being another name for the moving picture in German (and one that still figures in the name of many movie theatres to this day).[85] To film the illuminated city at night, then, is more than just a documentary exercise that has fascinated cinema since its silent beginnings. The 'play of lights' of the city becomes a mirror through which the cinematic medium can reveal and represent itself. In her article on Kracauer, Perivolaropoulou comments: 'In filming the nocturnal city lit up by luminous signs, those of large hotels, stations, bars, stadiums, places of entertainment, the cinema cannot but film itself.'[86] Giuliana Bruno, drawing on an early example of cinema's fascination with the illuminated urban space, Edwin Porter's 1905 *Coney Island at Night*, brilliantly expands on this nexus between the plastic luminosity of the city and cinematic projection:

> As the camera glides reflectively across the glittering urban surface, almost caressing the façades of the buildings, the film projects the atmosphere of an electrical landscape. In a play of refraction, the city itself becomes a 'projection', as if mirroring the qualities of the cinema. [. . .] We are reminded of Charles Baudelaire's description of the urban mass as a 'reservoir of electrical energy.' And so, as the urban imaginary turns into an absorbent canvas of radiant light projections, the screen becomes a surface encounter with the electrifying energy of urban culture.[87]

Captured in its 'difficult kind of beauty' or apprehended as a new language of forms, its weighty materiality assessed in the context of the new forms of dwelling that emerged in the course of the 1950s and 1960s or dissolved into a surface of light reflective of cinematic projection, architecture in New Wave film is the art that empowers cinema to express and reflect on its own modernity. Considered as 'the most incomplete art' in his *Aesthetic*, due to its heavy matter making it 'incapable of portraying the spirit in a presence adequate to it', Hegel predicts that, over time, architecture will be surpassed by other arts with less matter.[88] As the last to be admitted into the canon of the arts, cinema reckons with its pioneering ancestor, whose solid materiality is the matter that populates its own weightless projections. Conjoined, these two arts, that knew how to be in sync with their times, redefine twentieth-century modernity.

Notes

1. Baudelaire, 'The Swan' in *The Flowers of Evil*.
2. Debord, 'Les gratte-ciel par la racine'.
3. Eisenstein, Bois and Glenny, 'Montage and architecture' p. 117.
4. Bruno, 'Site-seeing: architecture and the moving image', p. 13.
5. Faure, *Fonction du cinéma*, p. 24.
6. For the proximity between cinema and architecture and on the relation between urban space and film see, *inter alia*, Bruno, *Atlas of Emotion* and *Public Intimacy*; Barber, *Projected Cities*; Jousse and Paquot (eds), *La Ville au cinéma*; Creton and Feigelson (eds), *Théorème*, 10 (2007), 'Villes cinématographiques, ciné-lieux'; Webber and Wilson (eds), *Cities in Transition*; Simond with Paviol, *Cinéma et architecture*; Pratt and San Juan, *Film and Urban Space*.
7. See for instance the differing positions in Brassart, 'Paris leur appartient' and Magny, 'Paris et la Nouvelle Vague'.
8. Magny, 'Paris et la Nouvelle Vague', p. 126. For discussions of the representation of Paris in New Wave films see also Brassart, 'Paris leur appartient' and Toubiana, 'Comment la Nouvelle Vague a filmé la ville'.
9. See Magny, 'Paris et la Nouvelle Vague', p. 128.
10. See de Baecque, *La Nouvelle Vague: portrait d'une jeunesse*, p. 83.
11. Bruneau, 'La Ville politique', p. 94.
12. Brassart, 'Paris leur appartient', p. 42.
13. Jones, *Paris*, p. 507.
14. Ibid. p. 507.
15. On urban renewal projects in Paris and its region see Scargill, *Urban France*, pp. 138–9; Jones, *Paris*, pp. 506–25; and Pinchemel, *La Région parisienne*.
16. See Jones, *Paris*, p. 506.
17. See Debord, 'Les gratte-ciel par la racine' and 'On détruit la rue Sauvage'; Lefebvre, *Le Droit à la ville*. For a discussion of the Situationists' thought on the modern city see Paquot (ed.), *Les Situationnistes en ville*.
18. Le Corbusier himself coined the catchphrase: 'A house is a machine for living in'.
19. Pinchemel, *La Région parisienne*, p. 31.
20. Chauvin, 'Nouvelle Vague'.
21. Cited in Toubiana, 'Comment la Nouvelle Vague a filmé la ville', p. 35. Toubiana comments that the film operates 'a rupture at once formal and aesthetic, that inscribes itself in the very interior of urban and architectural space' (p. 36).
22. Jacobs, *The Wrong House*, p. 307.
23. Brody, *Everything is Cinema*, p. 227.
24. See de Baecque, *Godard*, p. 280.
25. For an investigation of modern architecture in *Les Nuits de la pleine lune* and *L'Ami de mon amie* see my 'Between classicism and modernity'. For architecture and urban space in Rohmer's work see also Clerc, 'Rohmer l'urbain'.
26. Rohmer, *Le Celluloïd et le marbre*, p. 75.
27. DVD *Le Laboratoire d'Éric Rohmer, un cinéaste à la télévision*, CNDP 2012, accompa-

nying booklet, 'Fiches pédagogiques des films réalisés pour la télévision scolaire', p. 43.
28. Rohmer, *Le Celluloïd et le marbre*, pp. 52–4.
29. For a reading of the synthesis between nature and art, 'natural' environment and constructed reality effected in the film see Margulies, 'The changing landscape'.
30. DVD *Le Laboratoire d'Éric Rohmer*, booklet 'Fiches pédagogiques', p. 44.
31. Cf. also Clerc, 'Rohmer l'urbain', pp. 96–7. For an account of the Bechers' aesthetic see the article '1968a' in Foster et al., *Art Since 1900*, pp. 521–6.
32. The rare commentators of the film are divided between considering the whole of the film as ironic (Béghin, 'Métamorphoses du paysage', p. 18) or, on the contrary, taking the voice-over at face value (Puaux, 'Éric Rohmer', p. 790). Yet, the film is subtly traversed by irony, culminating in the clash between sound and image tracks in the last sequence that questions the functionalist architecture of the future.
33. DVD *Le Laboratoire d'Éric Rohmer*, booklet 'Fiches pédagogiques', p. 48.
34. Rohmer, *Le Celluloïd et le marbre*, p. 163.
35. Ibid. p. 76.
36. One of the founders of the Situationist movement, Ivan Chtcheglov, coined the term 'Continent Contrescarpe' for the area around the rue Mouffetard. See Marcolini, 'À quelle ville les situationnistes rêvent-ils?', p. 92.
37. Wilson, *Alain Resnais*, p. 91.
38. Cited in Monaco, *Alain Resnais*, p. 90.
39. Wilson, *Alain Resnais*, p. 101.
40. Ibid. p. 101.
41. Greene, *Landscapes of Loss*, p. 46.
42. See also Monaco, *Alain Resnais* and Benayou, 'Muriel'.
43. For the concept of 'non-lieu' see Augé, *Non-lieux*.
44. Lépingle, 'Entretien avec Noun Serra', p. 92.
45. The term 'pieds-noirs' refers to 'French citizens of European origin settled in North Africa until the time of independence' (Larousse, *Dictionnaire de Français*, https://www.larousse.fr/dictionnaires/francais/).
46. Bruno, *Atlas of Emotion*, p. 251.
47. Frodon, *L'Age moderne du cinéma français*, p. 207.
48. See Morrey, *Jean-Luc Godard*, p. 62.
49. Hensman, 'Oracles of suburbia', p. 444.
50. Guzzetti, *Two or Three Things*, p. 45.
51. Hensman, 'Oracles of suburbia', p. 444.
52. Guzzetti, *Two or Three Things*, pp. 173–5.
53. Guzzetti, *Two or Three Things*, pp. 247–9. While, in formal usage, the French 'grue' refers to crane, its colloquial meaning is 'woman of easy virtue' or 'hooker'.
54. Cited in Monaco, *The New Wave*, p. 178.
55. Quoted in Guzzetti, *Two or Three Things*, p. 47.
56. Gorz, 'The exit from capitalism', p. 10.
57. *Internationale Situationniste*, 6 (1961), 'Programme', p. 11.

58. Lefebvre, *Introduction to Modernity*, p. 119.
59. Morrey, *Jean-Luc Godard*, p. 63.
60. On the referencing of Marker, see Guzzetti, *Two or Three Things*, p. 73.
61. Guzzetti, *Two or Three Things*, p. 226.
62. Ibid. p. 229.
63. Heinich, 'Godard, créateur de statut', p. 313.
64. Godard, 'La Chance de repartir pour un tour', p. 411.
65. On the influence of Ponge on *Deux ou trois choses que je sais d'elle* see also Roud, *Godard*, p. 108.
66. Guzzetti, *Two or Three Things*, p. 349.
67. Kracauer, *Theory of Film*, p. 72.
68. Levin, 'Introduction', p. 20.
69. Kracauer, *Theory of Film*, p. 73.
70. Ibid. p. 72.
71. Pethő, *Cinema and Intermediality*, p. 101.
72. The term is coined from Giuliana Bruno's '*emotion*' (*Atlas of Emotion*, p. 9 and *passim*).
73. For a reading of urban space in *Cléo* see Pratt and San Juan, *Film and Urban Space*, pp. 77–89.
74. Pethő, *Cinema and Intermediality*, p. 102.
75. Ibid. pp. 103–22.
76. Ibid. p. 103.
77. Ibid. p. 103.
78. Ibid. p. 104.
79. Deleuze, *Cinema 2*, p. 2.
80. On Moholy-Nagy see Haus and Frizot, 'Figures of Style', p. 463.
81. Lépingle, 'Interview de Jérôme Pescayré'.
82. Kracauer, 'Publicité lumineuse', p. 66.
83. Ibid. p. 68.
84. Ibid. p. 68.
85. Perivolaropoulou, 'La Ville cinématographique', p. 17.
86. Ibid. p. 18.
87. Bruno, *Surface*, p. 59.
88. See Hegel, *Aesthetic*, p. 888. I owe this insight to Clotilde Simond and Sophie Paviol (*Cinéma et architecture*, p. 17).

CHAPTER FIVE

Still/Moving: Photography and Cinematic Ontology

> It is photography – enriched by the dimension of time and, thus, reaching its fullness – that seems to me to be [. . .] the cornerstone of the cinematic edifice, even more than the 'movement' our art shares with dance and theatre.
>
> Éric Rohmer[1]

> FAUX TO GRAPHE
>
> Jean-Luc Godard[2]

'What is cinema?' The question of film's specificity – in particular in comparison with other art forms – has preoccupied critics and filmmakers ever since the inception of the medium, with a particular urgency in classical film theory. Before the invention of digital, which throws up its own questions, the interrogation of cinema's nature was inseparably entangled with photography, due to the process of photochemical imprinting that both media share. Thus it is little surprise that Bazin's appositely named *What is Cinema?*, one of the foundational texts of the New Wave, should open with an essay on 'The Ontology of the Photographic Image' centred on photographic representation amid the wider reflection on the mutual influence between the arts that we have already encountered in several of his other essays. As a direct imprint of reality, Bazin argues, photography has opened up unprecedented possibilities for capturing life in all its likeness, thereby delivering the plastic arts from the 'resemblance complex' that has burdened them ever since the first mechanical system of reproduction: Leonardo da Vinci's *camera obscura*, one of the ancestors of the photographic camera. 'Simultaneously a liberation and a fulfilment', the critic proclaims, photography 'has freed Western painting, once and for all, from its obsession with realism and allowed it to recover its aesthetic autonomy'.[3] If, henceforth, photography satisfies our obsession with realism, its psychological appeal lies not so much in the perfecting of a representational process, but, rather, in the authentication of reality afforded by the photographic imprint:

> The objective nature of photography confers on it a quality of credibility absent from all other picture-making. In spite of any objections our critical spirit may offer, we are forced to accept as real the existence of the object reproduced, actually *re*-presented, set before us, that is to say, in time and space.[4]

As indicated in the title of his essay, Bazin is concerned above all with the 'species *photographic* image'[5] that encompasses both photography and film as lens-based media. Yet he nonetheless points to some essential differences between photography and film, especially concerning their treatment of time. Photography, he writes, 'does not create eternity, as art does, it embalms time, rescuing it simply from its proper corruption'.[6] Seen in such a perspective, cinema 'appears like the accomplishment in time of photographic objectivity':[7]

> The film is no longer content to preserve the object, enshrouded as it were in an instant, as the bodies of insects are preserved intact, out of the distant past, in amber. The film delivers baroque art from its convulsive catalepsy. Now, for the first time, the image of things is likewise the image of their duration, change mummified as it were.[8]

Stillness and movement, instantaneity and duration, past and present – in this seminal essay, Bazin teases out some of the paradigms that have come to inform theoretical discussions of the relationship between photography and film, from Roland Barthes to Raymond Bellour and Laura Mulvey, to name only three particularly prominent thinkers.[9] As a medium derived from photography, cinema shares with its ancestor an indexicality that, for Bazin, constitutes the essence of the photographic image, yet the two arts also fundamentally differ in their framing of time and motion. Indeed, so changed are the ways in which we apprehend the world when photographic images are animated in cinema, Barthes asserts in *Camera Lucida*, that we are faced with another art altogether: 'in the Photograph, something *has posed* in front of the tiny hole and has remained there forever [. . .]; but in cinema, something *has passed* in front of this same tiny hole: the pose is swept away and denied by the continuous series of images: it is a different phenomenology, and therefore a different art which begins here, though derived from the first one'.[10]

What makes photography's relationship to film unique compared to the other arts discussed in this book is not only its position as a technological ancestor, but its continued presence in the very materiality of film. Cinematic motion, as is well known, is created through the quick succession of single frames – also known as photograms – that pass through the projector, in standard modern cinema at a rate of 24 frames per second. Undistinguishable to the human eye, these still photographs that constitute the individual building blocks of the film strip are the umbilical cord that joins cinema to its ancestor, photography. 'The stillness of photography, its halt and hush, is never entirely shaken loose by sequential movement in and as film but is merely lost to notice', Garrett Stewart notes incisively. 'In the hairbreadth space between images, between staccato data, there flickers a gap, a join, a seam.'[11] The stillness of the single frame, in Laura Mulvey's words, 'provides cinema with a secret, with a hidden past that might, or might not, find its way to the surface'.[12]

The Lumière brothers' first public demonstration of the cinematograph cleverly played on the coexistence between stillness and movement that underpins cinematic projection: their 1895 screening at the Grand Café in Paris began with the projection of a still photograph suddenly brought to life by the cranking of the projector.[13] With the development of mechanical projectors and higher frame rates, the flutter between photograms that was still perceptible in early cinema gradually disappeared, erasing the photographic trace from human perception. Yet while mainstream cinema was keen to perfect cinematic illusion, avant-garde and modernist film found in the tension between movement and stillness inherent in the cinematic image a welcome source of experimentation. In *Man with a Movie Camera*, for instance, Vertov makes use of the freeze-frame (that is, a static shot that temporarily freezes the action obtained by printing multiple copies of the same frame) to draw attention to the materiality of film. Partaking in a wider investigation of the cinematic apparatus, the stop-motion effect of the freeze-frame triggers a self-reflexive moment in the film that gives visibility to the processes underlying filmic illusion.[14] Some five years before Vertov, René Clair in *Paris qui dort* (*Paris Asleep*, 1924) uses the freeze-frame technique in his sci-fi fable of Paris being put to sleep by a paralysing ray. As the scientist responsible for the experiment tampers with the lever of the arresting device, mobile pictures freeze and unfreeze, in what Annette Michelson has identified as a metacinematic pairing of the paralysis ray with the camera itself.[15] The freeze-frame device resurfaces in the course of the 1950s, precisely during the period which Deleuze pinpoints as the transition from the 'movement-image' (that is, a cinema still governed by action and narrative logic) to the 'time-image' (the new cinema of the post-war era that breaks with traditional narrative, focusing instead on the complex perception of time). Before becoming widespread in advertising and music videos, and films that emulate them, Bellour argues, the stilled image, 'has acted and still does act as a medium for the relentless search for another time, for a break in time into which modern cinema (this cinema of time that came into being after and because of the war, through neorealism and the Nouvelle Vague) has perhaps fallen while searching for its most intimate secret'. A time, he pursues further, 'that is also joined with that of photography, to which many have wanted at the same time to compare film, but from which they also forcefully sought to differentiate it'.[16]

Tacitly recalled in the stop-motion image of the freeze-frame, photography's umbilical relationship to film can also be evoked through the on-screen presence of photos, photo albums, or postcards, as well as a wider fascination with stillness that manifests in a director's style.[17] But what are the effects when the photographic thus erupts into the filmic, when the different phenomenologies of photography and cinema are being brought into play with one another? How does cinema benefit from such an encounter? Film, Barthes asserts in a seminal article on Eisenstein, can only reveal its richer ('third' or 'obtuse') meaning if it is broken down into its constituent still images: 'the filmic, very paradoxically, cannot be grasped in the film "in situation", "in movement", "in its natural state", but only in that major artefact, the still'.[18] In other words, in returning to its photogrammatic origin, film discloses precisely what makes it film; by way of stillness, it reveals its essence as a medium. Taking his cue from Barthes, Bellour develops the idea that the photograph enables cinema to look at and think about itself.[19] Reflecting on the encounter between photography and film more widely, he identifies the 1950s as a period when 'the cinema found new ways of twisting its neck around to look at itself, and of transforming itself using elements that apparently went against its nature of illusory spectacle founded on continuity and the illusion of movement'.[20] For Bellour the photographic, as a means to slow down the cinematic flow of images, affords the necessary time to add to the image: it transforms the 'hurried' spectator of cinema into a 'pensive' one.[21]

Poised between the freeze-frame experiments of the classical avant-garde and what Bellour identifies as the widespread use of still images in visual image culture since the 1980s, the New Wave holds a pivotal role in film's engagement with its parent medium. From Truffaut's influential freeze-frame ending in *Les Quatre cents coups* to Guy Gilles's fascination with photographs and Godard's use of photography as a self-reflexive tool, not to mention the photo-based films of Marker and Varda, photography is ubiquitous in New Wave films, both classic as well as lesser known. As another mirroring device, not unlike the theatre that we examined earlier, photography allows New Wave filmmakers to reflect on the specificities of their medium, to refine their understanding of the ontology of the cinematic image. Yet the encounter with the photographic, as we will see, also serves as a privileged means to grapple with social and political issues at a time when France and the world were undergoing a period of major change. Constructing a different temporality within the cinematic frame, by way of photography, New Wave films tackle matters that particularly mobilised intellectuals and artists of the late 1950s and 1960s: the vulnerability of communities left behind by modernisation, France's relations to its former colonial empire, the spectre of the Holocaust and the atrocities committed during the Indochina and Algerian Wars, not forgetting the Cuban Revolution as a beacon of hope for a more humane form of socialism. Focusing on a selection of films by Truffaut, Varda, Gilles, Godard and Marker, this chapter will explore the intersection between cinema and photography drawing on wider theoretical reflections concerning the two media's relations to time, memory, death and spectatorship.

IN THE BEGINNING WAS THE PHOTOGRAM

An adolescent runs steadily across a beach. His muffled footsteps in the wet sand mingle with the murmur of the waves, the sounds of nature amplifying whilst the diegetic music slows down markedly. Reaching the water, the boy wades in tentatively, turns, and, for a few metres, continues his run parallel to the shoreline before turning around and walking towards the camera. As he appears in medium shot, the image freezes while a rapid zoom closes in on the adolescent's face cut out against the vast expanse of the sea.

The first freeze-frame ending in the history of cinema, this final shot of Truffaut's *Les Quatre cents coups* is one laden with uncertainty. Antoine Doinel has arrived at the end of his journey: the sea he has been dreaming of discovering proves as indifferent to his fate as the mother with whom it is homophonous in French (*la mer/la mère*). A fugitive sought by the juvenile justice system, his situation appears hopeless. Some ten seconds before the actual ending of the film, the freezing of the image also brutally arrests time. Withholding any promise of closure or resolution, it suspends Antoine's fate in a troubling face-to-face between character and spectator.

From a strictly photomechanical point of view, the freeze-frame, consisting, as already mentioned, of a single photogram that is reprinted identically, does not actually stop cinematic motion. It merely creates an optical arrest. Yet, to the audience, the resulting still image has all the characteristics of a photograph. In stark contrast to Antoine's running away that, for the last four minutes or so, has kept spectators tightly sutured into the action, the freeze-frame marks an abrupt, uncomfortable halt. Snatched from the continuum of images, it compels us to examine details that may escape the eye if the action were ongoing: we notice the boy's turned-up collar, his hair ruffled by the wind. The stillness of the shot endows it with what Barthes has famously termed the *punctum* of photography, 'a detail [. . .] which attracts or distresses me', 'bruises me, is poignant to me'.[22] Bruising and perforating us,

Figure 5.1 The *punctum* of photography: freeze-frame ending in *Les Quatre cents coups* (François Truffaut, 1959).

the photogram of a boy forlorn, with little hope for the future, haunts us long beyond the 'Fin' superimposed on Léaud's face.

This singular ending of a film, which is often credited as the official beginning of the New Wave, pays homage to the medium of film through an interrogation of the cinematic image. Stripping the filmstrip back to its smallest, normally invisible unit – the single frame – Truffaut gives visibility to cinema's secret, the stillness that lurks unnoticed in cinematic projection. Serge Daney, drawing on a funerary metaphor, comments: '[It is] a way of returning the film to its skeleton of fixed images, like a corpse to the ashes that in any case it is (ashes to ashes, frames to frames . . .)'.[23] As a method of de-composition that breaks the mobile, deceptively 'living' images on screen down into their still components, the freeze-frame returns cinema to its origins. Its negation of movement evokes the sense of mortality that pervades all lens-based media, but which becomes particularly salient in photographic (or photogrammatic) stillness. It is precisely in this moment when cinema abdicates the forward thrust that binds it to life's duration that it attains its greatest affective charge: in its temporary return to the immobility of the photographic image, the freeze-frame lays bare a human vulnerability that *moves* us.

The last shot of *Les Quatre cents coups* was by no means Truffaut's only use of freeze-frames, even if he quickly lost interest in the technique, considering it too eye-catching.[24] Yet, in film history, his stark visualisation of the photogram in a work that officially put the new cinema on the map, marks an ending as well as a new beginning: out of a final fixed image, freezing a rebellious adolescent in a pose of flight on the shore of wide open waters, the young cinema that would brazenly assert its auteurist style, the New *Wave*, was born.

Photographic Pastness: The Melancholy Gaze

Beyond the freeze-frame, which most explicitly returns cinema to its photogrammatic syntax, the New Wave is in dialogue with photography in manifold ways. Inset into the filmic frame, photographs can have the function of an index or an ocular prop, such as, for instance, when Godard, in a cameo role in *À bout de souffle*, identifies the fugitive Michel thanks to a newspaper photograph and, in an ironic metacinematic turn of events, prompts the destruction of his filmic creation by denouncing him to the police. Inversely, in *Le Signe du lion*, the newspaper article announcing that the millionaire Pierre is missing contains no photograph, delaying the final recognition scene that will put an end to his vagrancy. Passers-by and even a journalist take pictures of Pierre, but fail to make a connection between the man the whole of Paris is searching for and the down-and-out he has become. Photos, especially in Godard's socio-critical fictions, warn of the artificial needs and desires created by the manipulative image culture of consumer capitalism linked to the wider danger of confusing the specular illusion of mass media with lived reality. In Resnais's *Hiroshima mon amour*, 'for lack of anything better' ('*faute d'autre chose*'), they are reduced to meagre testimonies, unable to speak the affective wounding and trauma caused by the atomic bombing. Photographs can take on the role of a fetish, particularly in Truffaut, where the promotional still from Bergman's *Summer with Monika* (1953) that Antoine and René steal from a cinema in *Les Quatre cents coups* and the slide of the Greek goddess that announces the appearance of Catherine in *Jules et Jim* become the contrasting poles of a liberated and an idealised femininity. Sequences in negative in *Une femme mariée* and *Alphaville* remind us of the photochemical process of the imprint that binds cinema to its photographic ancestor. In the latter, the quasi-obsolescent medium of photography, alongside literature, is associated with the individualistic cultural practices of the old world, in sharp contrast to the totalitarian regime's use of television as a means of collective brainwashing in Truffaut's *Fahrenheit*. Its ability to document and testify makes photography a privileged tool of resistance, yet it, in turn, can also be instrumentalised as a form of state control, as is shown in the scene in *Les Quatre cents coups* where Antoine has his photo taken by the police. Finally, to mention a more subterranean relation to photography, let us not forget that, failing to obtain fast enough film stock to allow location shooting without additional lighting, Godard shot his first feature, *À bout de souffle*, on taped-together pieces of Ilford HP5, a film designed not for cinematic use, but for photo reportage.[25]

While there is much scope in New Wave film for exploring what Garrett Stewart calls cinema's 'photographic subtext',[26] we will begin this enquiry with two directors who not only use photography as a recurrent motif in their works, but whose visual aesthetic is strongly inflected by the photographic medium: Agnès Varda and Guy Gilles. Both directors actively pursued photography, the former, as noted previously, as stage photographer for the Avignon festival and the *Théâtre National Populaire*, the latter as an amateur who amassed a large photographic oeuvre alongside his filmic work. Varda started exhibiting her photographs in the early 1950s, in the courtyard of her house in rue Daguerre, Paris.[27] Her photographs for the Avignon festival were shown *in situ* in a 2007 exhibition, *Je me souviens de Vilar en Avignon*, alongside an installation incorporating photographs, *Hommage aux justes de France*, in commemoration of the French civilians who saved Jewish lives during the Occupation; the photos she took during a visit to Cuba in 1962 to prepare her short *Salut les Cubains* and during her years spent in California in the late 1960s have equally been the subject of recent exhibitions. Her latest film, *Visages Villages* (*Faces Places*, 2017), documents her collaboration with French photographer and street artist JR.[28] Gilles's portraits of iconic stars and directors, including Jeanne Moreau, Alain Delon, Jean Marais, Johnny Hallyday and Orson Welles, were exhibited for the first time in 2014, in conjunction with the Cinémathèque française's retrospective of his films.[29] A selection of his wide and varied photographic practice, strongly resonant with his filmic work in its sensitivity to the poetry of the quotidian and its fascination with the object world, can be seen on an excellent website dedicated to his life and work, and in the collective volume *Guy Gilles, un cinéaste au fil du temps* as well as in Gaël Lépingle's documentary *Guy Gilles photographe* (2008).[30]

Both directors have let themselves be inspired by photography; indeed we could say that for both, photography and film are complementary ways of apprehending the world. Yet ultimately each values cinema over its photographic ancestor. Varda confesses that she quickly grew dissatisfied with the muteness of photography, which she considered a silencing of the female voice: 'Photography struck me as altogether too silent. It was kind of: "Look pretty and keep your mouth shut". Pretty photos, pretty frames, it already reeked.'[31] Gilles, while acknowledging his lifelong passion for photography, declares that 'filming remains [his] first and real job'.[32] Comparing the two practices, he insists on the movement inherent in all cinematic images, even in a fixed shot: only cinema, by giving visibility to even the slightest agitation within the filmic frame, such as the trembling of leaves, can convey 'the movement which is life'.[33] In many ways, Varda's and Gilles's filmic work, especially their early films, can be understood as attempts to breathe life into the stillness of photography. Or, to put it from the perspective of film, as endeavours to slow down cinema's forward thrust – what Bellour calls the medium's 'hysteria'[34] – to afford a more contemplative, thoughtful way of looking.

As we saw in Chapter 3, Varda's first feature, *La Pointe Courte*, draws on a hybrid layering of painting, theatre and photography, rooted in her training in the visual arts and practice as a professional photographer. Her second film, the short *L'Opéra Mouffe*, equally evinces an intermedial aesthetic with a special indebtedness to the pioneers of French photography. Poised between documentary and personal essay, *L'Opéra Mouffe* is framed as a theatrical experience, entered through the painted theatre decor of the credit titles where the director herself – stripped naked – occupies the role of spectator; and ended by the rolling down of a store shutter, followed by the final intertitle with the word 'curtain'. Alluding to Brecht and Kurt Weill's *Threepenny Opera* (1928), Varda's take on everyday life in one of the emblematic neighbourhoods of the *Paris populaire* is a spectacle both created and observed by a pregnant woman, whose plainly assumed subjectivity emotionally taints the images. Entirely without dialogue and divided into vignettes by handwritten intertitles, the film pays homage to silent era films, but, above all, invokes the rich legacy of early twentieth-century street photography, which has played an important role in alternative visual constructions of the French capital.

The black-and-white images of the winding rue Mouffetard with its withered, ramshackle buildings, open-air market displays and picturesque shop windows recall the photographic work of Eugène Atget (1857–1927), who, in the early decades of the twentieth century, archived the urban fabric and street scenes of the old Paris before they disappeared in the onslaught of modernisation. More oneiric sequences – most notably the ones entitled 'On nature' and 'On pregnancy' – place the film in the tradition of interwar avant-garde experiments by questioning the stability of optical vision and challenging perceptual habits. Defamiliarised in close-up and isolated from their habitual context, tracked by the camera or rotating around a horizontal axis, vegetables and plants take on a life of their own in images reminiscent of Surrealist photographers-cum-filmmakers Man Ray and Jacques-André Boiffard.[35] Dream-like slow motion sequences, on the other hand, recall the work of one of the most influential figures of the American avant-garde, who was also one of the pioneers of a female film language: Maya Deren.

The film narrative is permeated by frontal portraits of nameless passersby, snapped from the crowd in the mode of a street photographer. Some of the filmed subjects look right at the camera, ready, as it were, to have their picture taken. Marking a pause in the cinematic flow of images, these photography-like takes afford us the time to scrutinise the weary expressions and withered features of ordinary men and women whose faces speak of economic deprivation and personal adversity. These stark filmic portraits open a breach for the pensiveness which, for Barthes, is precisely what is lost in cinematic representation – hence his interest in the photogram:

> Last thing about the *punctum*: whether or not it is triggered, it is an addition: it is what I add to the photograph and *what is nonetheless already there*. [. . .] Do I add to the images in movies? I don't think so; I don't have time: in front of the screen, I am not free to shut my eyes; otherwise, opening them again, I would not discover the same image; I am constrained to a continuous voracity; a host of other qualities, but not *pensiveness*.[36]

Varda's aesthetic, inspired by photography, privileges moments of stillness in which the camera is allowed to linger on a shot, inviting a more thoughtful, empathetic engagement with the documented reality. Her photography-inflected images impel us to reflect on the hardships suffered by people on the margins of 1950s consumer society. Face to face with the filmed subjects, we are summoned to share their sorrows, to abandon the voracious consumption of images encouraged by the cinematic flow in favour of a more active affective involvement.

Only one sequence, entitled 'the dear departed', embeds actual photos into the filmic frame. At first lingering on a photo of three men shown full-screen, the camera zooms out to reveal a wall covered with photos and religious objects, cuts to a series of further photos, before ending on a full-screen image of a devotional object into which the photographic faces of a woman and a man have been inserted in a symbolic assignation of posthumous sainthood. Like carnival in the subsequent sequence, the devotion to the deceased is part of the popular rites and social practices that Varda documents with her characteristically fine humour and gentle irony. Yet in its direct association of photography with death – 'Photography is a kind of primitive theatre, a kind of *Tableau Vivant*, a figuration of the motionless and made-up face beneath which we see the dead', writes Barthes[37] – the sequence is also paradigmatic for the film's wider thematic stakes: inflected by the photographic, *L'Opéra Mouffe* casts a melancholy gaze on a fragile world on the cusp of disappearance.

Close to Varda in his shared love of popular culture and the quotidian, Guy Gilles similarly accords a particular role to photography in his portrayals of solitary outsiders, imbued with the fleetingness of time and the transience of human existence. Inspired, like the director of *L'Opéra Mouffe*, by Atget and the interwar Surrealist photographers, his careful compositions, sharp framing and *décadrage* effects reveal a photographic sensitivity, also manifest in his fascination with old-fashioned shop-window displays, the poetry of ordinary objects and the textures of the urban space that, as we saw in Chapter 3, constitute a recurrent motif in his films. In further resonance with Varda, his interest in gestures, the expressive body and still-life type compositions recalls that of the photographer, to such an extent that, in a tribute in *Cahiers du cinéma*, fellow filmmaker Jean-Claude Guiguet asks: 'So, filmmaker or not? Aesthete and photographer would be more accurate terms.'[38] The resemblance between Varda's early works and Gilles did not go unnoticed by the critic Jean-Louis Bory, who writes in a review of *Le Clair de terre*:

> The gamble of Guy Gilles (he stuck to it – as Agnès Varda once did, very fleetingly in *Opéra-Mouffe* or *Cléo de 5 à 7*), is to transform the ordinary into the extraordinary solely by the weight of looking. Thanks to film, the fragile and ephemeral escapes time, the forgettable escapes oblivion. That's what makes photography so invaluable, and it's not by chance that Gilles attaches a particular importance, which isn't just sentimental, to family albums, portraits, and yellowed postcards.[39]

A recurrent motif in Gilles's filmic oeuvre, photographs, vintage postcards, photo albums and newspaper clippings summon us into a world beyond the filmic frame, injecting the pastness of photography – what Barthes calls the medium's noeme of the 'That-has-been' or *'interfuit'*[40] – into the constitutive present tense of cinema. Pinned to walls, mounted in frames or filling up the entire plane of vision, the stillness of photographic objects intermittently stalls the cinematic flow of images, imbuing Gilles's screen worlds with the melancholy tone that Barthes identifies as being singular to photography. Photography, the critic writes, 'is *without future* (this is its pathos, its melancholy)'; cinema, by contrast, is 'protensive, hence in no way melancholic (what is it then? – It is, then, simply "normal", like life)'.[41]

The extended scene in *Au pan coupé* where the two lovers contemplate an old photo album found in a convenience store is emblematic of the director's obsession with the visual traces of passing time that permeate all of his work. Assembled over a period of some forty years, from 1907 to 1948, the album visually tells the life of a woman from a small village in the south-east of France, Marie Spinell, née Aubert. Private photographs and postcards in black and white or muted pastels evoke the simple pleasures and personal tragedies of Marie's life, caught up like all human existence in the destructive flow of time: 'It's the story of a life, our story [. . .] all lost away in time', muses Jean. Black-and-white photos of children bathing in the sea or playing in the street shown full-screen induce the couple to meditate about their destiny: are they still alive or already 'out of the world or close to it'? Suspending the portrayed subjects between an irretrievable past and an uncertain future, temporarily rescuing them from oblivion, yet also assigning them to a certain death, the photos cast a deadly shadow over the lovers' own present, soon to be upended by Jean's disappearance. Rupturing the filmic flow with the stillness of its images, the album becomes a premonitory sign of the corrosive force of time that threatens the happiness of the couple. In the slippage from the filmic to the photographic frame lurks what Stewart calls the 'deathwork of the still image':[42] the stasis of photography becomes a potent metaphor of death.

The photographic subtext that informs Gilles's filmic work is most prominently brought into relief in the autofictional *Le Clair de terre*, where the probing of the mnemonic values of photography extends into the plot of the protagonist's search for the traces of his childhood. A wanderer between two cultures who belongs to none, Pierre Brumeu returns to his native country to carve out an identity for himself and retrace memories of his late mother. Initially entitled *Où va le vent? Voyage en Algérie*,[43] the second part of the film was supposed to be set in Algeria, but was eventually transposed to Tunisia, as Gilles failed to obtain permission to film in time for the shooting. But the director's native country remains present, not only by way of references to the parents' Algerian origins, but through multiple visual signifiers. From the title credits, Pierre's desire to connect with his North African origins is aligned with photography, the medium that embalms and preserves time. Accompanied by the clicking sound of a camera as if they were in the process of being taken, old postcards from Algeria and Tunisia under French colonisation succeed one another in full screen, animated by transitional fades. These exoticising images of Maghrebi landscapes and cities, tainted by the gaze of the coloniser, are in turn intercut with vignettes of a group of American tourists, armed with cameras, on a visit through the Marais – a historical district, which, after the end of French rule in North Africa, became home to a sizeable community of Sephardic Jews. Past and present collide in this juxtaposition

Figure 5.2 *Nostalgérie*: colonial-era postcards in *Le Clair de terre* (Guy Gilles, 1970).

between the '*having-been-there*' of photography and the '*being-there*' of cinema,[44] announcing the *pied-noir* protagonist's double alienation from both his native Tunisia and his adoptive France, but also introducing a tension between, on the one hand, the rigidified vision of the past exhibited in the postcards and, on the other, the mobility of the cinematic image more apt at capturing transformation and change.

Having come to France at the age of six, in the wake of decolonisation, Pierre's remembrance of his childhood is largely constructed from photographs which substitute for real memories. Hence, perhaps, his fascination for all types of photographic objects – newspaper clippings, postcards, family photos, photos of stars – that adorn his walls and which he collects in antiques shops. As a device able to 'can' time, the photographic camera holds a privileged place in the young man's return to his roots, culminating in the sequence where Pierre and an old family friend (played by Edwige Feuillère) stumble upon a traditional street photographer in Tunis. Looking at the archaic device, she surmises, 'chances are it was the one that photographed you in your mother's arms'. No sooner said, the filmic camera examines the apparatus from various angles and in close-up. Like the title credits, the scene where the two have their photo taken is constructed around a tension between still and moving images. Less interested in the photographic end product, it focuses on the development of the photograph, captured in close-up as it gradually becomes visible in the developer bath. What is at stake here is the *becoming* of an image, a process which only the mobile images of cinema can render visible. In this enquiry into the different qualities of images, the spectrality of photography, which rigidifies the world into an uncanny fixity, is pitted against the mobility of film, which is able to grasp beings and things in their duration.

All through *Le Clair de terre* photography is thus associated with loss and death, nowhere more so than in the photograph of a friend who died under unclear circumstances, which Pierre's father sends his son. As emanations of the past, photographs call out to the protagonist, but, ultimately, they fail to accomplish the work of memory, which, like the development of a photo, must traverse time to filter slowly through consciousness. 'The Photograph does not call up the past (nothing Proustian in a photograph)', cautions Barthes. 'The effect it produces upon me is not to restore what has been abolished (by time, by distance), but to attest that what I see has indeed existed.'[45] In mnemonic terms, there is little to be expected from what Proust, cited by Barthes, calls these 'photographs of a being before which one recalls less of that being than by merely thinking of him or her'.[46] In *Le Clair de terre*, which Claude Mauriac calls 'the first Proustian film, undoubtedly',[47] it is dialogue with Proust's novel – not photography – that accomplishes the work of memory connecting the protagonist to his roots.

One year after *Le Clair de terre*, Gilles shot a poetic reflection on Proust, entitled *Proust, l'art et la douleur*, for French television. But already in the earlier feature, numerous echoes reference the Proustian universe, from the name of one of Pierre's former lovers (the editor Elstir) and the death of Jeanne (a barely dissimulated double of Proust's Albertine) to the bell tower of Combray and the Normandy sea resorts with their elegant summer vacationists. Far from seeking to adapt the Proustian novel, the director translates into cinematic terms the workings of what Proust famously calls 'involuntary memory', that is, the memory of the body (as opposed to the memory of the intellect termed 'voluntary memory') that alone can capture the true essence of a past moment. In *Search of Lost Time*, sensory stimuli such as sounds, perfumes and tactile sensations conjure up buried layers of the Narrator's past, which come to cohabit with his current self in a sudden flash of remembrance. Here, too, the tunes of an old ditty, the vivid colours and interleaved forms of Tunisian vernacular architecture or the velvet cover of a chair formerly in the possession of the Brumeu family bring back the sensuous textures of childhood.

In Gilles's signature-style sequences of rapid montage, which evoke the process of memory, images seem to collide with one another in a vertiginous dance of places, bodies, faces and objects. In these ecstatic moments of epiphany, thanks to the mobility of the cinematic image, past and present – retinal images and flashes of memory – fuse into what, with Proust, one can call 'a fragment of time in the pure state'.[48] A declaration of faith in cinema's resurrectional capabilities, *Le Clair de terre* – as is subtly referenced in its title, borrowed from André Breton's 1923 collection of poetry – returns to the building blocks of cinema with these photogrammatic flashes ('éclairs') that have the power to bring back the true essence of the past. 'The filmic apparatus', to cite a particularly judicious phrase coined by Stewart, 'disappears the photogram in the former's apparition as cinema.'[49]

TRUTH 24× A SECOND: COLONIAL OPPRESSION AND THE (PHOTO) SHOOT

In Varda and Gilles, as we have just seen, photography, while interrogating the ontology of the photographic image and shaping the directors' aesthetic, has above all a narrative function: incorporated into their films, photographic objects or references to the photographic apparatus help the directors work through a particular theme, be it the fleetingness of time, human vulnerability, or the process of memory. Godard's relationship to photographs, by contrast, is 'invariably analytical'.[50] In his aesthetics of collage, photography is not only ubiquitous as a self-reflexive tool that valorises cinema, but, in tune with the director's more politicised stance, it becomes a privileged means of commenting on the contemporary state of the world. Inserted into the filmic frame or arrested in freeze-frame, showcased in full screen as if it were a substitute for the cinematic image or zoomed into on a newspaper or billboard, pinned to the walls of the characters' dwelling places or captured in postcards, the photographic image is co-substantial to Godard's work. This sustained engagement with photography culminates in the book version of *Histoire(s) du cinéma*, in which film stills enter into dialogue with the manifold photographic traces of twentieth-century history. Indeed, so essential is photography to Godard's cinematic project that it can be considered the vantage point of what Serge Daney calls 'Godard's pedagogy', a pedagogy which 'has as its horizon, its limit, the enigma of enigmas, the sphinx of the still photograph: what defies intelligence, yet never exhausts it, what holds the look and the meaning, what fixes the scopic pulsion: restraint in action'.[51]

In a world increasingly dominated and manipulated by images, photography becomes a privileged tool for thinking about the truth value of images amid a wider reflection on the human condition that is at the core of the director's work. For Godard, Bellour observes, to take stock of the state of photography in the contemporary world is equivalent to thinking about the state of cinema: 'From the *Carabiniers* to *Photo et Cie* [. . .], Godard gave a literal and dizzying rundown of the state of photography in the contemporary world, and thus in film as well.'[52] While photography is so omnipresent in Godard's films that Campany rightly advances that 'the place of [the] photograph in Godard's work deserves a book study of its own',[53] it is in two works of the New Wave period, *Le Petit Soldat* and *Deux ou trois choses que je sais d'elle*, that the director develops his own ontology of the cinematic image in opposition to the photographic image.

Shot in 1960, Godard's second feature, *Le Petit Soldat*, was banned by the French authorities until 1963 because of its depiction of torture and references to the Algerian War. It was eventually released after the end of the war – a delay which, together with the film's much darker tone and ambivalent political stance, to some extent explains its mixed reception at the time. Photographs are intrinsic to the film's political plot, which pits members of the French paramilitary Secret Army Organisation (OAS), engaged in violent struggle to prevent Algerian independence, against their opponents from the Algerian National Liberation Front (FLN), on neutral Swiss territory. It is through the mediation of a fake street photographer that the agent Bruno (Michel Subor) receives coded messages from the OAS command, whereas the newspaper photo of the victim of a car bomb, scrutinised at length by the camera, quite literally puts spectators 'in the picture' about the paramilitary group's terrorist methods. Inversely, photos of OAS agents tortured to death by the FLN, used as a means to intimidate Bruno, denounce the use of torture by both groups. Unlike Resnais's *Muriel*, released the same year, which, as we saw in the previous chapter, refrains from showing images of torture, Godard not only gives visibility to the atrocities committed during the Algerian War; he shifts the emphasis from the widespread use of torture by the French military, which the French public discovered thanks to Henri Alleg's influential book *La Question* (1958), to the torture employed by the FLN. Ironically, Bruno's torturers cite from Alleg as if to validate their own methods. Riddled with paradoxes – not least the protagonist's collaboration with the OAS despite his admiration for the anti-fascist struggle of the Spanish Republicans – the film interrogates revolutionary ideals, refusing to submit to any binary, clear-cut opposition between the FLN's struggle for independence and the OAS's right-wing terrorism.

The gruelling photographs of victims maimed by terrorism and torture that punctuate the film are part of a wider questioning of the human condition via the photographic medium, culminating in the scene where Bruno contemplates the strange assembly of newspaper cuttings pinned to the walls of Veronica's (Anna Karina) bedroom. The camera glides from image to image, scrutinising scenes of armed conflict, execution or terror, while, in voice-over, Bruno recites German poet Wilhelm Hauff's poem *Reiters Morgenlied* (*A Cavalry Man's Morning-Song*, 1824) about a soldier stoically anticipating death in battle, used as propaganda during the Great War. The presence of Malraux's *La Condition humaine* (*Man's Fate*, 1933) on the bedside table hints at the brutal suppression of popular insurrection, developed in Bruno's musings about a 'handful of snapshots taken from around the world [that] pass by me like bad dreams: Panama, Rome, Alexandria, Budapest, Paris'. Navigated sequentially by the tracking camera, the photographs trace a patchy history of colonial oppression, state terror and failed revolutionary uprisings, reminding us, to use Barthes's words, that 'the age of the Photograph is also the age of revolutions, contestations, assassinations, explosions'.[54] These documentary images of war, conflict and insurrection contrast sharply with the photographs of stars posing for the camera that also adorn Veronica's walls in the indiscriminate collision of visual materials that is a trademark of Godard's aesthetics of heterogeneity.

That the image of the star is not altogether alien to a reflection on the nature of the photographic image becomes clear in the scene of the photo shoot where Godard formulates his theory of still versus moving images. To contextualise this scene it is useful to note that, in the 1950s and 1960s – that is, a period when fashion photographers such as Richard Avedon, Helmut Newton or David Bailey were at the height of their careers – the photo shoot makes its entry into cinema, figuring in iconic films centred on photography such as Stanley Donen's *Funny Face* (1957), inspired by Avedon (who provided some of the photos we see in the film), and Antonioni's *Blow-up* (1966), loosely based on the life of Swinging London photographer Bailey. Beyond their thematic preoccupation with stardom, glamour and the fashion industry, both of these films engage with the medium of film in a self-reflexive manner that resonates with Godard's variation on the photo shoot. In *Funny Face*, the manifold incorporations of photography (photography sessions, inset photographs, freeze-frames) expose film's materiality as a medium derived

Figure 5.3 The photo shoot in *Le Petit Soldat* (Jean-Luc Godard, 1963).

from photography.[55] Likewise the 'photogrammatic subtext' of *Blow-Up* makes Antonioni's film a quintessential meditation about its own medium.[56] Godard in many ways inverts the plot of Donen's film, where the bookish Jo Stockton (Audrey Hepburn), a passionate reader of existentialist philosophy, is transformed into an icon of feminine glamour by fashion photographer Dick Avery (Fred Astaire). His Veronica, behind the anodyne appearance of a photo model who seems to have few ideas about the world, turns out to be an undercover agent for the FLN – a turn of events all the more intriguing if we consider that Karina, who made her screen debut with *Le Petit soldat*, started her career as a cover girl for fashion magazines.

While in *Funny Face* photography unravels life (tying in with the film's Cinderella narrative),[57] in *Le Petit Soldat* the photo shoot insistently evokes death. Death permeates the two young people's conversation as they discover that each has violently lost close family members: Veronica her parents, shot during the war; Bruno his collaborator father, shot on Liberation Day. But the shiver of death also makes itself felt more tangibly during the photo shoot. As the character played by Karina turns to face the objective, we hear Bruno think in voice-over, 'suddenly I had the extraordinary sensation that I was photographing Death'. The photographic pose provokes the sudden shudder over what Barthes terms '*a catastrophe that has already occurred*'. 'Whether or not the subject is already dead, every photograph is this catastrophe.'[58] As an immobile representation that arrests the flow of life, for Barthes – and, in his wake, theorists like Christian Metz, Stewart and Mulvey – the photograph, unlike film, has a special kinship with death. If the person posing for the photograph senses the presence of death, it is also not lost on the photographer: 'The Photographer knows this very well, and himself fears [. . .] this death in which his gesture will embalm me.'[59] In cinema, by contrast, although there is still a photographic referent, 'this referent shifts, [. . .] it does not protest its former existence; it does not cling to me: it is not a *specter*.'[60]

Godard offers a visual demonstration of precisely this ontological difference through engaging the contrast between the deathly stillness of photography and the life-like mobility of film. Revealingly, it is when Veronica puts on a record – thus bringing yet another art form into the intermedial play – that her melancholy poses for the photographer morph into a joyous dance as she jumps up and down the bed and whirls around the flat to the sounds of a Haydn symphony. Bruno keeps pointing his camera at her, but such exuberant bounces can no longer be contained by the photographic apparatus. Only the filmic camera can do justice to this sudden eruption of life in a scene hitherto suffused by morbidity. As with painting and architecture which we discussed in previous chapters, Godard weighs up the cinematic medium against its artistic siblings in a sustained interrogation of the nature and limits of each medium. It is in the context of an implicit rivalry between media which permeates Godard's work – and which we already saw at work with regards to other art forms – that we need to consider the oft-cited definition of the *eidos* of both photography and film voiced by Bruno (whom we can take as a spokesperson for the director here) during the photo shoot: 'Photography is truth. And cinema is truth 24 times a second.'

Raymond Bellour, in a wider reflection on the role of photography in film, asks what Godard's statement may mean:

> Something impossible, since cinema hides what photography shows: each image for itself, in its naked truth, succumbing to the *défilement*. Unless cinema could, through this very *défilement*, get near this truth through various means, the safest and in any case the most striking being, one would imagine, to tell a story made of frozen moments, as soon as they have been shot [. . .]. This is what *La Jetée* does, two years after 'The Little Soldier' of the cinema revolution launched his formula.[61]

If *Le Petit Soldat* does indeed anticipate Marker's animation of photographs in *La Jetée*, as Bellour rightly points out, Godard's definition does, I believe, point to more than just the paradoxical nature of film as the spooling motion of images grounded in the stillness of the photogram. To fully understand what is implied in the director's maxim-like declaration we need, I will claim, to read it literally as well as figuratively. Cinema is truth 24× a second in the technical sense that the illusion of movement is created through the sequence of 24 photograms per second, which is standard for modern cinema projection. But, beyond this reminder of the secret presence of still images at the heart of cinematic movement, the multiplier '24×' also hints at cinema's amplification, indeed at its surpassing, of its photographic ancestor. In its capturing of the flux of time, cinema can yield *more* truth than a simple photographic image. Delivering photography of its inherent stasis, cinema potentiates the photographic image's value as an instrument for analysing and commenting upon reality.

It is pertinent to draw on Alain Badiou's conceptualisation of the interpenetration between cinema and the other arts here, first articulated at a time when the New Wave was still in its inception. In the 1957 article 'The False Movements of Cinema', later incorporated into the volume *Cinema*, the philosopher thus reflects on cinema's connection to its sister arts: 'The allusive quotation of the other arts, which is constitutive of cinema, wrests these arts away from themselves. What remains is precisely the breached frontier where an idea will have passed, an idea whose visitation the cinema, and it alone, allows.'[62] Badiou's designation of cinema as the *only* art capable of letting itself be traversed by ideas through the mediation of other art forms is strikingly close to Godard's belief in cinema as a thinking medium that dialogues with the other arts, yet which ultimately, in its capacity as a total work of art, is most apt for understanding and reflecting on reality.

For Godard, photography can always convey only a limited form of truth as it fails to adequately represent humans as thinking and feeling beings. These limitations are sharply brought into relief in *Pierrot le fou* when Marianne comments on a radio report of Viet Cong losses:

> We know nothing. They just say 115 dead. It's like photographs. They've always fascinated me. You see a still photograph of some man or other, with a caption underneath. He was a coward perhaps, or pretty smart. But at that precise instant when the photograph was taken, no one can say what he actually is, and what he was thinking exactly – about his wife maybe, or his mistress, his past, his future, or basketball. One never knows.[63]

In spite of its attempts to capture the inner lives of human beings, photography as a visual representation of outward appearances remains by necessity mute. Even propped up by written text ('a caption underneath'), it fails to give us adequate access to the *anima* of humans, to that which animates and infuses life in them. Without access to their inner thoughts and feelings, the depicted human beings remain unintelligible, rigidified in a deathly stillness even if still alive. 'Such is the Photograph: it cannot *say* what it lets us see', Barthes will say some fifteen years later in *Camera lucida*, a text that, in a curious circularity of concerns, cites Godard's own dictum: 'Not a just image, just an image.'[64]

Photography's lack as an inanimate, mute form of representation is dramatised further in *Deux ou trois choses* in a variation on the photo shoot where, as already in *Le Petit Soldat*, the filmic and the photographic intersect in the wider context of a colonial war. In the second of the film's prostitution scenes, the Vietnam correspondent John Faubus takes photos of Juliette and her friend Marianne, with the help of a light meter and a Widelux still camera. As Guzzetti notes, 'the image that the Widelux produces has proportions and perspective like those of Techniscope',[65] thus inviting a comparison between the moving cinematic image and the still image of photography. While Marianne engages in a sexual act with Faubus, Juliette meditates about the possibility of a person in Europe being able to think of another who is in Asia. Her thought processes are conveyed via six inserts of refilmed photographs of the Vietnam War, some taken from *LIFE*, others from a French magazine. The gruelling images of victims of napalm bombings, terrorised children, a wounded American soldier and Viet Cong prisoners and casualties are presented as mental pictures, yet, as a matter of fact, they were the first-hand witness accounts of Vietnam photographers like the fictional Faubus. Like the still photographs Marianne is referring to in *Pierrot le fou*, the images are mute, in stark contrast to the filmic scene into which they are inserted, which conveys Juliette's thought processes in voice-over. Guzetti comments, '[e]ven though we cannot know what the people in those photographs are thinking, we do know Juliette's thoughts and know them, moreover, partly through the inserted photographs. It is with respect to the possibility of such knowledge that film and photography differ.'⁶⁶

Thus, as in *Le Petit Soldat*, by pitting the photographer against the film-maker, and the mute, still image against the multi-track, kinetic medium film, Godard points to photography's ontological limitations as compared to its successor cinema. What is more, in a recurrent trope, photographing is linked to the act of killing by way of the non-diegetic sound that accompanies the Vietnam photographs reminiscent of both the firing of a machine gun and the clicking of a camera, interrupted by Marianne's exclamation 'America über alles!' If the analogy between taking photos and shooting is implied by aural means in this scene, it is spelled out in a voice-over commentary towards the end of *Deux ou trois choses*: 'There is no need of fortuitous events in order to photograph and kill people.' In the prostitution scene and beyond, Godard plays on what Susan Sontag has identified as two of the most ubiquitous fantasies surrounding the photographic camera: its symbolic function as both phallus and gun. Even though, Sontag writes,

> the camera/gun does not kill [. . .] there is something predatory in the act of taking a picture. To photograph people is to violate them, by seeing them as they never see themselves, by having knowledge of them they can never have; it turns people into objects that can be symbolically possessed. Just as the camera is a sublimation of the gun, to photograph someone is a sublimation of murder – a soft murder, appropriate to a sad, frightened time.⁶⁷

Within the wider analogy between prostitution, colonial oppression and consumer capitalism that Godard weaves in *Deux ou trois choses*, photography sides with the oppressor, symbolised by the American war correspondent Faubus. Substituting for the sexual act that is withheld from view, the photographs denouncing the atrocities of the Vietnam War point to a similarly dehumanising attitude towards women, reflected in Faubus's careless remark that 'a dead Vietcong costs the American treasury a million dollars. President Johnson could get himself twenty thousands girls like these two here for the same price', followed by his putting his still camera to his eye. In the extended analogy, the photo shoot, colonial oppression and the male act of taking sexual pleasure (in French slang 'tirer un coup', literally 'to fire a shot') intersect in a wider reflection on symbolic or actual acts of killing.

If, according to Godard's implied reasoning, photography's morbid arresting of life's flow makes it complicit with objectification, how about the film camera? Unlike in the later *La Chinoise* where the camera makes a self-reflexive appearance, in *Deux ou trois choses* it remains invisible, its own act of shooting hidden from view. Yet, it in turn becomes the object of an aggression when the child Christophe (Christophe Bourseiller) fires his toy gun directly at the audience, that is, implicitly, at the camera filming him. Despite their shared status as lens-based media, the director seems to exempt the cinema from the conjunction of violence in which he implies photography.[68] Presenting the two media as essentially different forms of apprehending the world, in spite of their shared technology, Godard designates cinema as the richer, but also more empathetic medium: where film endeavours to capture reality in its complex interplay between the visibility of outward phenomena and the inner – cognitive and affective – life of human beings conveyed by visual and aural means, photography turns the world into a morbid spectacle to be possessed and consumed. Such boundaries, as we will see now, will be undone by the hybrid form of the photo-film, the New Wave's most direct crossing-over between the arts.

FIGURES OF INTERSTITIALITY: THE 'CINEMATOGRAM'

Binding cinema to its parent medium of photography, freeze-frames, refilmed photographs and other photographic evocations serve to draw attention to the photogrammatic presence in the very materiality of film. As Stewart argues, the photogram makes a 'tacit appearance' in, essentially, two ways: it is either alluded to through a 'quoted' photograph or in the form of the stop-action image (i.e. the freeze-frame).[69] Yet, if all the films we have discussed so far in one way or another probe the qualities of the cinematic versus the photographic image, none of them fundamentally challenges the traditional assumption that cinema is characterised by movement while photography is the medium of stillness. It befell another filmmaker-cum-photographer (and also writer), Chris Marker, to unsettle the still/moving binary in the legendary *La Jetée* (1962), his science fiction about a time travel experiment constructed almost entirely from still images. Together with Marker's *Si j'avais quatre dromadaires* (*If I had Four Dromedaries*, 1966) and Varda's *Saluts les Cubains* (1963), which will be discussed in the final section, *La Jetée* explodes the traditional media boundaries of film, transforming our understanding of what cinema is.[70]

According to Marker's own account, he started experimenting with the animation of fixed images when he was a boy thanks to an optical tool called 'Pathéorama', with which he made a first film based on drawings of his cat. Showing the results to a school friend, he was quickly 'sobered up' by the latter's reminder that 'cinema is images that move, stupid. You can't make a film with still images.'[71] Thirty years later, *La Jetée* was to challenge this standard understanding of cinema as moving images, inaugurating a new *entre-deux* at the interstices between photography and film. As an experiment in dissolving traditional media boundaries, it follows earlier crossings into the domain of photography in *Lettre de Sibérie* (*Letter from Siberia*, 1958), a film which combines still photographs and animation sequences, and *Coréennes* (1959), a book composed of still photographs and text which Marker presented as a 'short film in a different medium'.[72] That film can take on many forms and, concomitantly, that traditional genre labels may be restrictive is made clear from the outset in *La Jetée*'s genre-bending subtitle 'photo-roman' ('photo-novel'), a term normally used to describe the novelisations of film that were popular between the 1940s and 1960s.[73]

La Jetée is often described as a film composed of photographs, though, in fact, it is actually made up of quite a variety of still images ranging from 'frames extracted from filmed footage' to 'documentary photos, archival images and staged narrative shots'.[74] Thus, even the materials on which it is based are hybrid, some of the still images having been derived from actual film, while the others are photographs in the strict sense of the word. As in a more traditional film, the images are edited into a narrative flow with classic cinematic transitions (in essence, a variation of straight cuts, dissolves and fades). The choice of images, pace, type and speed of the transition, combined with the overlaid sound (both diegetic and non-diegetic), endow individual sequences with their distinct rhythm and emotional charge. If editing is the principle source of movement in the film, its kinematic effect also results from the narrative organisation of sequences which, Catherine Lupton points out, 'are broken down into the recognisable patterns of classical narrative cinema, with establishing shots, eyeline matches, shot-counter-shot, close-ups and so forth, all working to create a sense of narrative coherence and momentum'.[75]

To give an example, when the protagonist (Davos Hanich) is submitted to his first time travelling experiment, the still images meticulously trace the different steps of the medical intervention, from the doctor's preparation of an injection, his ligaturing and disinfection of the 'patient's' arm to the moment when the needle pierces the skin, followed by the man's ensuing agitation and pain, culminating in a series of close-ups of his teeth biting the strings of his hammock. The progression of the action across distinct images, matched by the cinematic syntax, whispered dialogue and sound of the protagonist's accelerating heartbeat, as well as the omniscient narrator's (Jean Négroni) voice-over commentary, all contribute to the sequence's genuinely cinematic feel. Indeed, all through the film, the still images bristle with such vibrancy that Philippe Dubois proposes the term 'cinematogram' to account for their singular combination of stillness and movement, instantaneity and duration.[76]

As the medium of the 'it has been', photography is the ideal platform for Marker's science-fiction about a journey into the past from the vantage point of the future. Announced in the intertitles that align the film with both the silent era and the novel genre, *La Jetée* 'is the story of a man, marked by an image from his childhood': the image of a man collapsing on the jetty of Orly airport under the eyes of a woman. Set after the nuclear destruction of Paris during World War III, it recounts the time travelling experiments to which a prisoner of war is submitted by a group of scientists, who hope to access vital resources and energy through a journey into the future that is to be made possible by a preliminary return into the past. In a contaminated world where space is no longer accessible, their aim, as explained by the chief scientist, is 'to summon the Past and Future to the aid of the Present'. *La Jetée*'s dystopian plot, as several critics have noted,[77] is haunted by the trauma of the Nazi concentration camps (alluded to by way of the German dialogue of the doctors-scientists that appears all the more menacing for remaining untranslated), while also, more implicitly, giving voice to the outrage intellectuals and artists like Marker felt about the widespread use of torture during both the Indochina and the Algerian Wars (where, ironically, the French army used interrogation methods derived from the Gestapo). Over its apocalyptic images hovers the collective fear of nuclear annihilation post-Hiroshima and Nagasaki, which was to culminate in the Cuban missile crisis some eight months after the film's release.

In characteristic New Wave fashion, *La Jetée* doubles up as a fiction and a self-reflexive meditation about cinema, but here it is not via a film-within-the film or play-within-the-film structure (as, for instance, in *Le Mépris* or *L'Amour fou* discussed previously) that cinema contemplates itself, but, rather, through a return to its technological ancestor photography. The film's figurative dimension as an 'allegory of the cinematic apparatus'[78] is hinted at in the stated setting of the time travelling experiments under the Palais de Chaillot, an iconic Paris building which, in the early 1960s, was the storage space of Henri Langlois's Cinémathèque – that temple of cinema often referred to as the birthplace of the New Wave. The casting of the head of the Belgian Cinémathèque, Jacques Ledoux, in the role of chief scientist further emphasises the film's allegorical character,[79] suggesting that what is at stake here is above all an experiment in visuality. Moreover, in Marker's dense web of overlaid (at times conflicting) references, Sarah Cooper explains, the setting under the Palais de Chaillot harks back to the French occupation: 'The passages were used by members of the French resistance, and, in keeping with the photo-roman's blending of opposites (movement-stasis, life-death), the space is inhabited here by torturers whispering in German, thus pitting the resonance of resistance against the forces of occupation.'[80]

Commentators on the film tend to accept that the locations mentioned in voice-over correspond to the images we see. However, in a further complication of the relationship between word and image, the photos of the underground tunnels – just like those of the destruction of Paris in the preceding sequence (most of which are in fact archival photographs of other bombed-out cities) – are not what they purport to be. Far from depicting the subterranean galleries beneath the Palais de Chaillot, the second photograph of the subterranean space does in fact show a famous mythological site: the trapezoidal passage that archaeologists have identified as the entrance of the Sibyl's cave in Cumae, the ancient Greek settlement close to today's Naples. According to Greco-Roman mythology, the Cumean Sibyl, the most famous of the many sibyls of the ancient world, presided over the Apollonian oracle in an underground temple built by Daedalus. It is here that, under ritual possession by the god who brutally holds command over her body and mind, she is said to have pronounced her prophecies. Virgil describes her torments thus:

> Rather, as if Bacchus ruled her, she rages around in the cavern, hoping to buck the huge god from her breast. But he wearies her froth-flecked mouth even more, as he tames her heart's wildness, and shapes her with pressure. [. . .] She rolls up the truth in obscurity's riddles, rumbling the cavern with echoes. Apollo shakes hard on the bridle's reins as she raves, and he's raking her breast with his spurs to control her.[81]

In the *Aeneid*, the Sibyl prophesies further hideous wars to Aeneas. In the Christian tradition, she is regarded as a prophet of the last judgement and the coming of Christ, as conveyed in the opening lines of the thirteenth-century *Dies Irae*: 'Dies irae, dies illa,/ solvet saeclum in favilla,/teste David cum Sibylla' (That day of wrath, that dreadful day, shall heaven and earth in ashes lay, as David and the Sibyl say).

Substituted for the tunnels under the Palais de Chaillot, the photograph of the Sibyl's cave weaves a complex subterranean network of references that tie in with the film's resounding themes of apocalypse, torture and prophecy (even providing a link to the central locus of the airport and the bird imagery that traverses the film through the figure of Daedalus, the architect who flew with his own wings).[82] Acting as a bridge between the realm of the living and that of the dead – in the *Aeneid*, she accompanies Aeneas to Hades to help him find his deceased father Anchises – the Sibyl is a figure of liminality just like the protagonist of *La Jetée* who lives his own death twice over. On an allegorical level, she is a perfect figuration of the film's interstitial position between the oft-evoked deathliness of photographic stillness and the semblance of life created by cinematic motion. If Marker himself has claimed that the film is a

Figure 5.4 Figuring liminality: the Sibyl's cave in *La Jetée* (Chris Marker, 1962).

remake of Hitchcock's *Vertigo* (1958) – alluded to in several references[83] – the Cumean Sibyl also evokes another film generally acknowledged to be one of the inspirations for the New Wave: Rossellini's *Viaggio in Italia* (*Journey to Italy*, 1954), where a visit to the Sibyl's cave forms part of Katherine's (Ingrid Bergman) journey of self-discovery.

Inversely, the next photograph, with its depiction of rounded interiors and an archive-like storage space, conjures up the Bibliothèque Nationale, France's national library whose workings had been scrutinised by fellow Groupe Rive Gauche director Alain Resnais in his documentary short *Toute la mémoire du monde* (*All the World's Memory*, 1956) some six years earlier. Intriguingly, both Marker and Varda are listed as collaborators in the title credits (the former as 'Chris and Magic Marker') of Resnais's film. Varda can be glimpsed among other anonymous readers; Marker is referenced through a fake book in the 'Petite Planète' series of travel photo-books he edited at Éditions du Seuil, which is traced all the way through the library's complex processes from initial receipt to shelving.[84] Like *La Jetée*, Resnais's reflection on the storage of memory is laden with references to the Shoah (notably in the recurrent anthropomorphisation of the books as 'prisoners' and their stamped numbers recalling the tattoos of Holocaust victims, a trope which also resurfaces in the numbers that appear intermittently in *La Jetée*), to such an extent that Steven Ungar can read *Toute la mémoire du monde* as a supplement to Resnais's Holocaust documentary, *Nuit et brouillard* (*Night and Fog*, 1956).[85]

Layered with interconnected references ranging from classical mythology to the horrors of the Nazi death camps and torture in Indochina and Algeria,

La Jetée presents memory as a subterranean activity where the personal and the collective, individual trauma and shared tragedy intersect in a painful process of conjuring up the past. The protagonist's first images of remembrance, Lupton notes, 'have the fixed, elegiac, self-contained quality commonly associated with photographs'.[86] The voice-over designates them as 'a real bedroom, real children, real birds, real cats, real graves'. As an 'emanation of *past reality*', to use Barthes's term, they have the constative, authenticating function that the philosopher assigns to photography's double conjugation of reality and pastness.[87] These images of the man's personal recollection intermingle with those of statues in 'that museum which is perhaps that of his memory'. In a variation of the trope of stillness, their missing limbs or dented surface visually inscribe the passing of time.

In the early stages of the experiment, the photographs capture isolated moments of remembrance as a series of photographic takes. We see through the eyes of the protagonist aligned with the still camera lens, but we cannot see him. He only appears in the images of his own memory and these memories only coalesce into a narrative after one of the scientists declares jubilantly: 'Jetzt habe ich ihn soweit. Die Hälfte von ihm ist hier, die andere Hälfte ist in der Vergangenheit' (Now I have him right where we want him. One half of him is here, the other half is in the past). Like Gilles whose work we discussed previously, Marker exhibits a distinctly Proustian sensitivity in this depiction of involuntary memory as a fusion between past and present. It comes as no surprise, then, that the narrator's comment on the man and the woman sharing 'une confiance à l'état pur' (a pure trust) echoes Proust's famous description of involuntary memory as the experience of 'un peu de temps à l'état pur' (a fragment of pure time) from *Time Regained*. Some thirty years later, in *Immemory* (1997), a work at the intersection between Proust and Hitchcock, Marker will 'claim for the image the humility and powers of a madeleine',[88] referring once more to the resurrectional power that Proust assigns to the memory of the senses.

The collision between past and present in the workings of memory is effected most strikingly in the oft-commented scene that culminates in the film's only fragment of motion. As a series of close-ups of the sleeping woman (Hélène Chatelain) dissolve into one another at an accelerated pace, their overlap at first simulates and eventually becomes movement when, for a few seconds, the woman opens her eyes in a genuine moving-image shot. During this brief eruption of cinema into the stillness of photography, as Lupton puts it beautifully, 'it is the film that seems to wake up as she does'.[89] In this film of origins, in other words, we experience something akin to the birth of cinema.

Stewart offers an astute analysis of this 'cinematically "realised"' moment:

> Just before the photographic encroaches in this way upon the cinematic, the separate images have grown so nearly coincident with each other that they narrow to that differential spread [. . .] necessary to the process of 'animation'. Even before the filmic achieves its own cinematicity in a brief stretch of 'moving pictures,' then, its mechanisms have been rehearsed and asserted in what we might call again a pressure toward cinema.[90]

In a similar effect at the end of the film, when the man attempts to join the woman on the jetty of Orly airport, the rapid editing of images depicting him running towards her create a jerky simulation of movement. But in the film's narrative loop, his flight – that is, on an allegorical level, his attempt to break free of the confines of photographic time, and, thus, of the past[91] – is brutally halted as he is shot by one of the prison guards. In an inversion of the earlier waking-up sequence, the moment of his falling to his death is not conveyed through a motion-shot, but a series of still photographs. While both sequences play on the traditional association of photography with death and of cinema with life, they also further blur the boundary between stillness and movement by, on the one hand, showing photograms on the cusp of becoming a moving image, and, on the other, by decomposing movement into its discrete steps in an effect that recalls the experiments of Muybridge, one of the pioneers in the photographic study of motion.[92] As critics have noted, the image of the dying man around which the whole film revolves echoes Robert Capa's famous photograph of a Republican militiaman felled by a bullet, 'The Falling Soldier' (1936).[93] Capturing the moment in which the soldier, struck by enemy fire, collapses, his raised right arm letting go of his rifle, this iconic photo of the Spanish Civil War owes its reputation in part to its troubling suggestion of movement (indeed so striking is the composition that there is an ongoing controversy as to whether or not the photo may in fact have been staged).

In a seminal reflection on photographic and cinematic time, Peter Wollen has argued that *La Jetée*'s use of stills 'is to demonstrate that movement is not a necessary feature of film'.[94] Inversely, one may add, the film also challenges the preconception that photography is of necessity still. In a quintessential figuration of intermediality, *La Jetée* dissolves the border between the photographic and the cinematic, endowing each medium with the qualities that are traditionally associated with the other. In the path from all the photos that make up the story and the *one* photo that traverses the film, Bellour writes, '*La Jetée* seems to cover the entire breach opened up in cinema from its beginnings (if not from its origin) by the immobile presence of the photograph (both as body and as idea)'.[95]

ANIMATING PHOTOGRAPHY: DANCING BODIES, HYBRID FORMS

La Jetée is generally considered as the prototype of a number of films using stills that emerged in the 1960s and 1970s, most importantly Varda's *Salut les Cubains* and Marker's own *Si j'avais quatre dromadaires*, but also, in the US, George Lucas's photo-montage *Look at Life* (1965), produced for a course in animation while he was still a student at film school, and Alan Pakula's political thriller *The Parallax View* (1974). While *La Jetée* did of course prove hugely influential for any director working with photographs, its heterogeneous use of still images as well as its fictional mode distinguish it from Varda's and Marker's lesser-known photo-based documentaries with which we shall conclude this chapter. Made at an interval of some three years by directors who were close personal friends as well as fellow members of the Rive Gauche group, *Salut les Cubains* and *Si j'avais quatre dromadaires* are so closely connected through both their technique and their overlapping thematic concerns that they appear almost like a diptych, inviting us to read them in parallel.

Both Varda's exuberant portrait of post-revolutionary Cuba and Marker's poetic meditation on photography, society and socialism are travelogues based on still photographs. Varda took 4000 pictures, of which she selected 1500 for the film, on a trip to Cuba during the winter of 1962–3, that is, exactly four years after the overthrow of pro-American dictator Fulgencio Batista by the Cuban Revolution. The restless traveller Marker based *Si j'avais quatre dromadaires* 'on a series of photos taken just about everywhere in the world between 1956 and 1966'.[96] For both films, the photographs were filmed on an animation stand ('banc-titre') – that is, a device with a mounted camera used to film written or photographic documents or make animation – and both employ a dialogical format whereby different people comment on the images as if they were leafing through a photo album, offering different perspectives on the on-screen representations. In *Salut les Cubains*, the voice-over commentary spoken by Michel Piccoli tends to rehearse clichés (in the context of photography it is worth reminding ourselves that, in French, 'cliché' means both 'photo' and 'platitude'), while Varda offers a more personal, nuanced point of view; in *Si j'avais quatre dromadaires*, the photographer's somewhat utopian or over-idealistic positions are challenged by his two friends (the voice-over commentaries are delivered by Pierre Vaneck, Catherine Le Couey and Nicolas Yumatov). Furthermore, the two films use a technique that Marker introduced, but used very sparingly in *La Jetée*, most notably in the first photograph of Orly airport where the camera mounted on the animation stand moves transversally across the image until it fully comes into view. In *Salut les Cubains* and *Si j'avais quatre dromadaires*, the camera frequently scans, pans or zooms in or out to accentuate specific details, thus endowing the still photographs with movement. Beyond these formal similarities, these overlooked cinematic gems are linked by a shared desire for more compassionate forms of living and governance, at a pivotal point in the history of the Cold War – that is, after the Soviet invasion of Hungary in 1956 and the Khrushchev report of the same year denouncing the dictatorship and cult of personality of Stalin – when many leftist intellectuals and artists were compelled to reconsider their belief in Communism. As we will see, both Marker and Varda look to post-revolutionary Cuba as an example of a more human, impassioned form of socialism. In looking for alternative political and social models, their films trace bold new itineraries for a culturally diverse, connected world.

Although it was made three years after *Salut les Cubains*, our discussion will begin with Marker's *Si j'avais quatre dromadaires*, which is closer to *La Jetée* in terms of its editing and relation to photography, thus making it an ideal bridge between the two films. Lupton points out that the film constitutes some kind of retrospective of the photographs that Marker had amassed over a period of some ten years, 'but not in the usual form of an exhibition or book'.[97] Its literary references to Apollinaire's poem 'Le Dromadaire' – whose last line inspired the film's title – and to Cocteau's ballet *Les Mariés de la Tour Eiffel* align the film with an avant-gardist intermedial tradition: the modernist poet and art critic Apollinaire laid out the terms for a new relationship between word and image in his visual poetry, while Cocteau, an intermedial artist par excellence, criss-crossed between literature, theatre, painting and film. Marker also references his own *La Jetée*, evoked towards the end of the film in a series of dissolves simulating the smile of a woman that recall the waking-up sequence from the earlier film (though there is no genuine motion shot here).

A photo-film based on Marker's travels to some twenty-six countries, *Si j'avais quatre dromadaires* constitutes what, with Giuliana Bruno, one may call an 'atlas of life'.[98] Following the loosely associative pattern that characterises most of Marker's documentary work, it traces human experience across geographical borders and political fault lines, revealing commonalities between highly divergent countries and cultures. In its emphasis on Russia, China, North Korea, Cuba and the socialist Scandinavian countries, the film is true to Marker's left-leaning convictions. It is, however, by no means naive about the atrocities committed in the name of Communism, faced head-on in an extended sequence on the shortcomings of the 'two popular Revolutions' – that is to say, the Russian Revolution that led to the rise of the Soviet Union and the Chinese Communist Revolution that resulted in the establishment of the People's Republic of China. Poised after the Sino-Soviet split (the breaking of political relations between the USSR and the PRC that began in the late 1950s), the film interrogates a world where 'socialism is no longer the place of a single faith and fraternity', seeking to salvage central values such as compassion, solidarity and generosity from an increasingly fractured Communist ideal. Imbued by an internationalist spirit, Marker privileges moments of encounter: between the photographer and his photographed subjects, but also between people and cultures, as shown for instance in the images of the 1959 American National exhibition in Moscow, which for the first time brought Russians face-to-face with American consumer culture and contemporary art.

Marker's world is one that is connected, subject to constant exchange despite the tensions and divisions of the Cold War. It is a world where different cultures touch upon and interpenetrate one another rather like the photographs stitched together by the montage. In its endeavour to trace connections and exchanges between geographically distant and culturally diverse countries, Marker's project can be likened to what the Martinican philosopher and poet Édouard Glissant calls the 'Tout-monde' (Whole-world). In *Traité du Tout-Monde*, Glissant thus defines this seminal concept of his thought:

> I call Whole-world our universe as it changes and continues through its exchanges and, at the same time, our vision of it. The totality-world in its physical diversity and the representations that it inspires in us: we can no longer sing, tell, or work in the suffering of our only place, without plunging into the imaginary of this totality.[99]

Where Glissant, in his writings, develops a 'poetics of relation' that unearths the interpenetration of cultures and imaginaries while never losing sight of difference,[100] so Marker, in the cinematic medium – here via the intermediary of photography – makes connections across diverse countries and cultures, emphasising what unites rather than divides us in a common humanity. This relational vision, prescient of the Whole-world, counters any totalitarian or imperialist structures of domination and control.

The director finds a form for exploring relation in the city symphony genre, referenced in the first part of the film as 'the type of film that takes you from one dawn to the next saying things like it's six o'clock all over the world'. Triggered by a repetition of 'it's six o'clock', for some four minutes, the montage constructs its own city symphony as photos of the four corners of the world unfurl before our eyes, commented by the voice-over. Yet, where the city symphony films of the 1920s offered a kaleidoscopic portrait of daily life within one city (though Vertov famously shot *Man with a Movie Camera* in three different locations), here it is the whole world that surges in the dance of synchronous images. Though not followed through in any systematic way – which would be anathema to Marker's associative thinking

– the city symphony provides a pattern for exploring multiplicity and diversity beyond the confines of one urban space or traditional centre.

The film opens on a sustained theoretical meditation on photography that informs its thematic preoccupations. Like Godard in *Deux ou trois choses*, Marker plays on the analogy between taking a picture and shooting, but, in sharp contrast, insists on the photograph's preserving rather than annihilating powers: 'The photograph is the hunt, it is the instinct of the hunt without the desire to kill. It is the hunt of angels . . . You track, you aim, you shoot and – click! – instead of killing someone, you make them eternal.' At first, such a postulation seems to bring Marker closer to Bazin than to Barthes (who, as we have seen, associates photography with death). Yet, in reality, the director doubly refutes one of the central paradigms of Bazin's 'Ontology' essay we cited at the outset of this chapter: 'photography does not create eternity as art does, it embalms time.'[101] Unlike Bazin, who fails to apprehend photography in its artistic dimension (though he does not deny the photographer creativity) concentrating instead on its indexicality, Marker not only considers the medium as a way of creating eternity, but as an art *precisely* because it does not engage reality in a merely mimetic relationship. For Bazin, 'the photographic image is the object itself'.[102] For Marker, by contrast,

> [t]here is life, there is its double. Photography belongs to the world of the double. By getting closer to faces you have the impression of getting closer to their lives and their deaths as humans, while you get closer to their lives and deaths as images.

In his conception of photography as essentially an image, Marker thus ultimately reveals himself as closer to Barthes, who developed his theory of the constructedness of discourse (including artistic representations) in seminal texts such as *Mythologies* and *S/Z*. Where for Bazin, the aesthetic quality of photography lies 'in its power to lay bare the realities',[103] for Marker, as suggested in the voice-over of *Si j'avais quatre dromadaires*, the photographic impulse stems from a desire to 'bring the world together, reconcile it, make all the time zones level'. In essence, then, what we have here are two opposing conceptions of the photographic image, one realist (favouring mise-en-scène), the other modernist (favouring montage).

In *Si j'avais quatre dromadaires*, the photographic medium is self-reflexively foregrounded from the outset through the repeated figuration of a camera in the still photos: be it in the initial zoom into what appears to be a photographic lens in the first image, the presence of an ancient photographic device propped up in front of classical ruins, or of a Rolleiflex which we suppose to be Marker's own in subsequent photographs. In the voice-over commentary, photography is conceptualised as, essentially, a relation of looking. If the sculptor gives eternity to 'a certain face with a certain look', the photographer explains, the photographer in turn 'gives eternity to his own look on this look', while the spectator, the friend elaborates further, 'looks at the photo which looks'. In this triangular relation, then, three looks intersect: that of the photographer, of the photographed subject(s) and of the spectator. The second look (that of the subject), Lupton points out, is particularly prominent in the film 'through Marker's fondness for images of people who are themselves looking very intently at something'.[104]

Endowing his photographed subjects with the power to 'look back', Marker privileges a reciprocal relationship of looking, as is evidenced in recurrent portraits of people looking directly at the camera or interacting with the photographer, such as, for instance, in the photo of a Cuban hairdresser pointing his razor at Marker (whom we imagine behind the photographic camera) in a gesture of confrontation. Looking, in *Si j'avais quatre dromadaires*, becomes a crucial sign of openness to the world, a willingness to establish a relationship with the other, an engagement that can also take the form of resistance. Not everyone, the photographer sustains, is endowed with the look: 'There's no American look, no Scandinavian look, but there is a Black look, a Jewish look, a Russian look.' While, for Marker, the inner flame that is exteriorised in the look burns strong among the oppressed and the underprivileged, it disappears with material wealth: 'the light that shines among the poor [. . .] goes out among the rich'.

Imbued with a deep concern for what Frantz Fanon, in a colonial context, calls 'the wretched of the earth' (a term inspired by the opening lyrics of the left-wing 'International'), the film ends on the prophetic vision of a more harmonious, caring way of living. Over a montage of still images of couples tenderly interlocked and of animals showing signs of fondness, the voice-over heralds the advent of a more compassionate era:

> There is already a 'maquis', a clandestinity of happiness, a Sierra Maestra of tenderness. There is something which is advancing, through us, in spite of us, thanks to us when we have grace. And which announces for we do not know when the survival of the most loved.

References to the French resistance (evoked in the term 'maquis') and the Cuban Revolution (summoned through the Sierra Maestra where the revolutionaries around Castro fought their guerrilla war) insert this advance into a tradition of heroic struggle against oppression and injustice. But in its cross-cutting of images of humans and animals linked by a shared gestural language of care, the final montage also, crucially, moves away from the anthropocentric worldview that dominates cinematic representations up to this day.[105] No longer making a difference between humans and animals as regards their capacity for affection, the film ends on the photograph of a chimpanzee tenderly stroking a companion, put into motion in a combined tracking and zooming movement of the camera. In its fusion between the photographic and the cinematic, *Si j'avais quatre dromadaires* becomes an ideal vehicle for promoting encounters that transcend traditional boundaries and hierarchies, be they geographical, social, anthropological or medial. By way of an intermedial aesthetics that favours touch and encounter, the film imbues the photographic image, in the words of Cooper, 'with the breath of life that moves forward in time'.[106]

Turning now to Varda, we will see a shared set of concerns conveyed in a hybrid photo-filmic form, even if her *Salut les Cubains* is more overtly political. In her capacity as a professional photographer, Varda was initially invited by the ICAIC (Cuban Center for Cinematographic Art and Industry) to make a photobook to raise greater awareness of the Revolution, but decided to make a documentary based on photographs instead so as not to be encumbered by heavy equipment in her encounter with Cuba and its inhabitants. Travelling to the island shortly after the Revolution, she was one of many French visitors, most prominently Simone de Beauvoir and Sartre, Anne and Gérard Philipe, Henri Alleg and Charles Bettelheim, not forgetting Marker himself, whose *Cuba Sí* (1961) was still banned by the French authorities as she was preparing her film.[107] At the beginning of the 1960s, François Hourmant explains, Cuba became a 'new political mythology' celebrated by countless intellectuals, first and foremost Sartre, who gave an enthusiastic account of the Cuban Revolution in a series of articles entitled 'Hurricane over Sugar' (published in the popular daily *France-Soir* between June and July 1960). Aided by the charisma of its young leaders, the Revolution 'symbolised the struggle for emancipation of oppressed people at the very moment that the imperialism-third-world binary replaced the bourgeois-proletariat couple'.[108] Inspiring anti-colonial struggles across Africa and Latin America, Cuba enthralled leftist thinkers with its 'tropical' variant of socialism, giving rise to a new romanticism 'fuelled by idealism and passion, and inspired by the youth and brotherhood, the equality and sensuality of the body, the vitality and euphoria that surged from the island'.[109]

A 'committed testimony' made for didactic purposes,[110] *Salut les Cubains* reverberates with the vibrancy and enthusiasm of the early years after the Revolution – a time when what Giuliana Bruno calls Cuba's 'utopian texture' had not yet faded.[111] Varda herself has described the film as 'a didactic documentary treated like an entertainment', 'a giant conga, a giant cha-cha-cha to the rhythm of which Fidel Castro, Wilfredo Lam, Benny Moré and peasants and militia women and children and even cats danced and lived'.[112] She draws a quirkily sympathetic portrait of the island, rehearsing, as one would expect

Figure 5.5 Benny Moré dancing in *Salut les Cubains* (Agnès Varda, 1963).

from an official commission, the courageous struggle and achievements of the Revolution (notably the campaign against illiteracy, agrarian reform and gender equality), but also offering a refreshingly personal commentary. The film's main premise is playfully announced in the first minutes: the forward march of the Cuban people, the voice-over declares, 'is also a dance'. What is at stake, then, is to capture the Cuban movement 'in both senses of the word': as a political struggle, to be sure, but also, more literally, as that particularly sensuous way of moving which, for Varda, embodies the essence of Cuban culture. Looking at Cuba through this double lens, the film conjoins revolutionary politics and the dance in a celebration of an alternative kind of socialism, anchored, as it were, in the sensuality of the body.

Varda's upbeat portrait of the island is preceded by a prologue filmed in Paris in June 1963, during an exhibition marking the tenth anniversary of the start of the Revolution. As the camera follows a Cuban band around Saint-Germain-des-Prés, Varda herself as well as several of her friends come into view, among them Joris Ivens, Alain Resnais and Chris Marker, seen in the process of filming. While presenting the director as part of a 'family of cinema', the prologue also serves to align *Salut les Cubains* with earlier films on the island by Ivens and Marker.[113] On a formal level, its repeated use of freeze-frames combined with the triple focus on photographs from the exhibition (which will reappear later in the film), the musical performance and its filmic recording introduce a dialogue between photography, music and film that will constitute the defining syntax of the film.

The music for the film Varda brought back from Cuba provided the structure for the film's editing. Varda first selected photographs for filming on the animation stand, organising individual photos into sequences, and numbering and clipping them on preparatory sheets together with her comments. To synchronise with the images, the music was transformed into an optical sound strip, which can be measured in images (i.e. 24 images per second for a 35mm film), thus allowing her to calculate the number of images, following the rhythm of the music.[114] Based on the numbered photos and the number of images per photo, the animation stand operator made a 35mm film, after which she fine-tuned the duration of the images and of the voice-over commentaries. Varda explains that, from the outset, she shot photos as a series, 'knowing that these nearly identical photos would form a shot that would have been filmed continuously, a little jolted'.[115] This purposeful shooting of sequences in view of their animation, as well as the synchronisation of the images with the music, she asserts, distinguishes her documentary from Marker's *La Jetée*, making it closer to the animations of the Lodz Film School and the experimental works of Walerian Borowczyk and Jan Lenica, even though she did not intend to make an experimental film.[116]

Far from merely supporting the voice-over commentary, the photographs that underpin *Salut les Cubains* are the work of a professional with a sharp eye for composition, framing and mise-en-scène.[117] Some images, such as her iconic photo of Castro 'with stone wings', taken in the garden of a Havana restaurant, are held longer for viewers to fully appreciate their composition. Others, thanks to rapid editing, give the impression of movement. In a series of animations that punctuate the film, we see volunteers cutting the sugar cane, villagers undulating to the sounds of a rumba or the 'King of rhythm' Benny Moré doing a little song and dance routine move jerkily to Cuban rhythms. In their emphasis on popular music and dance, these animated choreographies intriguingly recall Bazin's analysis of the ways in which cinema was intuited long before its invention. In the landmark 'The Myth of Total Cinema', Bazin cites a passage from Villiers de l'Isle-Adam's *L'Eve future* in which the writer imagines mobile images two years before Edison began his research on animated photography:

> the vision, its transparent flesh miraculously photographed in color and wearing a spangled costume, danced a kind of popular Mexican dance. Her movements had the flow of life itself, thanks to the process of successive photography which can retain six minutes of movement on microscopic glass, which is subsequently reflected by means of a powerful lampascope.[118]

From today's perspective, Varda's take on Cuban life may seem somewhat exoticising, yet in its emphasis on cultural hybridity as one of the constituting features of modern Cuba her portrayal remains highly perceptive. Mindful of the different waves of colonisation and, in particular, of the island's place in the transatlantic slave trade, *Salut les Cubains* traces the African, Spanish and even French influences (through the French planters who took refuge in Cuba after the Haitian Revolution) that have shaped Cuba's diverse musical and dance styles, from rumba to tumba, conga, cha-cha-cha and danzón. The film is also attentive to the mixed ancestry of the Cuban population, with its Spanish and other European, African, Asian, Haitian and Jamaican origins as well as to its syncretism of African religions and Catholicism. This cultural and ethnic diversity, as Varda shows, finds expression in the hybrid artistic forms of Cuban artists, from Nicolás Guillén's 'incorporation of black rhythms into Spanish poetry' to Wilfredo Lam's tropical surrealism, shaped by both European modernism and his Chinese and Afro-Cuban heritage. Indeed, it is from this transculturation, rather than from any mythical unitary origin, that the island draws its creative energy and vitality. Perhaps the most durable message that emerges from *Salut les Cubains*, especially in light of the subsequent crumbling of the revolutionary ideal as the Castro regime took an authoritarian turn, is this celebration of *métissage* (the intermingling and cross-fertilisation of cultures)[119] that permeates the film – not only on a thematic level, but in its own hybrid form in-between photography, film and dance.

The last animated sequence of filmmaker Sarita Gómez dancing a cha-cha-cha with technicians and actors from the ICAIC, interspersed with earlier images of political leaders, children, artists and ordinary people, invites the whole of Cuba into a final, democratic dance. No longer steeped in melancholy or associated with death, far from embalming or arresting time, these exuberant images celebrating the island's joyous march into the future cement a new ontology of the photographic image where still and moving, past and present, animated and static are no longer opposites – a *kinematic* revolution!

Notes

1. Rohmer, *Le Celluloïd et le marbre*, p. 17.
2. Godard, *Histoire(s) du cinéma*, vol. 1, p. 197.
3. Bazin, 'The ontology of the photographic image', p. 16.
4. Ibid. pp. 13–14.
5. Ibid. p. 15.
6. Ibid. p. 14.
7. This is my own translation as Hugh Gray's 'the cinema is objectivity in time' (Bazin, 'The ontology of the photographic image', p. 14) is quite far from the original.
8. Bazin, 'The ontology of the photographic image', pp. 14–15.
9. For the relationship between photography and cinema see in particular Stewart,

Between Film and Screen; Bellour, *Between-The-Images*; Mulvey, *Death 24× a Second*; Beckman and Ma (eds), *Still Moving*; Campany, *Photography and Cinema*; Sutton, *Photography, Cinema, Memory*.

10. Barthes, *Camera Lucida*, p. 78.
11. Stewart, *Between Film and Screen*, p. 39 and p. 8.
12. Mulvey, *Death 24× a Second*, p. 67.
13. See Beckman and Ma, 'Introduction', p. 6.
14. For a detailed discussion see Stewart, *Between Film and Screen*, pp. 13–15 and Mulvey, *Death 24× a Second*, pp. 13–16.
15. Michelson, 'Dr Crase and Mr Clair', pp. 44–5.
16. Bellour, *Between-the-Images*, p. 133. For sake of proximity to the original and nuance, I have amended Allyn Hardyck's translation in a number of instances. Where this is the case, it is signalled as 'amended translation'.
17. Cf. Stewart, *Between Film and Screen*, p. 9.
18. Barthes, 'The third meaning', p. 65.
19. 'The photograph subtracts me from the fiction of the cinema, even if it forms a part of the film, even if it adds to it. Creating a distance, another time, the photograph permits me to reflect on cinema. With that I mean, all at the same time: to think that I am at the cinema, to think about cinema, to think while I am at the cinema' (Bellour, *Between-the-Images*, p. 89, amended translation).
20. Bellour, *Between-the-Images*, p. 106.
21. Ibid. p. 93.
22. Barthes, *Camera Lucida*, pp. 40 and 27.
23. Daney, Response to 'Questions sur: Photo et cinéma', cited in Bellour, *Between-the-Images*, p. 133.
24. In an interview of 1965 Truffaut states: '[the freeze-frame] can quickly get to be a gimmick. I stopped doing it as a visual effect after a few films. Now I use freeze frames as a dramatic effect. They're interesting provided viewers don't notice. It takes eight frames for a [still] shot to be noticed. A shot under eight frames is virtually unreadable. Unless it's a big close-up. So what I try to do now – in *La Peau Douce*, which I find satisfactory is to freeze the image only seven or eight frames instead of like here [Jeanne Moreau's frozen poses in *Jules et Jim*] which are frozen for thirty to thirty-five frames. So when it's a simple look frozen for seven frames it has real dramatic intensity. You can't say, just looking at it, unless you're an editor or a director, "Hey a freeze frame!" I'm interested in invisible effects now.' (Interview with François Truffaut in the short film *François Truffaut; ou, l'esprit critique* by Jean-Pierre Chartier, 1965, cited by Campany, *Photography and Cinema*, pp. 149–50, note 35).
25. See Campany, *Photography and Cinema*, pp. 34–5.
26. Stewart, *Between Film and Screen*, p. 59.
27. Chéroux, 'La dame de la rue Daguerre', p. 3.
28. 'Agnès Varda in Californialand', LACMA – Los Angeles County Museum of Art, 2014; 'Varda/Cuba', Centre Pompidou, Paris, 2015.
29. 'Guy Gilles Photographe', Galerie ART & MIS, Paris, 2014.

30. www.guygilles.com; Lépingle and Uzal (eds), *Guy Gilles*; Gaël Lépingle, *Guy Gilles photographe*, included in box set Guy Gilles, *L'Amour à la mer*, *Au pan coupé*, *Le Clair de terre* (Éditions Montparnasse and Lobster Films, 2008).
31. Varda, *Varda par Agnès*, p. 38 (cited in Ungar, *Cléo de 5 à 7*, p. 19).
32. See http://www.guygilles.com/v2/presse.php?id=3&idRessource=86&currentpage=documents.
33. Ibid.
34. Bellour, *Between-the-Images*, p. 92.
35. Steven Ungar also mentions Brassaï, Kertész, Cartier-Bresson, Stieglitz and Steichen as photographers with whom Varda shares a thematic and formal concern (*Cléo de 5 à 7*, pp. 25–7).
36. Barthes, *Camera Lucida*, p. 55.
37. Barthes, *Camera Lucida*, p. 32.
38. Guiguet, 'Hommage à Guy Gilles', p. 19.
39. http://www.guygilles.com/v2/presse.php?id=8&idRessource=3&currentpage=presse (accessed 2 October 2018).
40. Barthes, *Camera Lucida*, p. 77.
41. Ibid. p. 90.
42. Stewart, *Between Film and Screen*, p. 90.
43. Lépingle, 'Une Filmographie', p. 23.
44. See Barthes's distinction between the specific character of the two media in 'Rhetoric of the image', pp. 278–9.
45. Barthes, *Camera Lucida*, p. 82.
46. Ibid. p. 63.
47. Claude Mauriac, 'Le premier film proustien'.
48. Proust, *In Search of Lost Time*, VI, p. 224.
49. Stewart, *Between Film and Screen*, p. 24.
50. Campany, *Photography and Cinema*, p. 118.
51. Daney, 'Le terrorisé', cited in Bellour, *Between-the-Images*, p. 146 (amended translation).
52. Bellour, *Between-the-Images*, p. 146.
53. Campagny, *Photography and Cinema*, p. 130.
54. Barthes, *Camera Lucida*, pp. 93–4.
55. Sutton, *Photography, Cinema, Memory*, pp. 118–26.
56. See Stewart's reading of *Funny Face* in *Between Film and Screen*, pp. 298–305 and Jameson, *Signatures of the Visible*, pp. 194–7.
57. Sutton, *Photography, Cinema, Memory*, p. 120 and p. 123.
58. Barthes, *Camera Lucida*, p. 96 (emphasis in original).
59. Ibid. p. 14.
60. Ibid. p. 89 (emphasis in original).
61. Bellour, *Between-the-Images*, p. 173 (amended translation).
62. Badiou, *Cinema*, p. 92.
63. Cf. Guzzetti's analysis of Godard's distinction between photography and film in *Two or Three Things*, p. 267.

64. Barthes, *Camera Lucida*, p. 100 and p. 70.
65. Guzzetti, *Two or Three Things*, p. 250.
66. Ibid. p. 267.
67. Sontag, *On Photography*, pp. 14–15.
68. My argument here differs from Guzzetti, who asks himself whether the association 'photograph and kill' is meant of photography in general and whether it preserves the distinction between still photography and film postulated earlier. For Guzzetti, 'Godard does not resolve these questions so much as designate their importance in the shots and scenes that follow' (*Two or Three Things*, p. 305).
69. Stewart, *Between Film and Screen*, p. 9.
70. While Marker is generally acknowledged as the inventor of the photo-based film, let us note that Gilles claims precedence over *La Jetée* with his short *Histoire d'un petit garçon devenu grand* (1962, co-directed with François Reichenbach), which, in its original form, was similarly based on still photographs: 'It was a film made of still images (a little like La Jetée, but before that) with a single moving shot. Reichenbach wanted as few still frames as possible. He transformed the film. We argued and I took my name off the credits.' (Gilles, *Cinéma 64*, no 85, April 1964, cited in Lépingle and Uzal (eds), *Guy Gilles*, p. 235).
71. Booklet accompanying box set *Planète Chris Marker*, ARTE Edition, 2013, p. 6.
72. Lupton, *Chris Marker*, p. 40.
73. For the novelisation of films see Cléder, *Entre littérature et cinéma*, pp. 179–83 and Campany, *Photography and Cinema*, p. 83.
74. Campany, *Photography and Cinema*, p. 100.
75. Lupton, *Chris Marker*, p. 91.
76. Dubois, '*La Jetée* de Chris Marker', p. 34 and *passim*.
77. See Lupton, *Chris Marker*, p. 88 and Cooper, *Chris Marker*, pp. 50–1.
78. Stewart, *Between Film and Screen*, p. 105.
79. See Lupton, *Chris Marker*, pp. 94–5 and Cooper, *Chris Marker*, p. 50.
80. Cooper, *Chris Marker*, p. 50.
81. Virgil, *Aeneid*, p. 130 and p. 131. The translator, Frederick Ahl, uses a version of Virgil's ancient hexameter, but, for ease of reading, I haven't reproduced the line breaks.
82. Dubois reads the bird imagery in the film as a migratory form, linking the final image of the man's fall to Icarus ('*La Jetée*', p. 37).
83. See Lupton, *Chris Marker*, p. 95.
84. See Ungar, 'Scenes in a library', p. 6.
85. Ungar, 'Scenes in a library'.
86. Lupton, *Chris Marker*, p. 91.
87. Barthes, *Camera Lucida*, pp. 88–9 and p. 76.
88. Liner of original English edition of *Immemory*.
89. Lupton, *Chris Marker*, p. 95.
90. Stewart, *Between Film and Screen*, pp. 294–5.
91. Cf. Lupton, *Chris Marker*, p. 93.

92. On the link to chronophotography see Dubois, '*La Jetée*', p. 30.
93. On Capa's photograph as the source of Marker's still see Wollen, 'Fire and Ice', p. 112.
94. Wollen, 'Fire and Ice', p. 112.
95. Bellour, *Between-the-Images*, p. 153.
96. Title card for *Si j'avais quatre dromadaires*.
97. Lupton, *Chris Marker*, p. 103.
98. Bruno, *Atlas of Emotion*, p. 102.
99. Glissant, *Traité du Tout-Monde*, p. 176.
100. Glissant, *Poétique de la Relation*.
101. Bazin, 'The Ontology', p. 14.
102. Ibid. p. 14.
103. Ibid. p. 15.
104. Lupton, *Chris Marker*, p. 106.
105. For notable exceptions see for instance Robert Bresson's *Au hasard Balthazar* (1966), Michelangelo Frammartino's *Le quattro volte* (*The Four Times*, 2011), Godard's *Adieu au langage* (*Goodbye to Language*, 2014) and Pietro Marcello's *Bella e perduta* (*Lost and Beautiful*, 2015).
106. Cooper, *Chris Marker*, p. 64.
107. Hourmant, 'Cuba 1963', p. 153.
108. Ibid. p. 154.
109. Ibid. p. 157.
110. Ibid. p. 154.
111. Bruno, *Surface*, p. 211.
112. Archives Agnès Varda, cited by Vignaux, '*Salut les Cubains*', p. 151.
113. Vignaux, '*Salut les Cubains*', p. 148.
114. See Varda's interview with Karolina Ziebinska-Lewandowska, 'Socialisme et cha-cha-cha', pp. 9–10.
115. Ibid. p. 9.
116. Ibid. p. 9.
117. Cf. Chéroux, 'La dame de la rue Daguerre', p. 5.
118. Bazin, 'The myth of total cinema', pp. 20–1.
119. For *métissage* (or *mestizaje*) in the context of the Caribbean see Benítez-Rojo, *The Repeating Island*, p. 26 and *passim*.

Conclusion

> At the cinema, we get to the pure from the impure.
>
> Alain Badiou[1]

In a 1990 press conference, looking back at the emergence of the New Wave, Jean-Luc Godard reflects on the impetus behind one of the movement's defining discourses, auteurism. He states:

> I understand today that when we, the New Wave – and Truffaut first of all – defended the notion of the auteur, it was simply to say: it's not fair that Hitchcock, Howard Hawks or Sergei Eisenstein should be ranked below André Gide or Fyodor Dostoevsky. Eisenstein is more important than Mosfilm, and Howard Hawks is more important than Paramount, or in any case just as important. That was all. And then it became bigger than us.[2]

The birth of the New Wave, I have argued in this book, was inseparably intertwined with the movement's ambivalent positioning towards the other arts: first and foremost its main model and rival, literature (referenced once more here by Godard), but also the stage arts, the visual arts and architecture. Prominent in the theoretical discourses that paved the way for the New Wave – most importantly Bazin's landmark *What is Cinema?* and Rohmer's series of articles 'Le Celluloïd et le marbre', but also other foundational texts and interviews by New Wave directors – the other arts were instrumental in the cultural legitimation of the new cinema that emerged in France in the late 1950s. At a time when French cinematic production continued to be stifled by the industry-based model of the Tradition of Quality, the New Wave looked towards the traditional arts to enhance cinema's artistic credentials. It was by analogy with the literary author that the *Cahiers* critics defended auteurism as the expression of an intensely personal artistic vision. By extension, it was through sustained comparison with cinema's neighbouring arts that the movement forged the concept of art cinema as a cultural product on a par with literature, painting or theatre that obtains to this day. In its struggle for cinema's cultural legitimacy, the New Wave continued a path traced by the classical avant-garde, which similarly combined an intense critical activity with a highly innovative film practice. But, crucially, where the historical avant-garde of the 1920s upheld the ideal of a non-narrative, 'pure' cinema, the theoretician of the New Wave, André Bazin, promoted an 'impure cinema' that fully embraces the heritage of literature, the stage and painting, making its own the resources offered by the other arts.

Taking stock of the richly intermedial dimension of New Wave theory and practice, *Intermedial Dialogues: The French New Wave and the Other Arts* has provided a new critical optic through which to examine this legendary moment in film history. Shining a spotlight on the 'impure', intermedial nature of the New Wave, it proposes a theoretical framework for rethinking the New Wave and revisiting its films. As we have seen, New Wave cinema invokes a vast array of artistic practices and traditions, from the realist novel to the *Nouveau roman*, from Pirandello's 'metatheatre' to avant-garde theatrical performance, from Renaissance painting to twentieth-century sculpture, from functionalist architecture in the tradition of Le Corbusier to Surrealist photography. Summoning a diverse artistic legacy, New Wave directors were also particularly attentive to contemporary experiments in the other arts, notably literature and theatre, which became an inspiration for their own project of cinematic renewal. Unsurprising, perhaps, for a movement that was by no means homogenous, we have seen a huge variety in directors' attitudes toward the other arts, ranging from Varda's celebratory reworkings of artistic traditions to Godard's media rivalry, to highlight only the two extremes of a wide spectrum. Intermedial dialogue, I demonstrated, is by no means limited to the Left Bank Group, but can be traced across the different subgroups of the New Wave, including the 'Young Turks' and New Wave 'satellites', notably the 'secret child of the New Wave' Guy Gilles.

As Bazin posits in 'For an Impure Cinema', new hybrid forms are being generated at the crossroads of the arts: Robbe-Grillet's *ciné-romans* and Resnais's *cinematricalities*, Varda's *cinécriture* and Godard's cinemato*graphies*, Marker's *photo-roman* – to recall a few salient examples of the hybridisations we identified among a wide range of artistic interactions. Yet, while engaging in what Bazin terms 'intercourse between the arts',[3] the New Wave never lost sight of the idea of cinema. Reaching out to the other arts allowed directors to interrogate the question Bazin chose as the title for his seminal collection of essays, *What is Cinema?* For the essence of cinema, as later theorists of intermediality such as Jacques Rancière and Ágnes Pethő have pointed out, can be made visible only through dialogue with the other arts. It is in-between the arts, in what Rancière calls 'games of exchange' or Pethő 'media crossovers', that cinema is able to look at and reflect on itself.[4] Intermedial figurations such as the play-within-the-film, the *tableau vivant*, or the freeze-frame,

I argued, serve as mirroring devices, allowing New Wave filmmakers to examine the cinematic medium, while, at the same time, drawing attention to its inherent impurity.

The New Wave's reaching out to the other arts in the late 1950s and 1960s helped cinema to enter the history of art, but it is also witness to a new-found confidence; it testifies to a cinematic, indeed a cinephilic culture vibrant enough to creatively extend outwards rather than protectively fold in on itself. In an article of 1957 (that is, at a time when the New Wave was already burgeoning), Alain Badiou writes:

> The surest 'proof' that a cinematic culture exists can be found in the interpenetration of other styles of culture and cinema itself. There are films that cannot be understood without our having a sort of familiarity with some other art – literature, painting, or music – not because cinema is a pale reflection of the other arts but because there is nothing more fruitful for a mode of expression for which they weren't intended than the use of distinctive features of style or exposition.[5]

In mid-century, cinema could engage in a productive, mutually enriching relationship with the other arts, a relationship where film draws on the rich resources of the traditional arts, but also where these arts find a new outlet and lease of life through the mediation of cinema. The idea that cinema makes the other arts accessible to a wider audience was of course central to Bazin's notion of 'impure cinema', and it is one that resurfaces in the New Wave's intermedial practice, albeit, at times, with ironic twists as we have seen in the famous run through the Louvre in Godard's *Bande à part*. By referencing, absorbing and reframing the other arts, New Wave cinema divests them of their 'high art' character. It is pertinent to draw once more on Badiou here, who, pursuing his reflection on cinema as an impure art in a later article, argues that

> [c]inema *opens up* all the arts; it weakens their aristocratic, complex, and composite dimension. [. . .] As painting without painting, music without music, the novel without subjects, the theater reduced to the charm of the actors, cinema ensures the *popularization* of all the arts.[6]

For the philosopher, cinema operates 'at the border of art and non-art': 'cinema is a mass art because it democratises the process whereby art uproots itself from non-art by turning that process into a border, by turning impurity into the thing itself.'[7]

In light of Badiou's reflection, we are better able to grasp the New Wave's ambivalent position towards the other arts: on the one hand, invoking the neighbouring arts allowed the movement to overcome cinema's inferior status as what Rohmer calls 'a poor relative' and to enrich its themes and language;[8] on the other, its mixture of art and non-art constitute it as a mass medium. Herein lies the productive paradox of the New Wave: while positing film as art, it also asserts cinema's status as a popular medium better suited to reach a wide and diverse audience than the traditional arts – which, as Godard put it provocatively in the interview I cited in Chapter 1, had 'breathed their last'.[9] Drawing on a rich artistic legacy, but also fully embracing popular culture in all its manifold forms, cinema could became *the* predominant art of the twentieth-century: an art that combines unfettered vitality with alluring mass appeal.

Yet the new cinema of the late 1950s and 1960s would not have held such an appeal without it being so finely attuned to the fundamental social changes against which the New Wave is traditionally framed. Its intermedial forays, I argued, played a significant part in engaging some of the most central political, social and ideological issues of the time. In my readings of films, I have suggested that intermediality in New Wave cinema is not only an aesthetic category; it is a gateway to mediate crucial contemporary issues, from the traumatic legacy of the Second World War and the Holocaust to the more recent wounds of the Indochina and Algerian Wars, from the problems of mass housing to the condition of the 'modern woman', from the technocratic turn of Western societies to the lures of 1960s consumer culture. Intermedial strategies were harnessed to work through collective anxieties, be it the onslaught of consumer capitalism, the changing social fabric caused by gentrification or the widespread fear of nuclear catastrophe. As we have seen, for instance, with regards to architecture, in their willingness to confront an urban space in rapid mutation, New Wave directors asserted their own modernity; but their cinematic interrogation of modern architecture also engaged them in a wider debate about the impact of Gaullist modernisation projects on people's living conditions and affective lives.

The fracturing of the New Wave post-1968 did not bring an end to the intermedial exchanges that have concerned us here. Many New Wave directors have continued or even intensified their intermedial investments beyond the movement's historical parameters: one need only think of Rohmer's *L'Anglaise et le Duc* (*The Lady and the Duke*, 2001) with its digital incrustation of the filmic action into painted sets inspired by paintings of the Revolutionary era; of Godard's *Passion* and the multimedial *Histoire(s) du cinéma* which we traced as the horizon of his intermedial practice; of Marker's interactive CD-ROM *Immemory* (1998) or Varda's multimedia installation *L'île et elle* (*The Island and She*, 2006) – all of them pursuing a trajectory that was initiated during the New Wave period. In the era of digital, where other media are easily integrated, mixing between the arts is more frequent than ever. We are manifestly well advanced on the path towards a generalised hybridisation

Bazin predicted for the year 2050, when 'the (literary?) critic [. . .] would find not a novel out of which a play and a film had been "made," but rather a single work reflected through three art forms, an artistic pyramid with three sides'.[10] Exactly what forms and figures such intermedial encounters take in French and francophone cinema since the 1970s, what specific role they had to play in the altered cinematic landscape after the New Wave, that is a matter for another journey. As Guy Gilles suggests in the closing caption of *Le Clair de terre*: *à suivre*.

NOTES

1. Badiou, *Cinema*, p. 239.
2. Godard, 'Conférence de presse', p. 10.
3. Bazin, 'For an impure cinema', p. 60.
4. Rancière, *Film Fables*, p. 15; Pethő, *Cinema and Intermediality*, p. 66.
5. Badiou, *Cinema*, p. 31.
6. Badiou, *Cinema*, p. 238.
7. Ibid. p. 236 and p. 239.
8. Rohmer, *The Taste for Beauty*, p. 72.
9. Cf. also Bazin's comment at the end of 'For an impure cinema': 'The truth is there is here no competition or substitution, rather the adding of a new dimension that the arts had gradually lost from the time of the Reformation on: namely a public' (p. 75).
10. Bazin, 'Adaptation, or the cinema as digest', p. 26.

Bibliography

Abel, Richard, *French Film Theory and Criticism, 1907–1939: A History/Anthology*, vol. 1: 1907–28; vol. 2: 1929–39 (Princeton: Princeton University Press, 1988).
Abrigeon, Julien d', *Jean-Luc Godard, cinéaste écrivain: de la citation à la création, présence et rôle de la littérature dans le cinéma de JLG de 1959 à 1967*, <http://tapin.free.fr/godard> (accessed 2 October 2018).
Agamben, Giorgio, *Infancy and History: The Destruction of Experience* (London, Verso, 1993).
Albéra, François, 'Cultivons notre jardin. Entretien avec Jean-Luc Godard', *CinémAction*, 52 (1989), pp. 81–9.
Amiel, Vincent, 'Comme au théâtre! Notes sur la discontinuité des plans', *Double Jeu*, 7 (2010), pp. 39–43.
Andrew, Dudley, *André Bazin*, revised edn (Oxford: Oxford University Press, 2013).
Aragon, Louis, 'Qu'est-ce que l'art, Jean-Luc Godard?', *Les Lettres françaises*, n° 1096, 9 September 1965.
Arnheim, Rudolf, 'A new Laocoön: artistic composites and the talking film' (1938), in *Film as Art* (London: Faber and Faber, 1983), pp. 164–89.
Astruc, Alexandre, 'The birth of a new avant-garde: La Caméra-Stylo', in Graham with Vincendeau (eds), *The French New Wave: Critical Landmarks*, pp. 31–7.
Augé, Marc, *Non-lieux, introduction à une anthropologie de la surmodernité* (Paris: Seuil, 1992).
Aumont, Jacques (ed.), *Le Septième Art: le cinéma parmi les arts* (Paris: Léo Scheer, 2003).
Aumont, Jacques, *Matière d'images* (Paris: Images modernes, 2005).
Aumont, Jacques, *L'Œil interminable* (Paris: Éditions de la Différence, 2007).
Aumont, Jacques, Jean-Louis Comolli, Jean Narboni and Sylvie Pierre, 'Le temps déborde: enretien avec Jacques Rivette', *Cahiers du cinéma*, 204 (1968), pp. 7–21.
Aumont, Jacques, Alain Bergala, Michel Marie and Marc Vernet, *Aesthetics of Film* (Austin: University of Texas Press, 1999).
Badiou, Alain, *Cinema*, ed. Antoine de Baecque, trans. Susan Spitzer (Cambridge: Polity, 2013).
Baecque, Antoine de, *La Cinéphilie. Invention d'un regard, histoire d'une culture, 1944–1968* (Paris: Fayard, 2003).
Baecque, Antoine de, *L'Histoire-Caméra* (Paris: Gallimard, 2008).
Baecque, Antoine de, *La Nouvelle Vague: portrait d'une jeunesse* (Paris: Flammarion, 2009).
Baecque, Antoine de, *Godard. Biographie* (Paris: Grasset, 2010).
Baecque, Antoine de and Charles Tesson (eds), *La Nouvelle Vague. III. Petite Anthologie des Cahiers du cinéma* (Paris: Cahiers du cinéma, 1999).
Baecque, Antoine de with Gabrielle Lucantonio (eds), *La Politique des auteurs. Les Textes. IV. Petite anthologie des Cahiers du cinéma* (Paris: Cahiers du cinéma, 2001).
Baecque, Antoine de and Noël Herpe, *Eric Rohmer. Biographie* (Paris: Stock, 2014).

Banda, Daniel and José Moure (eds), *Le Cinéma: l'art d'une civilisation* (Paris: Flammarion, 2011).
Barber, Stephen, *Projected Cities: Cinema and Urban Space* (London: Reaktion, 2002).
Barthes, Roland, 'The Brechtian revolution', in Barthes, *Critical Essays*, trans. Richard Howard (Evanston, IL: Northwestern University Press, 1972), pp. 37–9.
Barthes, Roland, *S/Z*, trans. Richard Millar (New York: Farrar, Straus and Giroux, 1974).
Barthes, Roland, 'The third meaning: research notes on some Eisenstein stills', in *Image, Music, Text*, ed. and trans. Stephen Heath (London: Fontana Press, 1977), pp. 52–68.
Barthes, Roland, 'Rhetoric of the image', in Alan Trachtenberg (ed.), *Classic Essays on Photography* (New Haven, CT: Leete's Island Books, 1980), pp. 269–85.
Barthes, Roland, *Camera Lucida. Reflections on Photography*, trans. Richard Howard (London: Vintage, 2000).
Barthes, Roland, 'Pourquoi Brecht', in Barthes, *Ecrits sur le théâtre* (Paris: Seuil, 2002), pp. 162–5.
Baudelaire, Charles, 'The painter of modern life', in Baudelaire, *The Painter of Modern Life and Other Essays*, ed. and trans. Jonathan Mayne (London: Phaidon, 1964), pp. 1–40.
Baudelaire, Charles, *The Flowers of Evil*, trans. James McGowan (Oxford: Oxford University Press, 1993).
Bazin, André, *What is Cinema?*, ed. and trans. Hugh Gray, 2 vols (London: University of California Press, 1967–71).
Bazin, André, 'The ontology of the photographic image', in Bazin, *What is Cinema?*, vol. 1, pp. 9–16.
Bazin, André, 'The myth of total cinema', in Bazin, *What is Cinema?*, vol. 1, pp. 17–22.
Bazin, André, 'In defense of mixed cinema', in Bazin, *What is Cinema?*, vol. 1, pp. 53–75.
Bazin, André, 'Theater and cinema', in Bazin, *What is Cinema?*, vol. 1, pp. 76–124 (Part I: pp. 76–94, Part II: pp. 94–124).
Bazin, André, '*Le Journal d'un curé de campagne*', in Bazin, *What is Cinema?*, vol. 1, pp. 125–43.
Bazin, André, 'The evolution of the language of cinema', in Bazin, *What is Cinema?*, vol. 1, pp. 23–40.
Bazin, André, 'Painting and cinema', in Bazin, *What is Cinema?*, vol. 1, pp. 164–9.
Bazin, André, 'Adaptation, or the cinema as digest', in James Naremore (ed.), *Film Adaptation* (New Brunswick, NJ: Rutgers University Press, 2000), pp. 19–27.
Bazin, André, 'Le cas Pagnol', in *Qu'est-ce que le cinéma?* (Paris: Éditions du CERF, 2002), pp. 179–85.
Bazin, André, Jacques Doniol-Valcroze, Pierre Kast, Roger Leenhardt, Jacques Rivette and Éric Rohmer, 'Six characters in search of *auteurs*: a discussion about the French cinema' ('Six personnages en quête d'auteurs: débat sur le cinéma français', *Cahiers du cinéma*, 51, May 1957 (extracts)), in Jim Hillier (ed.), *The 1950s: Neo-realism, Hollywood, New Wave* (London: Routledge, 1997), pp. 31–46.
Beck, James H., *Italian Renaissance Painting* (Köln: Könemann, 1999).
Beckman, Karen and Jean Ma (eds), *Still Moving: Between Cinema and Photography* (Durham, NC: Duke University Press, 2008).
Beckman, Karen and Jean Ma, 'Introduction', in Beckman and Ma (eds), *Still Moving: Between Cinema and Photography*, pp. 1–19.
Béghin, Cyril, '*Métamorphoses du paysage* (1964): Usage pédagogique de l'ironie', *Cahiers du cinéma*, 588 (2004), p. 18.
Béghin, Cyril, 'Le Grand jeu', *Cahiers du cinéma*, 716 (2015), pp. 68–71.
Béghin, Cyril, 'C'est comme vous voulez. Entretien avec Michael Lonsdale', *Cahiers du cinéma*, 716 (2015), p. 75.

Bellour, Raymond, *L'Entre-images 2: Mots, images* (Paris: POL, 1999).
Bellour, Raymond, 'L'Autre cinéaste: Godard écrivain', in Bellour, *L'Entre-images 2: Mots, images*, pp. 113–38.
Bellour, Raymond, *Between-the-Images*, ed. Lionel Bovier, trans. Allyn Hardyck (Dijon: Les Presses du réel, 2012).
Bellour, 'The pensive spectator', in Bellour, *Between-the-Images*, pp. 86–97.
Benayou, Robert, 'Muriel, ou les rendez-vous manqués', in Stéphane Goudet (ed.), *Positif, revue de cinéma: Alain Resnais* (Paris: Gallimard, 2002), pp. 130–6.
Benhaïm, Safia, 'Le flâneur', *Vertigo*, 27 (2005), pp. 85–6.
Benítez-Rojo, Antonio, *The Repeating Island: The Caribbean and the Postmodern Perspective* (Durham, NC; London: Duke University Press, 1992).
Benjamin, Walter, 'Surrealism. The last snapshot of the European intelligentsia', in Benjamin, *Selected Writings*, trans. Rodney Livingstone et al., ed. Michael W. Jennings, Howard Eiland and Gary Smith, vol. 2, 1927–34 (Cambridge, MA: Harvard University Press, 1999), pp. 207–21.
Benjamin, Walter, *The Work of Art in the Age of Mechanical Reproduction*, trans. J. A. Underwood (London: Penguin, 2008).
Benoliel, Bernard, 'Le Temps d'un raccord: *Au pan coupé* (1967), *Le Clair de terre* (1970), *Proust, l'art et la douleur* (1971)', in Lépingle and Uzal (eds), *Guy Gilles: un cinéaste au fil du temps*, pp. 99–107.
Bergala, Alain (ed.), *Godard par Godard. Les années Cahiers (1950 à 1959)* (Paris: Flammarion, 1989).
Bergala, Alain (ed.), *Jean-Luc Godard par Jean-Luc Godard*, vol. 1, 1950–84 (Paris: Cahiers du cinéma, 1998).
Bloom, Harold (ed.), *Lugi Pirandello* (Broomall, PA: Chelsea House, 2003).
Bolter, Jay David and Richard Grusin, *Remediation. Understanding New Media* (Cambridge, MA; London: MIT Press, 2000).
Bonitzer, Pascal, *Décadrages: peintures et cinéma* (Paris: Éditions de l'Étoile, 1985).
Bontemps, Jacques, Jean-Louis Comolli, Michel Delahaye and Jean Narboni, 'Lutter sur deux fronts: entretien avec Jean-Luc Godard', *Cahiers du cinéma*, 194 (1967), pp. 12–27.
Brassart, Alain, 'Paris leur appartient: La Capitale française vue par la Nouvelle Vague', *Tausend Augen*, Hors Série 03 (2004), pp. 40–3.
Brecht, Bertolt, 'On Chinese acting', *Tulane Drama Review*, 6-1 (1961), pp. 130–6.
Brody, Richard, *Everything is Cinema. The Working Life of Jean-Luc Godard* (London: Faber and Faber, 2008).
Bruneau, Sonia, 'La Ville politique: 1968, Paris en utopie', *Théorème*, 10 (2007), pp. 93–103.
Bruno, Giuliana, 'Site-seeing: architecture and the moving image', *Wide Angle*, 19-4 (1997), pp. 8–24.
Bruno, Giuliana, *Atlas of Emotion: Journeys in Art, Architecture and Film* (New York: Verso, 2002).
Bruno, Giuliana, *Public Intimacy: Architecture and the Visual Arts* (Cambridge, MA: MIT Press, 2007).
Bruno, Giuliana, *Surface. Matters of Aesthetics, Materiality, and Media* (Chicago; London: University of Chicago Press, 2014).
Cabañas, Kaira M., *Off-Screen Cinema: Isidore Isidou and the Lettrist Avant-Garde* (Chicago: University of Chicago Press, 2014).
Campany, David, *Photography and Cinema* (London: Reaktion Books, 2008).
Canudo, Ricciotto, 'Reflections on the seventh art', in Abel, *French Film Theory and Criticism*, vol. 1, pp. 291–303.

Caratini, Fabienne, 'Le Fantôme du théâtre dans le cinéma de Jacques Rivette', *CinémAction*, 93 (1999), pp. 214–19.
Cardin, Aurélie, 'Les 4000 logements de La Courneuve: réalités et imaginaires cinématographiques. La représentation des "4000" à travers *Deux ou trois choses que je sais d'elle* (1967) de Jean-Luc Godard', *Cahiers d'Histoire*, 98 (2006), pp. 65–80.
Chabrol, Marguerite and Riphaine Karsenti (eds), *Théâtre et cinéma: le croisement des imaginaires* (Rennes: Presses universitaires de Rennes, 2013).
Chauvin, Jean-Sébastien, 'Nouvelle Vague', in Jousse and Paquot (eds), *La Ville au cinéma. Encyclopédie*, pp. 193–9.
Chéroux, Clément and Karolina Ziebinska-Lewandowska (eds), *Varda/Cuba* (Paris: Éditions du Centre Pompidou/Éditions Xavier Barral, 2015).
Chéroux, Clément, 'La dame de la rue Daguerre', in Chéroux and Ziebinska-Lewandowska (eds), *Varda/Cuba*, pp. 3–5.
Chion, Michel, *L'écrit au cinéma* (Paris: Armand Colin, 2013).
Cléder, Jean, *Entre littérature et cinéma: Les Affinités électives* (Paris: Armand Colin, 2012).
Clerc, Thomas, 'Rohmer l'urbain', in Sylvie Robic and Laurence Schifano (eds), *Rohmer en perspectives* (Paris: Presses Paris Ouest, 2013), pp. 95–111.
Colvin, J. Brandon, 'Explaining Varda's *Lions Love*: a European director responds to an American cultural marketplace', *Studies in French Cinema*, 16-1 (2016), pp. 19–31.
Cooper, Sarah, *Chris Marker* (Manchester: Manchester University Press, 2008).
Corvin, Michel, 'Une écriture plurielle', in de Jomaron (ed.), *Le Théâtre en France*, pp. 914–60.
Creton, Laurent and Kristian Feigelson (eds), *Villes cinématographiques, ciné-lieux* (Paris: Presses Sorbonne Nouvelle, 2007).
Dalle Vacche, Angela, *Cinema and Painting. How Art is Used in Film* (Austin: University of Texas Press, 1996).
Dalle Vacche, Angela, 'Jean-Luc Godard's *Pierrot le Fou*: Cinema as collage against painting', in *Cinema and Painting*, pp. 107–34.
Dalle Vacche, Angela (ed.), *The Visual Turn. Classical Film Theory and Art History* (New Brunswick, NJ: Rutgers University Press, 2002).
Daney, Serge, 'Le terrorisé (pédagogie godardienne)', *Cahiers du cinéma*, 262–3 (1976), pp. 32–9.
Daney, Serge, Response to 'Questions sur: Photo et cinéma', *Photogénies*, 5 (1982), n.p.
Daney, Serge, 'Truffaut, objectif plume', in *La Maison du cinéma et le monde. 3. Les Années Libé, 1986–1991*, ed. Patrice Rollet, with Jean-Claude Biette and Christophe Manon (Paris: POL, 2012), pp. 233–8.
Darke, Chris, *Alphaville (Jean-Luc Godard, 1965)* (London and Champaign, IL: I. B. Tauris and University of Illinois Press, 2005).
Debord, Guy, 'Les gratte-ciel par la racine', *Potlach*, no. 5, 20 July 1954.
Debord, Guy, 'On détruit la rue Sauvage', *Potlach*, no. 7, 3 August 1954.
Deleuze, Gilles, 'Three questions on *Six Times Two*', in *Negotiations. 1972–1990*, trans. Martin Joughin (New York: Columbia University Press, 1995), pp. 37–45.
Deleuze, Gilles, *Cinema 2: The Time-Image*, trans. Hugh Tomlinson and Robert Galeta (Minneapolis, MN: University of Minnesota Press, 1997).
DeRoo, Rebecca J., *Agnès Varda Between Film, Photography, and Art* (Oakland: University of California Press, 2018).
Derrida, Jacques, *Of Hospitality. Anne Dufourmantelle Invites Jacques Derrida to Respond* (Stanford: Stanford University Press, 2000).
Deschamps, Hélène, *Jacques Rivette: Théâtre, amour, cinéma* (Paris: L'Harmattan, 2001).
Didi-Huberman, Georges, *Passés cités par JLG* (Paris: Minuit, 2015).

Domarchi, Jean, Jacques Doniol-Valcroze, Jean-Luc Godard, Pierre Kast, Jacques Rivette and Éric Rohmer, 'Hiroshima, notre amour' ('Hiroshima, notre amour', *Cahiers du cinéma* 97, July 1959 (extracts)), in Jim Hillier (ed.), *The 1950s: Neo-realism, Hollywood, New Wave* (London: Routledge, 1997), pp. 59–70.

Dort, Bernard, 'L'âge de la représentation', in de Jomaron (ed.), *Le Théâtre en France*, pp. 959–1048.

Dosi, Francesca, 'Balzac et Rivette: l'énigme d'une rencontre', *L'Année balzacienne*, 12 (2011), pp. 337–67.

Douchet, Jean, *Nouvelle Vague* (Paris: Cinémathèque française/Hazan, 1998).

Dousteyssier-Khoze, Catherine, *Claude Chabrol's Aesthetics of Opacity* (Edinburgh: Edinburgh University Press, 2017).

Dubois, Philippe, '*La Jetée* de Chris Marker ou le cinématogramme de la conscience', *Théorème*, 6 (2002), pp. 8–45.

Dubois, Philippe, 'The written screen: JLG and writing as the accursed share', in Temple, Williams and Witt (eds), *For Ever Godard*, pp. 232–47.

Dulac, Germaine, 'The expressive techniques of the cinema', in Abel, *French Film Theory and Criticism,* vol. 1, pp. 305–14.

Eisenstein, Sergei M., with an introduction by Yve-Alain Bois, 'Montage and architecture' (*c.*1937), *Assemblage*, 10 (1989), pp. 110–31.

Elbhar, Robert, 'Éric Rohmer parle de ses *Contes moraux*', *Séquences: La Revue de cinéma*, 71 (1973), pp. 11–15.

Epstein, Jean, 'On certain characteristics of *Photogénie*', in Abel, *French Film Theory and Criticism,* vol. 1, pp. 314–18.

Faure, Elie, *Fonction du cinéma: de la cinéplastique à son destin social* (Paris: Denoël/ Gonthier, 1976).

Faure, Elie, 'The art of cineplastics', in Abel, *French Film Theory and Criticism,* vol. 1, pp. 258–68.

Fieschi, Jean-André and Claude Ollier, 'La Grâce laïque. Entretien avec Agnes Varda', *Cahiers du Cinéma*, 165 (1965), pp. 42–51.

Flaubert, Gustave, *Madame Bovary* (Paris: Gallimard, 'Folio', 1972).

Forret, Mélanie, 'Trois films du cinéaste Guy Gilles', *Il était une fois le cinéma*, <http://www.iletaitunefoislecinema.com/dvd/2053/trois-films-du-cineaste-guy-gilles> (accessed 2 October 2018).

Foster, Hal, Rosalind Krauss, Yve-Alain Bois and Benjamin H. D. Buchloh, *Art Since 1900: Modernism, Antimodernism, Postmodernism* (London: Thames and Hudson, 2004).

Frappat, Hélène, 'L'Angle du hasard. Entretien avec Bulle Ogier et Stéphane Tchalgadjieff', *Cahiers du cinéma*, 716 (2015), pp. 76–8.

Frémaux, Thierry, 'L'aventure cinéphilique de *Positif* (1952–1999)', *Vingtième siècle. Revue d'histoire*, 23 (1989), pp. 21–34.

Fried, Michael, *Manet's Modernism or, The Face of Painting in the 1860s* (Chicago: University of Chicago Press, 1996).

Frodon, Jean-Michel, *L'Age moderne du cinema français. De la Nouvelle Vague à nos jours* (Paris: Flammarion, 1995).

Gauteur, Claude, 'Un nouvel espoir du cinéma français: Jean-Daniel Pollet', *Arts*, no. 1, 17–23 December 1958.

Gilles, Guy, 'Ecrits personnels', 'Sur le cinéma', <http://www.guygilles.com/v2/index.php> (accessed 2 October 2018).

Giraud, François, 'La Picturalité dans le cinéma d'Agnès Varda: *La Pointe Courte* (1954), *Cléo de 5 à 7* (1961) et *Lions Love* (1969)', unpublished master's thesis, University Paris Sorbonne, 2013.

Giraud, François, 'Intermediality and gesture: idealising the craft of filmmaking in Agnès Varda's *Lions Love (. . . and Lies)*, *Studies in French Cinema*, <https://doi.org/10.1080/14715880.2018.1448957> (16 April 2018).

Glissant, Édouard, *Poétique de la Relation. Poétique III* (Paris: Gallimard, 1990).

Glissant, Édouard, *Traité du Tout-Monde. Poétique IV* (Paris: Gallimard, 1997).

Godard, Jean-Luc, 'Bergmanorama', *Cahiers du Cinéma*, 85 (1958), pp. 1–5.

Godard, Jean-Luc, 'Le Mépris', *Cahiers du cinéma*, 146 (1963), p. 31.

Godard, Jean-Luc, 'Joseph Mankiewicz, *La Maison des étrangers (House of Strangers)*', in Bergala (ed.), *Godard par Godard. Les années Cahiers (1950 à 1959)* (Paris: Flammarion, 1989), pp. 43–5.

Godard, Jean-Luc, 'Dictionnaire des cinéastes français', in Alain Bergala (ed.), *Godard par Godard. Les années Cahiers (1950 à 1959)*, pp. 89–91.

Godard, Jean-Luc, 'Tournage (*Les Cousins* de Claude Chabrol)', in Bergala (ed.), *Godard par Godard. Les années Cahiers (1950 à 1959)*, pp. 167–8.

Godard, Jean-Luc, 'Conférence de presse de Jean-Luc Godard (extraits)', *Cahiers du cinéma*, 433 (1990), pp. 10–11.

Godard, Jean-Luc, 'L'art à partir de la vie', in Bergala (ed.), *Jean-Luc Godard par Jean-Luc Godard*, vol. 1, pp. 9–24.

Godard, Jean-Luc, 'Truffaut représentera la France à Cannes avec *Les 400 coups*', in Bergala (ed.), *Jean-Luc Godard par Jean-Luc Godard*, vol. 1, pp. 193–5.

Godard, Jean-Luc, 'La Chance de repartir pour un tour', in Bergala (ed.), *Jean-Luc Godard par Jean-Luc Godard*, vol. 1, pp. 407–12.

Godard, Jean-Luc, 'Alfred Hitchcock est mort', in Bergala (ed.), *Jean-Luc Godard par Jean-Luc Godard*, vol. 1, pp. 412–17.

Godard, Jean-Luc, *Histoire(s) du cinéma* (Paris: Gallimard-Gaumont, 1998).

Godard, Jean-Luc and Youssef Ishaghpour, *Archéologie du cinéma et mémoire du siècle* (Tours: Farrago, 2000).

Gonzalez, Yann, 'Les Cicatrices intérieures de Guy Gilles', *Têtu*, 2005, <http://www.guygilles.com/v2/presse.php?id=5&idRessource=89&currentpage=presse> (accessed 2 October 2018).

Gorz, André, 'The exit from capitalism has already begun', *Cultural Politics*, 6-1, (2010), pp. 5–14.

Graham, Peter with Ginette Vincendeau (eds), *The French New Wave: Critical Landmarks* (London: British Film Institute, 2009).

Greenberg, Clement, 'Towards a newer Laocoon', in *The Collected Essays and Criticism*, ed. John O'Brian, vol. 1, *Perceptions and Judgments, 1939–1944* (Chicago: University of Chicago Press, 1986), pp. 23–38.

Greene, Naomi, *Landscapes of Loss. The National Past in Postwar French Cinema* (Princeton: Princeton University Press, 1999).

Greene, Naomi, *The French New Wave: A New Look* (New York: Wallflower Press, 2007).

Guiguet, Jean-Claude, 'Hommage à Guy Gilles', *Cahiers du cinéma*, 502 (1996), p. 19 <http://www.guygilles.com/v2/presse.php?id=5&idRessource=87&currentpage=presse> (accessed 2 October 2018).

Guzzetti, Alfred, *Two or Three Things I Know About Her* (Cambridge, MA; London: Harvard University Press, 1981).

Harrison, Nicholas, 'Readers as resistants: *Fahrenheit 451*, censorship and identification', *Studies in French Cinema*, 1 (2001), pp. 54–61.

Haus, Andreas and Michel Frizot, 'Figures of style: new vision, new photography', in Michel Frizot (ed.), *A New History of Photography* (Cologne: Könemann, 1998), pp. 456–75.

Hegel, G. W. F., *Aesthetics: Lectures on Fine Art*, trans. T. M. Knox, 2 vols (Oxford, Clarendon, 1975).

Heinich, Nathalie, 'Godard, créateur de statut', in Gilles Delavaud, Jean-Pierre Esquenazi and Marie-Françoise Grange (eds), *Godard et le métier d'artiste* (Paris: L'Harmattan, 2001).

Hensman, Ravi, 'Oracles of suburbia: French cinema and portrayals of Paris banlieues, 1958–1968', *Modern and Contemporary France*, 21-4 (2013), pp. 435–51.

Holmes, Diana and Robert Ingram, *François Truffaut* (Manchester: Manchester University Press, 1998).

Hourmant, François, 'Cuba 1963: Le Paradis révolutionnaire', in Chéroux and Ziebinska-Lewandowska (eds), *Varda/Cuba*, pp. 153–7.

Jacobs, Steven, *The Wrong House: The Architecture of Alfred Hitchcock* (Rotterdam: nai010, 2007).

Jacobs, Steven, *Framing Pictures: Film and the Visual Arts* (Edinburgh: Edinburgh University Press, 2012).

Jameson, Frederic, *Signatures of the Visible* (New York: Routledge, 1990).

Jeannelle, Jean-Louis, *Cinémalraux: essai sur l'œuvre d'André Malraux au cinéma* (Paris: Hermann, 2015).

Jomaron, Jacqueline de (ed.), *Le Théâtre en France* (Paris: Armand Colin, 1992).

Jomaron, Jacqueline de, 'En quête de textes', in de Jomaron (ed.), *Le Théâtre en France*, pp. 777–801.

Jones, Colin, *Paris, Biography of a City* (London: Allen Lane, 2004).

Jousse, Thierry and Thierry Paquot (eds), *La Ville au cinéma. Encyclopédie* (Paris: Cahiers du cinéma, 2005).

Kline, T. Jefferson, *Screening the Text. Intertextuality in New Wave French Cinema* (Baltimore; London: Johns Hopkins University Press, 1992).

Kracauer, Siegfried, *Theory of Film: The Redemption of Physical Reality* (Oxford: Oxford University Press, 1960).

Kracauer, Siegfried, 'Publicité lumineuse', in Kracauer, *Le Voyage et la danse. Figures de ville et vues de films*, ed. Philippe Despoix, trans. Sabine Cornille (Saint-Denis: Presses Universitaires de Vincennes, 1996), pp. 66–9.

Kreimeier, Klaus, 'Theatralität und Filmsprache in Godard's *À bout de souffle*', in Roloff and Winter (eds), *Theater und Kino in der Zeit der Nouvelle Vague*, pp. 103–10.

Lalanne, Jean-Marc and Jean-Baptiste Morain, 'Entretien avec Jacques Rivette – L'Art secret', *Les Inrockuptibles*, 19 March 2007, <http://www.lesinrocks.com/2007/03/19/cinema/actualite-cinema/entretien-jacques-rivette-lart-secret 1165507/> (accessed 2 October 2018).

Langlois, Henri, 'Jean Epstein (1897–1953)', *Cahiers du cinéma*, 24 (1953), pp. 8–31.

Léal, Brigitte, Christine Piot, Marie-Laure Bernadac, *The Ultimate Picasso* (New York: Harry N. Abrams, 2000).

Lefebvre, Henri, *Le Droit à la ville* (Paris: Seuil, 1968).

Lefebvre, Henri, *Introduction to Modernity*, trans. John Moore (London: Verso, 1995).

Léger, Fernand, 'Painting and cinema', in Abel, *French Film Theory and Criticism*, vol. 1, pp. 372–3.

Lépingle, Gaël, 'Interview de Jérôme Pescayré', March 2005, <http://www.guygilles.com/v2/presse.php?id=1&idRessource=41&currentpage=documents.> (accessed 2 October 2018).

Lépingle, Gaël, 'Une filmographie', in Lépingle and Uzal (eds), *Guy Gilles: un cinéaste au fil du temps*, pp. 9–37.

Lépingle, Gaël, 'Entretien avec Noun Serra (monteuse de *L'Amour à la mer*)', in Lépingle and Uzal (eds), *Guy Gilles: un cinéaste au fil du temps*, pp. 89–95.

Lépingle, Gaël, 'Arrêts sur images: *Le Clair de terre*, 1970', in Lépingle and Uzal (eds), *Guy Gilles: un cinéaste au fil du temps*, pp. 131–6.
Lépingle, Gaël and Marcos Uzal (eds), *Guy Gilles: un cinéaste au fil du temps* (Paris: Yellow Now, 2014).
Lépingle, Gaël and Marcos Uzal, 'Montage d'entretiens avec Guy Gilles', in Lépingle and Uzal (eds), *Guy Gilles: un cinéaste au fil du temps*, pp. 41–62.
Lessing, Gotthold Ephraim, *Laocoon: An Essay on the Limits of Painting and Poetry* [1766] (Baltimore: Johns Hopkins University Press, 1984).
Leutrat, Jean-Louis, *Des traces qui nous ressemblent* (Seyssel: Comp'Act, 1990).
Leutrat, Jean-Louis, *L'Année dernière à Marienbad* (London: BFI Publishing, 2000).
Leutrat, Jean-Louis, 'Godard's Tricolor', in David Wills (ed.), *Jean-Luc Godard, Pierrot le Fou* (Cambridge: Cambridge University Press, 2000), pp. 64–80.
Levin, Thomas Y., 'Introduction', in Siegfried Kracauer, *The Mass Ornament. Weimar Essays*, ed. and trans. Thomas Y. Levin (Cambridge, MA: Harvard University Press, 1995), pp. 1–30.
Libois, Jean-Louis, 'Théâtre, cinéma, l'autre-scène', *Double Jeu*, 7 (2010), pp. 17–23.
Lommel, Michael, '68er-Reflexionen. Zur Heterotopie und Theatralität des politischen Engagements in Godard's *La Chinoise*', in Roloff and Winter (eds), *Godard Intermedial*, pp. 67–84.
Lupton, Catherine, *Chris Marker: Memories of the Future* (London: Reaktion Books, 2004).
Magny, Joël, 'Paris et la Nouvelle Vague', *CinémAction*, 75 (1995), pp. 126–33.
Malraux, André, *Le Musée imaginaire* (Paris: Gallimard, 1996).
Malraux, André, *Esquisse d'une psychologie du cinéma* (Paris: Nouveau Monde, 2003).
Malraux, André, 'Le Premier art mondial . . . (1959)', in Banda and Moure (eds), *Le Cinéma: l'art d'une civilisation*, pp. 468–9.
Marcolini, Patrick, 'A quelle ville les situationnistes rêvent-ils?', in Paquot (ed.), *Les Situationnistes en ville*, pp. 87–100.
Margulies, Ivone, 'The changing landscape and Rohmer's temptation of architecture', in Leah Anderst (ed.), *The Films of Eric Rohmer. French New Wave to Old Master* (Basingstoke: Palgrave Macmillan, 2014), pp. 161–75.
Marie, Michel, *The French New Wave: An Artistic School*, trans. Richard Neupert (Oxford: Blackwell, 2002).
Martin, Adrian, 'Recital: three lyrical interludes in Godard', in Temple, Williams and Witt (eds), *For Ever Godard*, pp. 252–71.
Mary, Philippe, *La Nouvelle Vague et le cinéma d'auteur: socio-analyse d'une révolution artistique* (Paris: Seuil, 2006).
Mauriac, Claude, 'Le Premier film proustien', *Figaro littéraire*, <http://www.guygilles.com/v2/presse.php?id=8&idRessource=1&currentpage=presse > (accessed 2 October 2018).
McCabe, Colin, *Godard: A Portrait of the Artist at Seventy* (New York: Faber and Faber, 2003).
McHale, Brian, *Postmodernist Fiction* (London: Methuen, 1987).
Michelson, Annette, 'Dr Crase and Mr Clair', *October* 11 (1979), pp. 30–53.
Monaco, James, *The New Wave: Truffaut, Godard, Chabrol, Rohmer, Rivette* (New York: Oxford University Press, 1976).
Monaco, James, *Alain Resnais, The Role of Imagination* (London: Secker and Warburg, 1978).
Morrey, Douglas, *Jean-Luc Godard* (Manchester: Manchester University Press, 2005).
Moullet, Luc, 'Contingent 65 1 A', *Cahiers du cinéma*, 166 (1965), pp. 56–63.
Mulvey, Laura, *Death 24× a Second* (London: Reaktion Books, 2005).
Murcia, Claude, *Nouveau roman – Nouveau cinéma* (Paris: Nathan, 1999).

Nagib, Lúcia and Anne Jerslev (eds), *Impure Cinema. Intermedial and Intercultural Aproaches to Film* (London: I. B. Tauris, 2014).

Nagib, Lúcia, 'The politics of impurity', in Nagib and Jerslev (eds), *Impure Cinema. Intermedial and Intercultural Aproaches to Film*, pp. 21–39.

Narboni, Jean, 'Le Temps de la critique: entretien avec Éric Rohmer', in Éric Rohmer, *Le Goût de la beauté*, ed. Jean Narboni (Paris: Cahiers du cinéma, 2004), pp. 11–37.

Neupert, Richard, *A History of the French New Wave Cinema*, 2nd edn (Madison, WI: University of Wisconsin Press, 2007).

Nussbaum, Valentin, 'Classic=modern: Godard's *Bande à part*, McTiernan's *The Thomas Crown Affair* and the question of cinematic modernity', *Shida Studies in Art History*, 1 (2011), pp. 285–330.

Ostrowska, Dorota, *Reading the French New Wave: Critics, Writers and Art Cinema in France* (New York: Wallflower, 2008).

Paech, Joachim, 'Die Spur der Schrift und der Gestus des Schreibens im Film', in Roloff and Winter (eds), *Godard Intermedial*, pp. 41–56.

Paech, Joachim, 'Das Kino als Bühne (in Filmen der Nouvelle Vague)', in Roloff and Winter (eds), *Theater und Kino in der Zeit der Nouvelle Vague*, pp. 11–39.

Païni, Dominique, *Le Cinéma, un art plastique* (Crisnée: Yellow Now, 2013).

Paolucci, Anne, 'Anne Paolucci on Pirandello's exploration of theater as a medium', in Bloom (ed.), *Lugi Pirandello*, pp. 55–8.

Paquot, Thierry (ed.), *Les Situationnistes en ville* (Gollion: Infolio, 2015).

Paraskeva, Anthony, 'Samuel Beckett, Alain Resnais and French Modernist Cinema', *Forum for Modern Language Studies*, 50-1 (2014), pp. 30–9.

Perivolaropoulou, Nia, 'La Ville cinématographique, Siegfried Kracauer', *Théorème*, 10 (2007), pp. 13–24.

Pethő, Ágnes, *Cinema and Intermediality: The Passion for the In-Between* (Newcastle: Cambridge Scholars, 2011).

Peucker, Brigitte, *The Material Image: Art and the Real in Film* (Standford, CA: Stanford University Press, 2006).

Pichard, Hervé, 'L'oubli et la mémoire: sauvegarder et montrer les films de Guy Gilles', <http://www.cinematheque.fr/article/34.html> (accessed 2 October 2018).

Pinchemel, Philippe, *La Région parisienne* (Paris: Presses universitaires de France, 1979).

Poe, Edgar Allan, 'The Oval Portrait', in *The Fall of the House of Usher and Other Writings* (Harmondsworth: Penguin, 1986).

Pratt, Geraldine and Rose Marie San Juan, *Film and Urban Space: Critical Possibilities* (Edinburgh: Edinburgh University Press, 2014).

Proust, Marcel, 'Classicisme et romantisme', in Pierre Clarac and Yves Sandre (eds), *Contre Sainte-Beuve*, précédé de *Pastiches et mélanges* et suivi de *Essais et articles* (Paris: Gallimard, 'Pléiade', 1971).

Proust, Marcel, *In Search of Lost Time*, ed. Christopher Prendergast, 6 vols (London: Allen Lane, 2002).

Puaux, Françoise, 'Éric Rohmer', in Jousse and Paquot (eds), *La Ville au cinéma. Encyclopédie*, pp. 789–93.

Rancière, Jacques, *Film Fables*, trans. Emiliano Battista (Oxford: Berg, 2006).

Rajewsky, Irina O., 'Intermediality, intertextuality and remediation: a literary perspective on intermediality', *Intermédialités*, 6 (2005), pp. 43–64.

Rivette, Jacques, 'Conférence de presse (extraits), Cannes 1991', *Cahiers du cinéma*, 445 (1991), p. 34.

Robbe-Grillet, Alain, *L'Année dernière à Marienbad* (Paris: Minuit, 1961).
Rohmer, Éric, *The Taste for Beauty*, trans. Carol Volk (Cambridge: Cambridge University Press, 1989).
Rohmer, Éric, *Six contes moraux* (Paris: Cahiers du cinéma, 1998).
Rohmer, Éric, *Le Goût de la beauté*, ed. Jean Narboni (Paris: Cahiers du cinéma, 2004).
Rohmer, Éric, *Le Celluloïd et le marbre suivi d'un entretien inédit avec Noël Herpe et Philippe Fauvel* (Paris: Léo Scheer, 2010).
Rohmer, Éric, 'Architecture d'apocalypse', in Rohmer, *Le Celluloïd et le marbre*, pp. 69–80.
Rohmer, Éric, 'Avant-propos', in Rohmer, *Le Celluloïd et le marbre*, pp. 11–23.
Rohmer, Éric, 'Deuxième entretien: "Le Siècle des peintres"', in Rohmer, *Le Celluloïd et le marbre*, pp. 109–26.
Rohmer, Éric, 'Le Siècle des peintres', in Rohmer, *Le Celluloïd et le marbre*, pp. 37–45.
Roloff, Volker, 'Theater und Theatralität im Film', in Roloff and Winter (eds), *Theater und Kino in der Zeit der Nouvelle Vague*, pp. 5–9.
Roloff, Volker and Scarlett Winter (eds), *Godard Intermedial* (Tübingen: Stauffenburg, 1997).
Roloff, Volker and Scarlett Winter (eds), *Theater und Kino in der Zeit der Nouvelle Vague* (Tübingen: Stauffenburg, 2000).
Ropars-Wuilleumier, Marie-Claire, *Ecraniques. Le Film du texte* ([Lille]: Presses universitaires de Lille, 1990).
Ropars-Wuilleumier, Marie-Claire, *Le Temps d'une pensée: du montage à l'esthétique plurielle*, ed. Sophie Charlin (Saint-Denis: Presses universitaires de Vincennes, 2009).
Ropars-Wuilleumier, Marie-Claire, 'L'instance graphique dans l'écriture du film. A bout de souffle, ou l'alphabet erratique', in Ropars-Wuilleumier, *Le Temps d'une pensée: du montage à l'esthétique plurielle*, pp. 101–30.
Ropars-Wuilleumier, Marie-Claire, 'Totalité et fragmentaire: la réécriture selon Godard', in Ropars-Wuilleumier, *Le Temps d'une pensée: du montage à l'esthétique plurielle*, pp. 153–66.
Roud, Richard, *Godard*, 3rd edn (London: British Film Institute, 2010).
Sand, Luce, 'Entretien avec Alain Resnais', *Jeune cinéma*, 31 (1968), pp. 2–8.
Scargill, D. I., *Urban France* (London: St Martin's Press, 1983).
Schapper, Antoine, *Jacques-Louis David 1748–1825*, catalogue de l'exposition (Paris: Musée du Louvre/ Éditions de la Réunion des musées nationaux, 1989).
Schmid, Marion, 'Between classicism and modernity: Éric Rohmer on urban change', *French Studies*, 69-3 (2015), pp. 345–62.
Simond, Clotilde with Sophie Paviol, *Cinéma et architecture. La relève de l'art* (Lyon: Aléas, 2009).
Simsolo, Noël, *Dictionnaire de la Nouvelle Vague* (Paris: Flammarion, 2013).
Sipière, Dominique and Alain J.-J. Cohen (eds), *Les Autres arts dans l'art du cinéma* (Rennes: Presses universitaires de Rennes, 2007).
Smith, Alison, *Agnès Varda* (Manchester: Manchester University Press, 1998).
Smock, Ann, 'The honor of poets', in Denis Hollier (ed.), *A New History of French Literature* (Cambridge, MA: Harvard University Press, 1994), pp. 948–53.
Sontag, Susan, *On Photography* (London: Penguin, 1980).
Sontag, Susan, 'Theatre and film', in *Styles of Radical Will* (London: Vintage, 1994), pp. 99–122.
Sontag, Susan, 'Godard', in David Rieff (ed.), *Essays of the 1960s and 70s* (New York: Library of America, 2013), pp. 414–50.
Stam, Robert, *Literature Through Film: Realism, Magic and the Art of Adaptation* (London: Wiley-Blackwell, 2004).
Stewart, Garrett, *Between Film and Screen* (Chicago: University of Chicago Press, 1999).
Styan, J. L., 'J. L. Styan on Pirandello's innovations', in Bloom (ed.), *Lugi Pirandello*, pp. 80–3.

Sutton, Damian, *Photography, Cinema, Memory. The Crystal Image of Time* (Minneapolis, MN: University of Minnesota Press, 2009).
Temple, Michael, James S. Williams and Michael Witt (eds), *For Ever Godard* (London: Black Dog Publishing, 2004).
Thiher, Allen, 'Postmodern dilemmas: Godard's *Alphaville* and *Two or Three Things that I Know About Her*', *Boundary 2*, 4-3 (1976), pp. 947–64.
Toubiana, Serge, 'Comment la Nouvelle Vague a filmé la ville', in Nasrine Seraji and Jessie Magana (eds), *Architecture et cinéma* (Gollion: Infolio, 2015), pp. 18–46.
Truffaut, François, 'Ali Baba et la "Politique des auteurs"', *Cahiers du cinéma*, 44 (1955), pp. 45–7.
Truffaut, François, 'A certain tendency of French cinema', in Graham with Vincendeau (eds), *The French New Wave: Critical Landmarks*, pp. 39–63.
Turim, Maureen, 'Three way mirroring in *Vivre sa vie*', in Tom Conley and T. Jefferson Kline (eds), *A Companion to Jean-Luc Godard* (Chichester: Wiley Blackwell, 2014), pp. 89–107.
Ungar, Steven, *Cléo de 5 à 7* (London: BFI, 2008).
Ungar, Steven, 'Scenes in a library: Alain Resnais and *Toute la mémoire du monde*', *SubStance*, 41 (2012), pp. 58–78.
Uzal, Marcos, 'Les Couleurs du temps', in Lépingle and Uzal (eds), *Guy Gilles: un cinéaste au fil du temps*, pp. 186–94.
Vanoye, Francis, *L'Adaptation littéraire au cinéma* (Paris: Armand Colin, 2011).
Varda, Agnes, *Varda par Agnès* (Paris: Cahiers du cinéma, 1994).
Vignaux, Valérie, '*Salut les Cubains* d'Agnès Varda ou cinécriture et cinéma politique', in Chéroux and Ziebinska-Lewandowska (eds), *Varda/Cuba*, pp. 147–51.
Vincendeau, Ginette, 'Introduction: fifty years of the French New Wave: from hysteria to nostalgia', in Graham with Vincendeau (eds), *The French New Wave: Critical Landmarks*, pp. 1–29.
Virgil, *Aeneid*, trans. Frederick Ahl (Oxford: Oxford University Press, 2007).
Wall-Romana, Christophe, *Jean Epstein* (Manchester: Manchester University Press, 2013).
Webber, Andrew and Emma Wilson (eds), *Cities in Transition: the Moving Image and the Modern Metropolis* (London: Wallflower, 2007).
Wiles, Mary M., *Jacques Rivette* (Urbana: University of Illinois Press, 2012).
Wilson, Emma, *Alain Resnais* (Manchester: Manchester University Press, 2006).
Winter, Scarlett, 'Kino-Schauspiel. Zur Theatralität in den Filmen von Resnais', in Roloff and Winter (eds), *Theater und Kino in der Zeit der Nouvelle Vague*, pp. 41–52.
Winter, Scarlett and Susanne Schlünder (eds), *Körper-Ästhetik-Spiel. Zur filmischen écriture der Nouvelle Vague* (Munich: Wilhelm Fink, 2004).
Wollen, Peter, 'Fire and ice', *Photographies*, 4 (1984), pp. 118–20.
Ziebinska-Lewandowska, Karolina, 'Socialisme et cha-cha-cha: Cuba 1963 vue par Agnès Varda. Entretien réalisé par Karolina Ziebinska-Lewandowska', in Chéroux and Ziebinska-Lewandowska (eds), *Varda/Cuba*, pp. 7–12.

Index

Note: page numbers in *italics* indicate illustrations; n indicates notes

À bout de souffle (Godard), 6, 17, 26, 38, 43, 75, 106, 128, 132, 155, 169
Abel, Richard, 12–13, 14, 54, 109
Adamov, Arthur, 55
adaptation, 17–22
Aeschylus, 66, 71
Agamben, Giorgio, 72–3
Aimer, boire et chanter (Resnais), 57
Akerman, Chantal, 70
Algerian War, 45, 114, 130, 139, 141–2, 146, 177–8, 186, 207
Alleg, Henri, 178, 196
Alphaville (Godard), 29, 34–9, *38*, 41, 81, 132–3, 169
L'Ami de mon amie (Rohmer), 87, 134
Amiel, Vincent, 61
L'Amour à la mer (Gilles), 114, 115–19, 144–6, 156–7, *157*
L'Amour en fuite (Truffaut), 28
L'Amour existe (Pialat), 131, 148
L'Amour fou (Rivette), 61–2, 66–70, 74, 186
L'Amour par terre (Rivette), 61
L'Anglaise et le Duc (Rohmer), 207
animation, 9, 181, 184, 185, 191, 198
L'Année dernière à Marienbad (Resnais), 23–4, 26, 57–61, *58*
Anouilh, Jean, 57
anti-illusionism, 64, 74–5
Antonioni, Michelangelo, 155, 179–80
Apollinaire, Guillaume, 26, 38, 43, 110, 139, 192
Aragon, Louis, 36, 38, 43, 105
L'Arbre, le maire et la médiathèque (Rohmer), 134

architecture, 127–62, *136*, *140*, *145*, *148*
Arnheim, Richard, 113
Aron, Raymond, 147
L'Arrivée d'un train en gare de la Ciotat (Lumière), 98
art brut, 120
Artaud, Antonin, 70, 72, 74
Ascenseur pour l'échafaud (Malle), 6, 131–2
Astruc, Alexandre, 3, 14–15, 19, 116
Atelier de recherches et d'études d'aménagement (AREA), 151
Atget, Eugène, 171, 172
Au pan coupé (Gilles), 114, 115, 119, 120–2, *120*, 141, 173–4
Aumont, Jacques, 88, 90, 105
Aurenche, Jean, 19–20
auteurism, 3, 13–17, 21, 27, 61–73, 204
avant-garde, 2–4, 7–8, 12–15, 23, 25, 45, 54, 55, 61, 66, 70, 72, 78, 80, 82, 86, 109, 113, 120, 165, 166, 171, 205
Avedon, Richard, 112, 178–9
Ayckbourn, Alan, 57

Badiou, Alain, 181–2, 204, 206–7
Baecque, Antoine de, 82, 105–6
Bailey, David, 178–9
Le Ballon rouge (Lamorisse), 128
Balzac, Honoré de, 26–34, *30*, 70, 73, 110, 139
Bande à part (Godard), 6, 20, 44–5, 46, *46*, 47, 85n, 91–4, *92*, 105, 106, 206
La Bande des quatre (Rivette), 61
Barthes, Roland, 22, 34, 35, 45, 74, 82, 105, 164, 166, 171–2, 173, 175, 178, 180, 182, 189, 194

Baudelaire, Charles, 117, 119, 127, 137–8, 153, 158
Bazin, André, 4, 5, 6, 18–19, 41, 54–5, 60–1, 65, 78, 86–7, 88–90, 93, 117, 121, 163–4, 194, 198, 204, 205, 206, 208, 208n
Beauvoir, Simone de, 196
Becher, Bernd, 137
Becher, Hilla, 137
Beck, Julian, 72
Becker, Jacques, 19, 128
Beckett, Samuel, 55, 60–1
Béghin, Cyril, 70, 72
Bellour, Raymond, 47, 165–6, 170, 177, 181, 190, 200n
Belmondo, Jean-Paul, 128
Benhaïm, Safia, 117
Benjamin, Walter, 117, 118, 153
Benoliel, Bernard, 122
Bergman, Ingmar, 169
Bergson, Henri, 35–6
Bernard, Luc, 114
Bernstein, Henri, 57
Berto, Juliet, 72
Bettelheim, Charles, 196
Bildungsroman, 28–9, 81
Blow-up (Antonioni), 179–80
Blumenfeld, Erwin, 158
Boiffard, Jacques-André, 171
Bolter, Jay David, 106
Bonfanti, Antoine, 145
Le Bonheur (Varda), 99–101
Bonitzer, Pascal, 97
Les Bonnes femmes (Chabrol), 155–6
Borges, Jorge Luis, 35–6
Borowczyk, Walerian, 198
Bory, Jean-Louis, 173
Bost, Pierre, 19–20
Bourseiller, Antoine, 73
Bradbury, Ray, 20, 34, 39–41
Brassaï, 120
Brassart, Alain, 129, 133–4
Braunberger, Pierre, 114
Brecht, Bertolt, 24, 55, 64, 74–7, 80, 82, 171
Bresson, Robert, 16, 19, 24, 64
Breton, André, 70, 118, 176
Brialy, Jean-Claude, 115, 157
Brigitte et Brigitte (Moullet), 133, 146
Brook, Peter, 55, 63, 71, 72, 73

Bruneau, Sonia, 129
Bruno, Giuliana, 146, 159, 192, 196
Buchloh, Benjamin, 112

Cabañas, Kaira M., 45–6
Cahiers du cinéma, 2–3, 5, 23–5, 29, 33, 61–2, 66–7, 72, 74, 81, 88, 109, 115, 128, 133, 134, 172–3, 204
Calmettes, André, 54
caméra-stylo (Astruc), 3, 14
Canaletto, 98
Cannes Film Festival, 1–2, 5, 9n
Canudo, Ricciotto, 1–2, 54, 57
Capa, Robert, 190
Les Carabiniers (Godard), 20, 47, 75–7
Carné, Marcel, 128, 131, 153
Carroll, Lewis, 32
Casa Malaparte, 132
Cayrol, Jean, 22, 141–3
Céline, Louis-Ferdinand, 27, 36, 110
Centre International de Recherches Théâtrales, 71
Cézanne, Paul, 87, 152
Chabrol, Claude, 5, 16, 17, 28–9, 154, 155–6
Chagall, Marc, 116
Le Chant du styrène (Resnais), 22
Chardère, Bernard, 2–3
Chauvin, Jean-Sébastien, 131
La Chinoise (Godard), 47, 77, 78–82, *79*, 85n, 184
Chrétien de Troyes, 27
Chronique d'un été (Rouch and Morin), 139, 147, 154
cinécriture, 16, 49, 205
cinéma vérité, 128, 139
Cinémathèque française, 170, 186
cinematic ekphrasis, 108
'cinematogram', 184–90
cinemato*graphies*, 41–9, 205
cineplastics, 12, 86
ciné-roman, 24, 205
cité des 4000, 147–52, *148*
city symphony films, 155
Clair, René, 128, 165
Le Clair de terre (Gilles), 114, 115, 117, 119, 122, 156, 157–8, 173, 174–5, *174*, 208
Clarke, Shirley, 104
Cléder, Jean, 15, 17
Cléo de 5 à 7 (Varda), 95, 98

Cocteau, Jean, 19, 34, 78, 110, 192
Cœurs (Resnais), 57
Cold War, 192–3
Colette, Sidonie-Gabrielle, 20
collage, 81, 105
Colvin, J. Brandon, 101
Coney Island at Night (Porter), 159
Constantine, Eddie, 34–5
consumer culture, 43, 70, 112, 151, 169, 193, 207
Cooper, Sarah, 186, 196
Coppola, Francis Ford, 155
Corneille, Pierre, 93
Cortázar, Julio, 20
Les Cousins (Chabrol), 28–9, 154, 157
Coutard, Raoul, 35, 80, 92, 128
Cuba, 170, 191–2, 196–9
Cuba Si (Marker), 196
cultural legitimacy, 2–4, 7, 15, 204

Dalí, Gala, 36
Dalí, Salvador, 36
Dalle Vacche, Angela, 7, 47, 106
dance, 6, 197, *197*, 199
Daney, Serge, 26, 168, 177
David, Jacques-Louis, 91, 93
Davis, Miles, 6
Debord, Guy, 56, 80, 127, 130–1
Delacroix, Henry-Charles, 147
Delerue, Georges, 6
Deleuze, Gilles, 113, 157, 165
Delluc, Louis, 109
Demy, Jacques, 6, 101, 114, 115–16
Deren, Maya, 171
DeRoo, Rebecca, 95, 97, 99
Derrida, Jacques, 45, 113
Les Désastres de la guerre (Kast), 88
Descartes, René, 15
Les Deux Anglaises et le continent (Truffaut), 28
Deux ou trois choses que je sais d'elle (Godard), 20, 35, 47, 49, 85n, 129, 132, 147–52, *148*, 177, 182–4
Diderot, Denis, 21, 65
Didi-Huberman, Georges, 27, 43, 52n, 105, 112
Dine, Jim, 69
La Diversité du paysage urbain (Rohmer), 151

Domicile conjugal (Truffaut), 26
Donen, Stanley, 179–80
Dort, Bernard, 72
Dostoevsky, Fyodor, 16
Dreyer, Carl Theodor, 40, 109
Dubois, Philippe, 42, 185
Dubuffet, Jean, 120
Duchamp, Marcel, 118
Dullin, Charles, 66
Duras, Marguerite, 22–3, 24, 25, 119
d'Urfé, Honoré, 27

Eggeling, Viking, 12
8 ½ (Fellini), 21
Eisenstein, Sergei, 127, 166
'electropolis', 156–9
Elliott, Grace, 27
Éluard, Paul, 22, 36–9, *38*, 41
Emmer, Luciano, 88
L'Enfant Sauvage (Truffaut), 28
Les Enfants du Paradis (Carné), 128
Les Enfants terribles (Melville), 78
Entretien sur le béton (Rohmer), 134, 138
Epstein, Jean, 108–9

Fabian, Françoise, 71
'facingness', 98, 107
Fahrenheit 451 (Truffaut), 20, 34, 39–41, *40*, 133, 169
Fanon, Frantz, 195
Faulkner, William, 26, 27, 151
Faure, Elie, 12, 86, 127
Fauvel, Philippe, 27, 87, 137
Fellini, Federico, 21
Une femme est une femme (Godard), 106
Une femme mariée (Godard), 43–4, 106, 109–13, *111*, 169
Festivals 1966, Cinéma 1967 (Gilles), 115
Le Film est déjà commencé? (Lemaître), 85n
film-within-a-film, 21, 40, 66–7, 70
flâneur, 117, 127, 152–9
Flaubert, Gustave, 43–4, 109
Fluxus, 69
Fragonard, Jean-Honoré, 65
freeze-frame, 165–8, *168*, 200n, 205–6
Fried, Michael, 98
Friedrich, Caspar David, 88
Frodon, Jean-Michel, 147

Funny Face (Donen), 179–80
Fusco, Giovanni, 6

Gance, Abel, 19
Gauguin, Paul, 87
Gaulle, Charles de, 130–1, 153
Gavarry, Pierre, 135
Le Genou de Claire (Rohmer), 87
Germania anno zero (Rossellini), 81
Gide, André, 20, 27
Gilles, Guy, 5, 113–22, 129, 141, 144–6, 156–8, 166, 170, 172–6, 202n, 205, 208
Giraud, François, 123n, 124n
Giraudoux, Jean, 73, 139
Giroud, Françoise, 3
Glissant, Édouard, 193
Godard, Jean-Luc, 1, 5, 6, 12, 16–17, 20, 21–2, 25, 26–7, 28–9, 34–9, 41–9, 52n, 53, 63, 65, 73–82, 85n, 91–4, 100, 105–13, 115, 116, 122, 128, 129, 132–3, 147–52, 163, 166, 169, 176–84, 194, 204, 205, 206, 207
Goethe, Johann Wolfgang von, 82
Gómez, Sarita, 199
Goodis, David, 20
Goodman, Nelson, 156
Gorz, André, 150
Goya, Francesco, 102
grands ensembles, 130, 147–52
Greenaway, Peter, 48
Greenberg, Clement, 113
Grien, Hans Baldung, 95
Grotowski, Jerzy, 55, 72, 73
Gruault, Jean, 75
Grusin, Richard, 106
Guardi, Francesco, 98
Guernica (Resnais and Hessens), 22, 88
Guiguet, Jean-Claude, 172–3
Guillén, Nicolás, 199
Guillevic, Eugène, 120
Guitry, Sacha, 54
Guzzetti, Alfred, 148, 151–2, 182–3, 202n

happenings, 69–70
Hauff, Wilhelm, 178
Haussmann, Georges Eugène, Baron, 138, 140

Hegel, Georg Wilhelm Friedrich, 86, 90, 159
Heine, Heinrich, 40
Heinich, Nathalie, 152
Hensman, Ravi, 148–9
Henze, Hans Werner, 142–3
Herpe, Noël, 27, 87, 137
Hessens, Robert, 88
Hiroshima mon amour (Resnais), 1, 6, 22–5, 141, 142–3, 155–6, 169
L'Histoire d'Adèle H. (Truffaut), 28
Histoire(s) du cinéma (Godard), 43, 105, 106, 107, 177, 207
Hitchcock, Alfred, 131, 188, 189
Hitchens, Dolores, 20
Hollywood, 101, 132
Holmes, Diana, 39
Holocaust, 188, 207
L'Homme qui aimait les femmes (Truffaut), 28
Hopper, Edward, 87
Hourmant, François, 196
Hugo, Victor, 134

Ibsen, Henrik, 60
ICAIC (Cuban Center for Cinematographic Art and Industry), 196, 199
Immemory (Marker), 189, 207
Impressionism, 99–101
improvisation, 71, 73, 83n
impure cinema, 4, 6, 18–19, 49, 55, 65, 89, 205–6, 208n
Ingram, Robert, 39
Ionesco, Eugène, 55
Irish, William, 20
Ishaghpour, Youssef, 44, 49
Isou, Isidore, 46
Italian neorealism, 128
Ivens, Joris, 197

Jacobs, Steven, 88, 102, 106, 132
James, Henry, 21
Jane B. par Agnès V. (Varda), 102
Le Jardin qui bascule (Gilles), 115
La Jetée (Marker), 34, 181, 184–90, *188*, 191–2, 198, 202n
Le Joli Mai (Marker), 129, 139–41, *140*, 142, 147, 151, 154, 156
Jones, Colin, 130
Joppolo, Beniamino, 20, 75

Jouané, Patrick, 114
Journal d'un combat (Gilles), 121
Joyce, James, 26–7
JR, 170
Jules et Jim (Truffaut), 20, 169, 200n

Kalfon, Jean-Pierre, 66, 70
Kaprow, Allan, 69
Karina, Anna, 36–7, 65, 73–4, 107–8, 109, 180
Kast, Pierre, 23, 25, 88
Kennedy, Robert F., 101
Klee, Paul, 87, 106, 110
Kleist, Heinrich von, 27
Kline, T. Jefferson, 13
Kracauer, Siegfried, 153, 158–9
Kreimeier, Klaus, 75

Labarthe, André S., 66–7, 68, 70
Lacan, Jacques, 45
Lafont, Bernadette, 71, 73
Lam, Wilfredo, 199
Lamorisse, Albert, 128
Lang, Fritz, 21–2
Langlois, Henri, 109, 116, 186
Le Bargy, Charles, 54
Le Corbusier (Charles-Édouard Jeanneret), 130, 205
Le Couey, Catherine, 191
Léaud, Jean-Pierre, 72, 80, 115, 157, 168
Ledoux, Jacques, 186
Leenhardt, Roger, 19
Lefebvre, Henri, 130–1, 151
Left Bank Group, 5, 22, 115, 205
Léger, Fernand, 12
Lemaître, Maurice, 46, 85n
Lenica, Jan, 198
Lennon, John, 70
Leonardo da Vinci, 163
Lépingle, Gaël, 114, 115, 170
Lessing, Gotthold Ephraim, 113
Letonturier, Louis Paul, 138
Lettre de Sibérie (Marker), 185
Lettrism, 45–6, 66, 85n
Leutrat, Jean-Louis, 58, 106, 113
Libera, Adalberto, 132
La Ligne de mire (Pollet), 16

Lions Love (. . . and Lies) (Varda), 99, 101, 102–5, *104*
'liquid city', 155
literature, 12–52; *see also* poetry
Living Theatre, 55, 72, 81
Lodz Film School, 198
Lommel, Michael, 79
Lonsdale, Michael, 72
Look at Life (Lucas), 191
Louvre, 91–4, *92*, 206
Loyer, François, 138
Lucas, George, 191
Lumière, Louis and Auguste, 93, 98, 127, 165
Lupton, Catherine, 185, 189, 192, 195
La Luxure (Demy), 114

Ma nuit chez Maud (Rohmer), 27
Made in U.S.A. (Godard), 49, 106
Magny, Joël, 128
Maillol, Aristide, 111, 112
Malatesta, Sigismondo Pandolfo, 96
Malclès, Jean-Denis, 116
Malina, Judith, 72
Mallarmé, Stéphane, 65
Malle, Louis, 6, 131–2
Malraux, André, 1–2, 5, 9n, 14, 18, 43, 52n, 86, 91–2, 93–4, 106, 116, 130, 152, 178
Man Ray, 171
Man with a Movie Camera (Vertov), 165, 193
Manet, Édouard, 98, 107, 109
Mankiewicz, Joseph, 16
Marc'O, 55, 66
La Mariée était en noir (Truffaut), 20
Marker, Chris, 5, 27, 34, 129, 139–41, 142, 147, 151, 166, 181, 184–90, 191–8, 202n, 205, 207
La Marquise d'O (Rohmer), 88
Mary, Philippe, 2, 16, 30
Masculin féminin (Godard), 20, 45
Matisse, Henri, 87–8
Maupassant, Guy de, 20
Mauriac, Claude, 175
Mayakovsky, Vladimir, 79
McClure, Michael, 101
McHale, Brian, 80
McQuire, Scott, 155
media rivalry, 27, 106, 181, 205

Méliès, Georges, 13–14
Mélo (Resnais), 57
Mélodie en sous-sol (Verneuil), 129
Melville, Herman, 17
Melville, Jean-Pierre, 17, 78, 128
memory, 184–90
Le Mépris (Godard), 20, 21–2, 47, 100, 106, 132, 157, 186
Méril, Macha, 110–12, 115
metalepsis, 8, 61, 76, 80
Métamorphoses du paysage (Rohmer), 134, 135–8, *136*, 140
metatheater, 68–9, 205
Mies van der Rohe, Ludwig, 138
mise-en-abyme, 8, 22, 26, 32, 59, 61, 62, 64, 68–70, 74, 80, 108, 111
Les Mistons (Truffaut), 20, 115
Mnouchkine, Ariane, 55, 63, 71
Modernism, 95, 98, 101, 132, 199
Modigliani, Amadeo, 64, 116
Moholy-Nagy, László, 158
Molière (Jean-Baptiste Poquelin), 110
Mon Oncle (Tati), 131
Mondrian, Piet, 87
Monet, Claude, 101
Monfort, Silvia, 96–7, 98–9
Montand, Yves, 139
Moravia, Alberto, 16, 20, 22
Moré, Benny, *197*, 198
Moreau, Jeanne, 115, 200n
Morin, Edgar, 139, 147
Morrey, Douglas, 151
Moullet, Luc, 133, 146
Mühl, Otto, 69–70
Mulvey, Laura, 165
Muriel, ou le temps d'un retour (Resnais), 129, 141–4, 145–6, *145*, 148, 149, 178
Murillo, Bartolomé Esteban, 98
music, 6, 12, 157, 198
Muybridge, Eadweard, 190

Nadeau, Maurice, 15
Nagib, Lúcia, 12
'new towns', 8, 134
Nietzsche, Friedrich, 35–6
Noiret, Philippe, 96, 98–9
Nouveau roman, 22–6, 27, 28, 205
Nuit et brouillard (Resnais), 22, 188

Nuit et jour (Akerman), 70
Les Nuits de la pleine lune (Rohmer), 87, 134
Nussbaum, Valentin, 92–3

Ogier, Bulle, 66, 73
Oldenburg, Claes, 69
Ono, Yoko, 70
L'Opéra-Mouffe (Varda), 102, 140, 171–3
Ophuls, Max, 19
Orphée (Cocteau), 34
Ostrowska, Dorota, 10n
Out 1, 5, 31–4, *33*, 61, 63, 66, 70–3, *71*

Paech, Joachim, 42, 108
Pagnol, Marcel, 54
painting, 86–126
Pakula, Alan, 191
Paolucci, Anna, 68
The Parallax View (Pakula), 191
Paraskeva, Anthony, 59, 60
Parent, Claude, 134, 138
Les Parents terribles (Cocteau), 78
Paris nous appartient (Rivette), 30–1, 34, 61, 62–6, *63*, 70
Paris qui dort (Clair), 165
Paris vu par . . . (Chabrol et al.), 132
Pascal, Blaise, 27, 35–6
Passion (Godard), 106, 113, 207
The Passion of Joan of Arc (Dreyer), 40, 109
Pauline à la plage (Rohmer), 87–8
Paysages urbains (Rohmer), 134
La Peau douce (Truffaut), 31, 200n
Péguy, Charles, 65
Perivolaropoulou, Nia, 159
Pescayré, Jérôme, 158
Pethő, Ágnes, 7, 48, 108, 112, 153, 155, 156, 205
Petit à petit (Rouch), 31, 133
Le Petit Soldat (Godard), 47, 106, 156, 177–81, *179*, 182–3, 194
Peucker, Brigitte, 98, 105
Philipe, Anne, 196
Philipe, Gérard, 94, 196
photo shoot, 176–84, *179*
photogram, 9, 164–8, 171, 176, 180, 181, 184, 190
photography, 94–5, 112, 137, 158, 163–203
photo-roman, 185, 205

Pialat, Maurice, 131, 148
Picasso, Pablo, 48, 87, 101, 102–4, *103*, 105, 110, 124n
Piccoli, Michel, 191
Piero della Francesca, 96–8, *96*
Pierrot le fou (Godard), 20, 27, 29, 45, 46–9, *48*, 77–8, *77*, 105, 106, 182
Pigeat, Jean-Paul, 151
Pinchemel, Philippe, 131
Pirandello, Luigi, 61–73, 74, 79, 205
Pitoëff, Georges, 57
Planchon, Roger, 75
Plato, 137
Playtime (Tati), 147
play-within-the-film, 57–60, *58*, 66–7, 70, 77, 186, 205–6
Poe, Edgar Allan, 21, 107–9, 112
Poèmes électriques (Gilles), 158
poetry, 2, 5, 14, 36–9, 41, 46, 48, 86, 91, 109, 120, 122, 134–6, 138, 170, 172, 176, 192, 199
La Pointe courte (Varda), 5, 95–9, *97*, 102, 171
Pollet, Jean-Daniel, 16, 133
Ponge, Francis, 152
Pons, Maurice, 20
Pop Art, 105, 112–13
Porter, Edwin, 159
Pouillon, Fernand, 140
Preminger, Otto, 61
Proust, l'art et la douleur (Gilles), 115, 176
Proust, Marcel, 20, 26, 27, 93, 116, 118–19, 126n, 158, 175–6, 189
Psycho (Hitchcock), 131
punctum, 167–8, *168*
La Punition (Rouch), 154
pure cinema, 2, 4, 12, 86, 205

4 aventures de Reinette et Mirabelle (Rohmer), 88
Les Quatre cents coups (Truffaut), 1, 29–32, *30*, 154, 157, 166, 167–8, *168*, 169
Queneau, Raymond, 22, 45

Racine, Jean, 66, 81, 82
Rado, James, 101, 103
Ragni, Gerome, 101, 103
Rancière, Jacques, 77, 82, 205
Raphael, 88

Reichenbach, François, 202n
La Religieuse (Rivette), 21, 61, 65–6, 73
Renaissance painting, 94–8
Les Rendez-vous de Paris (Rohmer), 88
Renoir, Jean, 18, 19, 61, 128
Renoir, Pierre-Auguste, 99, 105, 106
Resnais, Alain, 1, 5, 6, 22–6, 53, 57–61, 76, 78, 88, 129, 141–4, 145–6, 149, 169, 178, 188, 197, 205
Richter, Hans, 12
Rimbaud, Arthur, 46, 48
Riva, Emmanuelle, 115
Rivette, Jacques, 5, 21, 24, 25, 28, 30–4, 61–73, 73–4, 76, 78, 112, 115
Robbe-Grillet, Alain, 23, 24, 58–9, 205
Roché, Henri-Pierre, 20
Rohmer, Éric, 5, 6, 21, 23–4, 25, 27–8, 31–2, 53, 86–8, 129, 134–9, 140, 143–4, 151, 163, 204, 206–7
Roloff, Volker, 56
Romney, Jonathan, 62
Ropars-Wuilleumier, Marie-Claire, 21–2, 43
Rossellini, Roberto, 75, 81, 188
Rouch, Jean, 31, 129, 132, 133, 139, 147, 154
Rozier, Jacques, 116
Ruttmann, Walter, 12, 155

Sadoul, Georges, 105, 112–13
Salut les Cubains (Varda), 6, 170, 184, 191–2, 196–9, *197*
Sartre, Jean-Paul, 196
Savel, Francis, 120–1
Scénario du film Passion (Godard), 42
Schiffman, Suzanne, 31
Scorsese, Martin, 155
scriptwriters, 13–20
sculpture, 91, 101, 102–5, 111–12, 113, 137, 205
Seberg, Jean, 128
Ségur, Comtesse de, 21
self-reflexivity, 4, 9, 21, 43, 62, 76, 82, 98, 104–5, 115, 154, 165, 166, 176, 179, 184, 186, 194; *see also* film-within-a-film; mise-en-abyme; play-within-the-film
Serra, Noun, 115, 145
Seyrig, Delphine, 115

Shakespeare, William, 62–3
Si j'avais quatre dromadaires (Marker), 184, 191–2, 194–6
Sibyl's cave, 187–8, *188*
Le Signe du lion (Rohmer), 132, 134, 140, 155, 169
silent film, 44, 108
Simsolo, Noël, 4–5, 114
Sisley, Alfred, 105
Situationist International, 130–1, 140, 151
Smoking/No Smoking (Resnais), 57
Solal, Martial, 6
Soleil éteint (Gilles), 114
Sontag, Susan, 26–7, 77, 82, 83n, 85n, 183
Sophocles, 93
La sortie de l'usine Lumière à Lyon (Lumière), 127
sound revolution, 12–13, 54
Sous les toits de Paris (Clair), 128
Soutine, Chaïm, 116
Staël, Nicolas de, 87
Stam, Robert, 23
Stanislavski, Konstantin, 74
Stendhal (Marie Henri Beyle), 139
Stéphane, Nicole, 20
Stevenson, Robert Louis, 21
Stewart, Garrett, 165, 169–70, 173–4, 176, 184, 189–90
Stora, Jean-Pierre, 114, 157
Styan, J. L., 68
Sully, Thomas, 107
Summer with Monika (Bergman), 169
Surrealism, 14, 36–7, 38, 41, 70, 118, 120, 171, 172, 199, 205
Survage, Léopold, 12

tableaux vivants, 101–5, 106, 172, 205–6
Tambuté, Clément, 147
Tati, Jacques, 19, 131, 147
Taylor, Elizabeth, 107
television, 32, 66–7, 115, 129, 134–5, 138, 151
Terrain vague (Carné), 131, 153
theatre, 53–85
Théâtre du soleil, 71
Théâtre national populaire (TNP), 55, 66, 81, 95, 170

Theatre of Cruelty, 70
Theatre of the Absurd, 55
theatrum mundi, 56, 60–1, 78, 82
Thiher, Allen, 35, 37
Tire-au-flanc 62 (de Givray and Truffaut), 114
Tirez sur le pianiste (Truffaut), 20
Titian, 88, 102
Toute la mémoire du monde (Resnais), 188
Tradition of Quality, 2–3, 13, 14, 16, 18, 19–20, 64, 128, 153, 204
Triple Agent (Rohmer), 88
Truffaut, François, 1, 2, 5, 14, 15, 16, 17, 18, 19–20, 21, 26, 28, 29–31, 34, 39–41, 114, 115, 133, 154, 166, 167–8, 169, 200n

Ungar, Steven, 98, 188
urban modernisation, 8, 128–31, 140–1, 143, 150–1, 171, 207
Uzal, Marcos, 121

Va Savoir (Rivette), 61
van Eyck, Jan, 87
Van Gogh (Resnais), 88
Vaneck, Pierre, 191
Vanoye, Francis, 24
Varda, Agnès, 5, 6, 16, 57, 94–105, *97*, *104*, 106, 113, 116, 140, 154–5, 166, 170, 171–3, 184, 188, 191–2, 196–9, 205, 207
Velázquez, Diego, 102
Vertigo (Hitchcock), 188
Vertov, Dziga, 139, 155, 165, 193
Viaggio in Italia (Rossellini), 188
Victor Hugo, architecte (Rohmer), 134
Viennese Actionism, 69–70
Vierny, Dina, 112
Vietnam War, 70, 77, *77*, 149, 150, 182–3
Vilar, Jean, 55, 66, 81, 95
Visages Villages (Varda), 170
Villiers de l'Isle-Adam, Auguste de, 198
Vincendeau, Ginette, 4
Virgil, 187
Virilio, Paul, 134, 138
Viva (Janet Susan Mary Hoffmann), 101
Vivien, Pierre, 142, 144, *145*, 149
Vivre sa vie (Godard), 43–4, 47, 106, 107–9, 112

Vlady, Marina, 148–9
Vous n'avez encore rien vu (Resnais), 57

Wagner, Richard, 37, 57
Walter, Marie-Thérèse, 103–4
Warburg, Aby, 90
Warhol, Andy, 101
Weekend (Godard), 20, 85n
Weill, Kurt, 171
White, Lionel, 20
Wiles, Mary, 65–6, 68
Wilson, Emma, 142
Winter, Scarlett, 57, 59
Wollen, Peter, 190
World War II, 36, 39–41, 139, 141–2, 170, 186, 207
'written screen', 42–9

'Young Turks', 5, 13, 16, 21, 22, 28, 31, 33, 115, 205
Yumatov, Nicolas, 191

Zola, Émile, 43, 92, 107, 109

EU representative:
Easy Access System Europe
Mustamäe tee 50, 10621 Tallinn, Estonia
Gpsr.requests@easproject.com

www.ingramcontent.com/pod-product-compliance
Lightning Source LLC
Chambersburg PA
CBHW071838230426
43671CB00012B/1996